I WAS,
I AM,
I WILL BE

By John Coventry and Trish Faber

Copyright © 2016 Trish Faber & John Coventry
All rights reserved.
Wonder Voice Press
ISBN-13: 978-0-9877188-6-0

ACKNOWLEDGEMENTS

From JOHN

This was never a story I thought I would ever tell. Many of the events happened so long ago, and many of the memories I wanted to keep buried in one small corner of my mind forever.

It's very important for me to let the reader know that in no way do I think I am a good person or have led a good life or been honest or kind…I have been neither. I have done so many things and have hurt so many people that I love and care for, never intentionally, nevertheless, I have made some shocking mistakes. I do not want to come out of this with a halo above my head. I am no saint.

What you are about to read is my true real story, inspected and fact-checked by two Attorneys and international investigators.

I have to first thank Trish Faber, my co-writer, who right from the start, not only had total faith in the book that we wrote together, but asked for nothing in return for the long hours that she put in. This book would not have been possible without her and I owe her a great debt of gratitude.

And finally, I'd like to thank my family and friends, starting with my Father and Mother. I am only sorry they are not alive to read this, although both experienced it firsthand. In fact, much of the story was written from the original masses of notes that my father compiled some thirty years ago. I am not going to name any names, but to those few who stuck with me and continue to do so, you know who you are. Thank you so very much. I love you all.

Enjoy the read - it was quite a journey!
John

From TRISH

First, I would like to thank John for having the courage to tell his story and entrusting me with guiding his hand through the process. It's been a wonderful, enlightening experience and I can't thank him enough for putting his faith and trust in me. I look forward to seeing where this adventure leads for the both of us!

Second, I have to thank my family and friends. You've all been so encouraging and faithful, not just with this project, but with everything I've done. I cherish your love and thank each and every one of you! I really couldn't have done it without you and I can't express how important you all have been in my life.

A special thanks to my "big sista" who is my best friend, sounding board, and general go-to girl. You know how much you mean to me. And of course to my Father, who, well just manages to put up with me on a daily basis. I know it sometimes isn't easy…

And for my beloved Mom - I love you and I miss you - always!

Thanks again everybody and happy reading!
Trish

PROLOGUE

*"**I Was, I Am, I Will Be**". The first time I heard the expression it meant nothing to me. Just seven little words strung together like an ancient Chinese riddle. I had no idea the power or the prophecy hidden deep within the simplicity of the phrase. In the end, those words would haunt, torture and terrorize me - forever a symbol of a passion disenchanted by romantic ideology.*

"You've certainly gotten yourself into one hell of a mess this time John," I said tossing the book on the table.

I'd been at the Central Library in Liverpool since noon doing some reading and research. This would be my first trip to Ireland and from the tone of Peter Barrington's voice on the telephone; I knew it wasn't for pleasure. Brian wanted to see me and when Brian summons you to his house, you don't say no. Not unless you wanted to end up with a face split open and smashed like an overripe tomato crushed on the pavement. I suppose that was more promising than winding up in a body bag or floating belly up in the Thames River with a bullet through your neck.

That's what the IRA did without even blinking an eye. It was all there in black and white. "Bloody Friday" the bombing of Belfast in 1972, where over twenty bombs went off in the crowded City center killing nine and injuring over 130 people – innocent people – some of them severely. Then there was the "Kings Mills Massacre" of January 5th, 1976. I opened the periodical and re-read the passage describing the carnage:

"The talk on the minibus that night was no different than normal. There had been talk earlier in the factory that day about the killing of

the young Reavey brothers from Whitecross. It horrified us all. We passed through Whitecross village shortly after 5.30 p.m. and when our minibus was stopped, a short distance up the road past Kingsmills crossroads, we thought it was the army. A group of about 12 armed men, unmasked but with their faces blackened and wearing combat jackets, surrounded the vehicle and ordered us all out on to the road. Even then few of us thought there was anything amiss. One man, with a pronounced English accent, did all the talking and proceeded to ask each of us our religion. Our Roman Catholic work colleague was ordered to clear off and the shooting started. It was all over within a minute and after the initial screams there was silence. I was semi-conscious and passed out several times with the deadly pain and the cold. A man appeared on the scene. He was in a terrible state and was praying loudly as he passed along the rows of bodies. He must have heard my groans and came across to comfort me. I must have been lying at the roadside waiting on the ambulance for up to 30 minutes. It was like an eternity and I can remember someone moving my body from one side to the other to help ease the pain". What was done that night was a sheer waste, a futile exercise that advanced no cause."[1]

Being a native Englishman, I knew all about the exploits of the Irish Republican Army. Intent on ending British sovereignty in Northern Ireland, the IRA wanted Irish lands united as one. The idea of Irish Republicanism was centuries old and the conflict with Britain was intense and complicated. British sentiment for the Irish was one of mistrust and scorn. Of course, that was a generalization, but the increased violence and killing of innocent people by the IRA wasn't helping the image too much.

The thought of maybe being involved with a group of people so violent and inhumane made the insides of my stomach crawl with fear and disdain. I wasn't positive that

---

[1] (Belfast Newsletter, January 5, 1986 – 10 years after the event).

Brian was a member of the IRA, but I certainly had my suspicions based on all the circumstantial evidence. The drugs, the shipments of crates containing God knows what – the rumours about what he'd done in the past and what he's capable of doing at any given moment. He just had that aura of evil. The way he commanded a room with his sheer size, barking orders, almost daring someone to step out of line and challenge his authority. I think he took immense sick pleasure in making people squirm, terrifying them until they broke down like babies and did whatever he wanted.

I flipped through a new bunch of newspaper clippings the librarian set on the table. Bombings, shootings, and more bombings.

"The IRA has admitted killing the three men found by the army at different roadsides in South Armagh last night. They claim the men were informers for MI5 and the Royal Ulster Constabulary (RUC) Special Branch and they had been tried and killed by the IRA. In a style typical of IRA ritual killings the bodies were found in ditches, naked and hooded with evidence of beatings and single bullets through the backs of the heads."[2]

Was that why Brian wanted to see me in Ireland? So he could put a bullet in my head? Would I be next in line for execution? Did he know? How could he? I'd been so careful. God help me if he did. My mind was racing with questions I couldn't answer. I've seen and done some things I'm definitely not proud of and gotten myself mixed up in some very dicey business. I honestly don't know how it all happened. I guess life just puts you on a path and it's up to you to choose the right one when you're at the intersection. Unfortunately, it's quite easy to hit a bump in the road, lose control, and fly face first into the ditch. In my case, I always

---

[2] (BBC News July 2).

seemed to land in a pile of shit.

I tried to make good decisions, I really did, but it didn't take me long to recognize that one bad decision could wipe out a lifetime of good. Trying to cover up the first bad decision with a second and third, only sends you spiraling further into your pit of despair. Yet it seems no matter how hard you try to change things and move forward, people will always judge you by that one mistake. I'm not going to tell you I'm an angel. I've told my share of lies, cheated people out of money, and been a downright arrogant bastard in my younger days. And I've kept secrets...so many secrets...from family, from friends, from authorities. I feel horrible for having kept those secrets, but at times, it's hard to know just who to trust.

I was in deep. With Brian, with Peter Atwood, with Nigel, with Michelle. I just needed to find a way out, to slip away in the middle of the night, and disappear. Easier said than done. If it wasn't the government guys tailing me then it was some greasy thug on Brian's payroll. I'd never felt this trapped before in my life. I couldn't go home to Townfield and hide out. Peter Atwood and Nigel took care of that with their unannounced visits to my father's drawing room. Besides, I wouldn't dream of putting my family in any more danger. The government cronies were a pain in the ass but Brian and his bunch wouldn't hesitate to pour some gas, toss a match and burn the house to the ground.

If Brian ever found out I was working undercover for the British Government, I'd be a dead man for sure. I had to be extremely careful with everything I did and said, and honestly, I wasn't sure how much longer I could keep up the game. Unfortunately, I just couldn't pick up my ball and go home because I was tired of playing. This was a high stakes game of drugs, terror, and espionage. On both sides, the players were hard-nosed professionals, and the consequences of failure were death, jail or the muddied waters in between.

Looking back, serving my time in jail for the government fraud probably would have been a walk in the park compared to the life I was living now. At least then, I could have counted down the days until my release. I could have planned for my future. Now, I have no idea what my future holds. The government has me by one ball, Brian has me by the other, and they're both pulling as hard as they can.

CHAPTER ONE

Letting Andy and Craig talk me into the government scam was definitely a stupid mistake. No matter what anyone says, there is no such thing as easy money. There are always strings attached and there are always consequences – I found that out the hard way. All three of us were unemployed at the time and looking for a source of income. Andy heard that the British Government was offering financial aid to any start-up company who hired new staff from the ranks of the unemployed, and suggested we start a Staff Recruitment business.

Over the next few weeks, the three of us discussed the idea and Andy researched exactly how the Department of Trade and Industry plan worked.

"So here's what happens," he said. "Every time a new company is formed and hires unemployed people, they're eligible to apply for government assistance to help pay the wages."

"Like receiving a grant for each employee then?" said Craig.

"Absolutely," answered Andy. "And the sum is quite substantial for each employee you claim…and you're also able to claim any taxes paid for company equipment, computers, and what not."

"So what are we going to do with the staff we hire?" I asked. "I mean what is the company going to do?"

Andy's cheeks rose in a mischievous grin. "That's the beauty of it John. Our company isn't going to *do* anything…we're just going to set it up so it looks like we are."

From the beginning, I didn't think it was the best idea. Swindling the guy next door out of a few bucks was one thing, trying to scheme Her Majesty's Government out of a sizeable sum of money was quite another. But Andy and Craig were just so damn convincing with their arguments. I should have known better, but the thought of some quick money when your pockets are bare was just too hard to pass up. My morals went straight out the window and I agreed to help.

I knew defrauding the government was a crime but really, there were no outsiders involved, no one was going to get hurt or lose any of their own money. I guess in my eyes committing a "white collar crime" didn't seem all that bad. A year earlier, I'd have never dreamt I'd be involved in this sort of activity, but a year ago, I had a job and an income. Things and attitudes can change in an instant.

I didn't have to resign as Managing Director of Sim and Coventry, the family business, but I just couldn't stand the constant bickering and bashing of heads with my brother. Every decision I made was challenged or met with scorn. Sim and Coventry Limited was old and behind the times in so many ways. A fixture on the Liverpool business scene since 1845, it dealt with imports and exports. Profits were good and the business had a solid, upstanding reputation, but it hadn't really evolved and taken advantage of modern technology or even a fresh coat of paint. Office walls stained a yellowish-brown sludgy colour from decades of wafting cigar and cigarette smoke weren't exactly an enriching or inspiring environment for staff members still plunking away on manual typewriters. For the last forty years, every company memo issued by my father's secretary had the same raised "g" and "y". The Company was stuck in the past and I was more a man of the future.

I liked change and didn't mind taking a few risks. Maybe I just had a little more entrepreneurial spirit than my brother did. Young and single, I was a regular dashing British gentleman with notions of grandeur. I loved Sim and Coventry and had great pride in the company, but I just couldn't stay any longer. I knew Max had no intentions of leaving, so with a heavy heart I resigned my position, and at thirty-five years of age, set off to make a name for myself in the business world, without the crutch of the family name or the family money. Had I known then, what my future held, I might have just stuck it out. Hindsight is a bitch.

After leaving Sim and Coventry, I took a job as a travel agent at "Cosmopolitan Travel", a small agency in Liverpool. That led to a job with "RDR Travel" in Wilmslow, a small village south of Manchester. When "RDR Travel" ran into financial trouble, I seized the opportunity for myself and offered to buy the company. Not having any other options, the owner reluctantly agreed to my terms. Next, I made a trip to see Alex Schaeffer, the owner of "Cosmopolitan Travel", to persuade him to sell me the branch and offices in Liverpool. Soon, I was the proud owner of two travel agencies and a suite of offices. I was definitely on my way up.

Needing a personal assistant, I hired a young man from Liverpool named Richard Carrington. Bright and energetic, we hit it off immediately. A few months after he started, he came to me with a business idea. He suggested we pool our resources – my money and his contacts and knowledge – and start a record manufacturing company called "Ryker Records Ltd". While the main intent of the company was to physically press and produce records, Richard talked me into signing an artist named Paul Young, and recording and releasing his single.

When Young's single failed to make any impact on the "UK Top 200", Richard had the crazy idea of recording and producing a single for ourselves, under the name of "Funkmaster". We added our vocals to some "heavy" type of electronic music and much to my surprise, the song, "War Dance" cracked the "UK Top 100" and gave the company a hint of success and much needed exposure. An invite to the Cannes Music Festival in France followed, where we lounged on a yacht, hob knobbing with music industry types and tasting the sweet nectar of the luxurious life.

Unfortunately, "Ryker Records" needed more than one semi-hit record to pay the bills. The equipment was old, slow and forever breaking down and we still had a staff of employees – one of whom was Andy Trafford – to pay. In a financial mess, the only way out was to liquidate company assets and file for bankruptcy. Not wanting to face the consequences, Richard Carrington fled to the United States, leaving me to face our creditors alone. During this terrible time, Andy Trafford was one of the only people who stood by and supported me.

When most of my friends in the "record business" deserted me, Andy took pity and introduced me to many of his friends, including Craig. With the demise of the record company (which also included the travel business), I felt like a total failure, my confidence shot. Andy told me not to worry, that things would get better. He was the sort of friend a person needed in dark times, someone who enjoyed going out, having a bit of fun, and refreshing the spirit.

Spending time with Andy, Craig and their friends opened my eyes to a whole different lifestyle. Parties and small gatherings where copious amounts of marijuana took top billing was the norm and many of their friends were drug dealers selling on the street. I smoked cigarettes and drank alcohol but I'd never gotten into the drug scene. Didn't like the smell and didn't really see the purpose. I did however learn some tricks of the drug trade. Like how a wall in a house sometimes isn't a wall at all, and that bricks can be hollow. Being around Andy, Craig and their buddies gave me great insight into the ingenious methods and lengths one goes to hide and protect their drugs.

Andy was about 7 years younger than I was and lived with his mother in Wallasey, not too far from Liverpool. About 5'7" with a medium build, he fancied himself somewhat of a suave superstar with the ladies. I remember him calling me on the phone once while he was apparently screwing some girls' brains out. Such a classy fellow. His shiny blue Escort convertible and gray cloth peaked cap only added to his contrived debonair image. His words were fast and slick, just like his car, and I hopped on for the ride, really, not even questioning where we were headed. But I make no excuses, at the time, I was more than happy to strap on my seatbelt.

We leased some office space in the city of Ellesmere Port, a large industrial town about twenty kilometers south of Liverpool, created our company, and started applying for government grants on employees that never existed. With the dye cast, there was no turning back. We applied for tax rebates on an umpteen number of items the company was supposed to have purchased, and like clockwork, the government rebate cheques rolled in. Andy and Craig were ecstatic. I was astounded the government didn't send an agent out to check on the legitimacy of the business before the cheques hit the mail. At first, the cheques were small, like in the hundreds, but it didn't take long before they hit the tens of thousands. The money just kept coming.

Andy and Craig pranced around with grins down past their balls but my stomach grew weary and nervous with each passing day. The government might be slow but they weren't stupid. Sooner or later, someone in the Department of Trade was going to start asking questions. I wanted to shut things down, divide up the profits and be on my way. I'd made enough money to get myself going again in a legitimate business, and if we played our cards right and didn't do anything to raise suspicion; we might just get away with it.

After a long heart to heart with Andy, he agreed it was time to close down operations. Craig was furious and wanted to keep running the scam. Money was a drug and he just couldn't get enough. A few days before we were set to fold the company, a representative from the Department of Industry paid the office a visit. Of course, I happened to be the only one there at the time. Lucky me.

He was a tallish man with a graying moustache and thinning brown hair who certainly fit the profile of a government pooch. By the crinkled net of curious wrinkles on his brow, I knew he wasn't in the mood to chat about the weather. He flashed his credentials and asked if he could look around. We were dead.

"So where's your staff?"

"Oh they're all out at the moment…running errands…taking an extra-long lunch. You know how people can be." I didn't know what else to say.

He smirked as a sarcastic chuckle slipped from the corner of his chapped mouth. "Yes I know exactly how people can be."

Surveying the nearly empty space, he made a few notes in a thick blue binder and left. My heart dropped, lodging somewhere between my lungs and my stomach, making breathing a difficult task. There was no way that man wasn't going to report us. I still believed that if we moved fast enough, dissolved the business, and just disappeared, we might get away with it. I could lay low for a while, stay out of trouble and in time, everything would be okay. And it might have, if Craig hadn't been such a greedy jackass.

A few weeks later, Andy called to tell me Craig had started up another fake business. I honestly couldn't believe he would be that stupid but I guess the lure of the big dough had gotten the best of him. Even worse, as soon as Craig got his first rebate cheque, he went to the bank and demanded they give him the total amount in cash. The idiot spent every penny on lavish clothes, expensive jewelry, and fancy dinners. So much for keeping things quiet.

His bank manager became suspicious at the sudden influx of cash into Craig's account and called the police. It didn't matter; the government agents were already hot on his trail. A few days later, Craig was arrested. I was scared shitless and figured they'd be coming for me next. I decided to disappear and figured South Africa would be as good a place as any. It was far away and had a good exchange rate, so my money would last longer. I also didn't think any South African banks would bother asking me too many questions, especially about the large cash deposits I'd need to make.

Very carefully, I started planning my escape. I didn't want to raise suspicion by clearing out my bank accounts in one fell swoop, so I made small cash withdrawals from all of my accounts as often as I could, and hid the money in a case in my room. A second passport was a must, just in case British authorities confiscated the first.

A grey sheet of rain pounded against the car window as I drove to the passport office in Liverpool. Putting on some James Bond charm, I explained to the attractive blond woman behind the counter that I had to go on a business trip to China and Taiwan, and since both countries hated each other, the British government recommended I get a second passport – one to present in China and the other to present in Taiwan. That way, each country's stamp of approval wouldn't appear on the same passport and my travel plans wouldn't be compromised.

The office seemed to buy my story and issued me a second legal passport under the same name. I kept one passport on me at all times, and the other, I hid in my father's study behind a book on Winston Churchill. I continued to stockpile funds and prepare for my getaway. The thought of leaving my family and my home almost killed me but freedom seemed to be a much better option than a lengthy prison sentence. If only I'd had a damn crystal ball.

A few days after apprehending Craig, the authorities caught up with Andy. Both were charged with "deception". Two down, one to go. I was feeling the heat and the kettle was about to boil over. Things had gotten crazy and I needed a chance to clear my head and calm my nerves. My parents were away for a few days visiting friends along the coast and it was a good thing. I hadn't yet told them what had happened or that I was planning to leave for South Africa in the next week or so. I figured the less they knew the better off they would be. I had just come back from taking a walk in the orchards on the family estate when a pounding shook the old wooden front door.

"Hello, can I help you?"

"Are you Mr. John Coventry?"

"Yes I am."

He held out his hand. "My name is Peter Atwood. My partner and I are from Her Majesty's Department of Customs and Excise. We'd like to have a few words with you if we could."

"Of course, come in." My heart sank to the bottom of my toes. This was it, the moment I had been trying to escape.

My arrest was imminent. The Customs and Excise Department has wide sweeping powers in the United Kingdom and unlike the police, don't need a warrant to enter the premises. I invited them into the drawing room, all the while pretending I didn't have a clue as to why they were there.

"Helen," I said to the housekeeper, "would you mind putting on a pot of coffee for our visitors?" I took a seat in my father's oversized leather chair, crossed my legs, and rubbed the side of my nose with the back of my hand, pretending this was just a typical visit on a typical day.

"Have a seat please gentlemen," I said pointing to the sofa. The two men sat down and Peter Atwood placed his well-worn briefcase in front of him.

"Nice place you have here," he said looking around the room.

"Thank-you…yes Townfield has been in the family for generations. The estate itself has a much-storied history. In fact, right out there in the orchards was the exact spot King William and his army pitched their tents on their way to fight the Irish in the Battle of the Boyne in 1690. You'd be amazed at the sort of artifacts found over the years."

Peter raised his eyebrows, "Really? What sorts?"

"Well cannon balls, clay pipes and clay pots…some other personal goods. My father has a record of everything around here somewhere. And that wood flooring in the front hall? Original with the house…we're all amazed it's lasted this long." A half-hearted laugh escaped through the rapid heaving of my lungs.

"That's really quite interesting, Mr. Coventry," grinned Atwood, "but I think you know we're not here for a history lesson."

The housekeeper set an antique wooden tray on the table

and poured the steaming coffee into the three mugs without breaking stride or losing a drop.

"Thank-you Helen," I said with a smile. "Would you mind closing the door on your way out?"

"Certainly sir," she answered sneaking a glimpse at Atwood's unkempt fingernails.

I waited until I heard the click of the door handle before answering Atwood. "Actually," I said taking a sip of my coffee, "I have no idea why you're here."

The other man laughed while Atwood bent down and unlocked his briefcase. He took out a file folder and held it in the air in front of him.

"Maybe this will help jog your memory." He opened the file and began reading. "Name, John Coventry. Born, May 9th, 1951 in Brookfield, in Wirral Cheshire to parents John and Evelyn. Has a younger brother named Max." He looked up from his papers. "So far so good?"

I nodded. "Seems accurate."

He nodded and continued reading. "In the past year you opened a new business. Is that correct?"

Shit…here it comes. "Yes that's correct."

"And you and your associates applied and received rebates and tax breaks for the hiring of staff and purchase of new equipment?"

"Yes that's correct."

"But you never actually hired any staff or purchased any of that equipment did you Mr. Coventry?"

I was caught. He knew it and I knew it. There was no point in lying anymore but I didn't want to say anything more without a lawyer present.

"I'd prefer not to answer that question."

He looked annoyed and his large forehead grew red with anger but his voice stayed calm. "Okay then, maybe I need to be a bit more specific." He read through the entire list of staff names and purchases we lied about. He seemed to know everything right down to the tiniest detail. There was no way I was getting out of this jam, even with a lawyer present. I was heading to jail.

He stopped reading and took a long drink from his coffee cup. "Very good coffee by the way. Just how I like it, strong and full of flavour. Not many people get it right, but your housekeeper…I just may have to take her home so she can make my coffee."

I wasn't really in the mood for small talk and I couldn't quite figure what Atwood was up to. Why hadn't they arrested me yet? I didn't give a shit whether or not he liked the coffee. He flipped through some more pages, then stood up and strode around the room. A shorter man with a medium build and receding blondish hair, his blue suit looked a size too big and the sleeves came down to the middle of his fingers. Obviously, he'd never employed the help of a tailor. He had these huge rimmed glasses and blue eyes that never seemed to look right at you – one was always a little off. It was unnerving.

"So what do you know about the drugs?" he asked.

"Nothing really," I answered. "Andy and Craig smoked a lot of pot but I never saw too much else." I was keeping my mouth shut on this one; I was already in enough trouble.

"You know nothing? I find that a little curious."

"I don't do drugs and I've never had anything to do with them," I answered. "I'm not sure what more I can tell you."

The wine glasses hanging from the cocktail bar clinked precariously as he marched across the handcrafted wooden floor and slammed the file folder on the oak coffee table. His left eye twitched as if the circuit from his brain was overloading.

"I think you know a lot more than what you're telling us. Like names and places."

"I only know Andy, Craig and a few of their friends. I'm telling you, I never got involved."

"Well I guess that makes you a fucking angel doesn't it," he glared. "Do you have any idea how much trouble you're in right now? You will spend a very long time in prison, meet some lovely new friends who won't hesitate to kick the bloody shit out of you if the mood strikes. And what about your beloved house? They'll be no more pleasant walks out in the orchard looking for artifacts or any of this wonderful coffee." He took another sip and paused, giving his fiery red cheeks a chance to calm down. "John, you seem like a fine gentleman…you really do and I like you. I think you've made a few very dim-witted mistakes and gotten yourself muddled up with some bad people. I don't think jail is your kind of place."

I had to agree with him. The thought of spending years in jail made me sick to my stomach. I hated confrontation of any sort and I knew I didn't have the type of personality to survive the rigors of prison. Being some guys' bitch wasn't an appealing prospect. What a total fool I'd been. First committing the crime, and then thinking I could get away with it. I'd disgraced my family and myself. I certainly was sorry for what I'd done, but there wasn't a thing I could do to change it. At least I didn't think so.

"Here's the thing," he said pushing up his glasses. "We might just be able to help you, if you're willing to help us with a few things."

I didn't like where this conversation was heading. Atwood had a weird snarl on his lips like a cat ready to pounce. I needed a drink. I poured myself a very large scotch from the cocktail bar at the end of the room. I wasn't about to offer my guests any, I wasn't that much of a gentleman. Taking a large swig, the liquid burned as it rushed down my throat. It felt like my last blood and testament before being led to slaughter.

"What do I have to do?" I asked.

"Oh splendid John! You've made the right choice."

I took another drink, quickly wiping away the drop of scotch escaping down my chin. "I didn't say I was going to do anything…yet. Tell me what you want."

"Well to start…I want to know all the names and addresses of those people you've met who are dealing drugs. Times, dates, places…anything you can remember. There's no such thing as too much detail."

We talked for the better part of the day and I told them everything I knew about Andy's drug friends. The fake walls, the hollow bricks, who I thought was dealing and those who were just using. Atwood and his partner took notes the entire time. Helen brought in some sandwiches and a fresh pot of coffee, so we took a short ten-minute break. The process was exhausting. If Atwood wasn't happy, he'd snap at me with his sharp voice.

"Details John! I need details! How do you expect me to help you when you're giving me drivel like this?"

"I'm telling you everything I know!" I yelled. "It's not like I had a bloody camera or a tape recorder with me."

"All right," said the other man. "Let's everybody keep a cool head."

Atwood drilled me a while longer, constantly re-reading his notes, and asking for clarification. Finally, he put down his pen and closed up his notebook.

"I think we're about done here John."

"Are you sure?" I answered. "I mean…don't you want to know who was sleeping with who or who shit three times a day?"

Atwood laughed. "There's no need for sarcasm, Mr. Coventry. The more information we have, the better we can help you."

"So how exactly are you going to help me?"

"Well…if everything you've told us here today checks out, then I'll have a word with the judge in your trial and try and make things as easy as possible for you."

"That's it?" I asked. "You'll try and make things easier? What the hell is that supposed to mean?"

"Be patient John," Atwood answered. "You've given us a great deal of information. Let us process it and we'll be in touch. We'll show ourselves out. Thank you for your time."

I was glad they were gone. It gave me some time alone to think and sort through what had just happened. Thoughts of South Africa still lingered in my head but I needed a few more days to clear out my accounts. I had to be careful since the government was probably tailing me now. One wrong step and any good will Atwood offered would surely be in the toilet. I was just going to have to wait it out. I poured myself another scotch and lit a cigarette. My life was a fucking mess.

CHAPTER TWO

For the next couple of days, I was on pins and needles, hardly sleeping, or eating. I continued withdrawing small amounts of cash and hiding the money in the briefcase wedged at the back of my closet. I wasn't taking any chances. One well-placed phone call from Peter Atwood, and I'd be denied access to all my assets and bank accounts. The power of the government is a frightful thing. I was sitting in the drawing room chatting with my parents when the doorbell rang.

"John," said Helen popping her head in the room. "The gentlemen from the other day are back to see you."

My father gave me a concerned look, "What gentlemen?"

"Oh it's nothing," I said quickly getting off my chair. "Just going over the details of a business venture that's all."

"Anything you need my help with?" he asked.

"At the moment I'm not really sure." Truth be told, keeping the whole incident from my parents was tearing me up inside. We'd always been open and honest with each other but until I knew for sure what was going to happen, I thought it best to keep them in the dark.

Peter Atwood and his partner were waiting for me in the front hall.

"Hello John," said Peter holding out his hand. "So nice to see you again."

I ignored his hand and pushed open the front door. "Let's talk outside." The men followed me onto the porch. "Okay so what's going on?"

"Actually John, it's such a nice day and you have such a

brilliant property, I say we go for a walk." Atwood started down the stairs and followed the cobblestone path leading to the gardens.

I was anxious and annoyed that he was taking his time. "So am I going to jail or what?"

Atwood smiled. "I'm very pleased with you. Everything you told us checked out. That's a good start."

"A start?" I said. "I thought that was it."

He looked at his partner and laughed. "Oh John you're so naïve. You actually think the Government is going to let you off that easy after you and your friends made off with a substantial amount of their money? Which I might add hasn't been accounted for either?" His voice dripped of sarcasm and disdain.

"Okay fine, I get it. What do you want me to do?"

"Your job is to become friends with those friends of Andrew and Craig's…the ones who were dealing the drugs and such. I want you to infiltrate the group and make yourself an intimate member, keeping your eyes and ears open at all times. Of course, I'll expect a detailed report every few days. We'll meet at the Midland Hotel in Manchester. If this works out and you do a good job, then we might really be able to help you with any court action taken against you in the matter of the fraud case. If you don't help us, then we certainly can't help you and you'll be prosecuted to the full extent of the law."

I couldn't help but scoff, "I see you've given me a multitude of options." I wanted to wipe the smirk off Atwood's face with a quick backhand. "Fine…I guess I have no choice but to agree. I'll do my best to find out everything I can, but I hope you realize I'm no undercover agent."

"On the contrary John," he said raising his eyebrow. "You're *my* undercover agent." He slapped me on the back and turned to walk away. "I'll be in touch. In the meantime, go make some new friends."

I collapsed into the lawn chair and watched them walk away. I'd just made a deal with the devil, who'd asked me to make an even riskier deal with another devil. Getting mixed-up with drug runners and heaven knows what else not only worried me; it scared me to death. South Africa was looking better and better all the time.

I sat in the garden forever, just thinking and watching the fish swim so effortlessly in the pond. If I ran, there was the distinct possibility I would never return home, to my family, to my beloved Townfield. I didn't know if that was something I could live with for the rest of my life. I already felt like such a disappointment to my parents, especially my father. He worked so hard for the family, and at every opportunity, I seemed to blow it.

My father worked at the family firm just as his father Hubert had done before. When I joined at the age of twenty-five, followed by my brother, it carried the family tradition forward. Around 5'9" very slender with a tanned complexion, my father controlled his mop of jet-black hair with a comb through of Vaseline. Family rumours attribute the tanned complexion of my father (and me) to an affair many, many generations ago during the time of the Spanish Armada. No one knows for sure but it does seem odd that every once and a while a Coventry baby is born without the typical fair skin and mousey brown hair.

Dad loved his work. Six days a week, he would always be the first one in the office and the last one to leave. With stacks of papers here there and everywhere, his office was an organized mess, although he was meticulous about keeping notes and documenting everything – just in case. A thick layer of dust and smoke from his insatiable habit covered the whole lot, yet he forbade anyone to clean or re-arrange his papers. Despite being very careful with money and expenses, he was incredibly generous to his family and we never wanted in any way. I idolized my father, always have, always will.

The relationship between my parents was amazing and I can honestly say I never heard them argue even once. They were kind, loving, and extremely supportive of each other and us kids. "Right or wrong, the family always comes first" my father used to say. Thankfully, he kept that promise because there were many times over the years I called on my parents for support, guidance, and goodwill, and not once did they ever shut me out or turn me away. Their love carried me through many a dark day and even darker night.

The tightening in my chest told me I couldn't keep my secret any longer. I had to tell them about the charges and Peter Atwood. Sooner or later, they were going to find out and I wanted them to hear it from me, not some policeman knocking on the door ready to take me away in handcuffs. I sensed they already had a feeling something was wrong but every time they asked, I just lied and told them "not to worry, everything was fine." I owed them an explanation. I owed them the truth.

My father was still sitting in the drawing room when I returned.

"What was that all about son?" he asked. "You look quite pale. Are you feeling okay?"

I slouched down in the leather chair opposite his. "I need to talk to you and Mother. I have something to tell you."

The crinkles in his brow deepened, pushing his brown eyes into a squint as he folded up his newspaper and set it on the side table.

"Come, come, then…into the dining room. I'll go find your mother."

Family conferences always took place in the dining room with my mother present. He pulled his leather armchair up to the head of the table and readied his pen. My father loved these conferences and discussions, whether they were about finances, politics, or other pressing family matters. He would put forth one point of view on the subject, discuss it thoroughly, then bring in the opposing point of view and discuss it in detail. Then he'd go back to the original point of view, and so forth until he was sure he'd gotten it right. The process could be long and tedious but no one could ever accuse him of not thinking things through. Sometimes I wish I'd inherited more of that trait from him.

His bookkeeping was excellent and at any given moment, he could tell you exactly how much money, down to the penny, was in each of his and my mothers' bank accounts. It was truly incredible. He didn't trust banks or bankers and when the bank statement came every month, he would sit down and with great care go over every transaction to make sure it was correct and matched his own. He never owned a credit card, a debit card, or a cheque guarantee card and said that if anyone wasn't satisfied with his word and his cheque, then they need not have his money.

All great old houses have their secret rooms and Townfield was no exception. Tucked away in one of the five cellars was a little space my father used as the family strong room. There he kept his meticulous notes and records hidden away under lock and key. Each member of the family, going back for generations, had their own file marked with their initials. Many of the papers had yellowed with age, only slightly dimming the ink from the ancient goose feather quills.

Nothing was left to chance with my father, everything was recorded in these notes and kept forever; wills, birth certificates, death certificates, financial information. Anything he deemed relevant survived behind those four walls. Alarmed and booby-trapped like a fortress, entrance to the thick wooden main door was safeguarded by a master key, which my father kept safe and sound in his pocket. I'd always thought the numerous notes he took were a complete and utter waste of time. How wrong I was.

The weight of their sympathetic eyes bearing down on my own guilt-ridden ones jostled the contents of my stomach, inching them up my throat like a caterpillar climbing a tree. My father ripped the covering off a fresh pack of cigarettes, placed one in his mouth, and flicked the switch on his gold-plated lighter. A few short puffs and the end glowed a bright orange ember. He passed the lighter to my mother.

I had no idea where to begin. How was I going to tell the two people I loved most in the world, that I'd messed up royally and there was a good possibility I was going to jail for a long time if I didn't agree to go undercover for the British Government? The words seemed unreal in my head, how the hell was I going to say them out loud?

"Okay John," said my father. "Something's being going on with you lately, we've both noticed you haven't been yourself and now these men show up at the door today. Enough with it…let's have it."

Pride isn't the easiest meal to swallow but I gulped hard, got it down, and started talking.

"So that man today was from the Customs and Excise Department then?" said my father.

"Yes…and he wants me to go undercover to discover as much about the drug runners as I can." My mother's hand shot up from the table to catch her gasp. "In return, they'll do what they can to help make my fraud case as easy as possible."

"I see," said my father. The entire time I talked, he'd taken notes. "Now let me get this straight..." He went through his papers and reiterated some of the main points. I did my best to answer him fully and truthfully. Finally, he set the papers down and looked me square in the eye.

"I think it's best we call a lawyer." He wasn't cross or angry and most of all he didn't judge me for what I'd done. "I'll do whatever I can to help you John. You have our full support. Whatever you need...advice, money, whatever...we're here. Right or wrong, family always comes first."

Finally telling my parents the truth about what'd been happening the last few months was like lifting a concrete block off my chest. Snuffing out his cigarette, my father pulled back his chair, picked up his stack of papers and disappeared to the drawing room to call his lawyer and set up an appointment. My mother just looked at me, her empathetic smile melting away my fear of her disappointment and disapproval.

"Let's go in the garden and we'll have Helen bring us some tea." She clutched my hand in hers. "It'll all work out."

A charming woman who has always been very kind and generous to me, my mother has lived her life with that "make the best out of it" and "pull yourself together" attitude. I appreciated the fact she didn't intend to lecture me or tell me what I did was wrong. God knows I'd already beaten myself up enough for both of us. I was just grateful to have her love and her support. While we waited for Helen to bring the tea, we took a walk around the property and reminisced about times when life didn't seem so complicated.

The main gates of Townfield are at the apex of a triangle with three roads running by its side. Opened and closed electronically from the main house further up the white pebbled drive, the large black iron gates with their golden tips mark the entrance to the driveway of the grand old estate. Lined with rare Espalier pear and apple trees on one side and regular variety fruit trees on the other, the driveway welcome's visitors to the oasis of the property. The Espalier fruit trees were very, very old, their branches trained by generations of gardeners to reach out to the next tree like outstretched arms and fingertips.

To the right of the drive lies a separate orchard filled with beautiful apple and Victoria plum trees. Those trees provided a great refuge from my Grandmother Poldy on the occasions when a young lad needed to climb a tree in a hurry to escape his wrongdoings. It was also in this orchard that I pitched a tent with Max, my younger brother for our very first all night campout. Further up the drive was the gorgeous pond garden, designed by my father, and home to over one hundred and fifty goldfish, frogs, and newts. During the summer months, we'd all sit by the pond feeding the fish and having our afternoon tea. It was a wonderful place, so peaceful and serene. I miss those times when we'd all be together, talking, laughing, and just spending time as a family. I was very lucky to have such a place to grow up in – so carefree and full of adventure. As a boy at Townfield, there was never a dull moment.

Down a little bit more along the driveway was the main lawn, an expansive patch of grass bordered by an equally large flowering garden that bloomed from the first drop of spring dew to the first chilled winds of winter. An amazing sight to see, it was easy to get lost if you didn't know your way through the smaller cobblestone paths and mazes of beauty. A final sweep toward the front of the house revealed the prized rose garden, six large beds of brilliant roses, their different shades providing a rainbow backdrop to the tall flagpole that proudly flew the flag of St. George, the flag of England, and never the Union Jack. A gigantic willow tree grew on the main lawn and I can remember many an afternoon spent swinging on its branches and relaxing in its shade.

Four large handcrafted stone steps gave way to the big black wooden door marking the entryway to the house and the main hallway with its original wooden block flooring. On one wall, the huge portrait painting of "Aunt Rebecca", one of my ancestors who lived in the 1700's beckoned guest's hello, while on the opposite wall hung a painting of the Battle of Trafalgar, where Lord Nelson defeated the Franco-Spanish fleet during one of the Napoleonic Wars. The paintings, artifacts, and general demeanor of the décor gave a sense of how deep the Coventry family roots ran in English society.

Two days after the family conference in the dining room, my father and I had a meeting with the lawyer in Liverpool. His constant removal and scratching at the side of his head gave me the impression I was in some pretty deep shit.

"I'll make some enquiries on your behalf," he said. "But I have to tell you from a legal perspective, it doesn't look good. You'll be facing a prolonged jail sentence…that much is for sure."

We went over my options but I knew in my heart I had no choice but to cooperate with Atwood and the government. At this point, fleeing the country would only make matters worse.

Later that day my father and I were sitting in the drawing room having a drink when the lawyer called back. He confirmed Craig and Andy were in custody awaiting trial and that police had issued a warrant for my arrest on the charge of "deception". Even though I was expecting the charge, the news still felt like a jagged knife to the chest. Now it was official. I was a wanted man. Knowing my future was in the hands of someone else wasn't a pleasant feeling. Stupid ass! I had no one to blame but myself. I'd gotten into this mess and I was going to have to pay the price to get myself out. I'd run out of time and I'd run out of excuses. I telephoned Peter Atwood to confirm our first meeting at the Midland Hotel and braced myself for an uncertain and unwanted future. Very wary of my clandestine meeting with the Customs and Excise people, my father didn't want me going alone and was quite concerned for my safety.

"I will go to these meetings with you John," he said. "They won't know I'm there but I promise I'll be sitting somewhere close by and watching the entire time. I don't trust them."

"I'm not entirely sure I trust them either," I answered. "It'd be nice seeing a friendly face, even if it is just a passing glance."

"So it's a deal then?"

"It's a deal."

"Splendid." He took a large gulp of his gin and tonic and adjusted his bottom to a more comfortable position in his chair. "When is the meeting?"

"Saturday."

Steeped in tradition and luxury, The Midland Hotel is one of the main hotels in the heart of Manchester. Built around the turn of the twentieth century, it's played host to a slew of business deals and is a destination point for celebrities and many of the worlds' wealthy and elite. My father and I arrived early for the meeting and parked in a side lot. The plan was for me to enter the hotel first and find a table in the lounge. He would hang back in the car and wait fifteen minutes before he entered the hotel from a separate entrance.

Out of the corner of my eye, I watched him pull open the front doors and walk through the main foyer.

Peter Atwood couldn't have picked a more ideal location for the meetings then the lounge at the Midland Hotel. It was three steps up to get to the main lounge and five more stairs to sit on the top platform. My father found a table on the platform, giving him an unimpeded view of the main lounge area, including my table. He nonchalantly took the newspaper out of his briefcase and started to read. No one would have suspected a thing. I couldn't help but smile; it was as if he was born for this undercover life.

I, on the other hand, was quite nervous and couldn't stop checking my watch. At exactly three o'clock, Peter Atwood strode into the lounge in his ill-fitting suit and muddy shoes, looking out of place in the splendor of the hotel. He glanced around the lounge, spotted my table, and had a seat.

"Here's the deal John." His voice was just above a whisper and I had to lean in closer than I wanted. His breath smelt like a mish mash of garlic, onions, and over-fried fish. It was all I could do not to back away in disgust. "I want you to get close to a group of people in Wallasey and Birkenhead. Start out by giving a man named Peter Barrington a call. Do you know who he is?"

I nodded. "I've met him on several occasions."

"Excellent," said Atwood. "He's not the one we're interested in but we're hoping he introduces you to some other, more important people."

"So what do I say to Peter Barrington? You want me to just call him up out of the blue?"

"Take it nice and easy…be real casual. Ask him if he wants to get together for a drink. Whatever you do, don't be nervous like you are right now. People like Barrington and his buddies can smell fear in a heartbeat. They'll wonder why you're afraid and start asking you questions you can't answer. Once that happens, it's over…and if we have to pull you out of there because you've fucked up…then start picturing yourself in an eight by ten cell." He wiped his mouth with the handkerchief from his left blazer pocket. "So my suggestion to you? Don't fuck up!" He said the words slowly and deliberately like I was still in the third grade or something.

I hated the way he spoke to me in that condescending voice of his. Give a man a badge and he thinks he can run the goddamn world, talking to people any way he pleases. Thinks he's all high and mighty but he's no different from anyone else. Judging by the looks of him he probably goes home at night to an empty flat, where his only friend is a stray cat named Bennie who persistently pisses on the floor. Making others seem small is his only means of empowerment.

"Peter Barrington has a large circle of friends," he continued. "Get to know these friends, especially three girls who live together in a house in Wallasey…it's close to Barrington's place. It's here you'll more than likely meet those next in the chain of command. In particular, there's a man named Brian who runs a scrap dealership in Birkenhead. He's a man of definite interest. Find out all you can and meet me back here in one week at eleven am." He took a business card out of his pocket. There was no name, just two numbers. "Here's my office number and my home number. If you need me at all, any time of the day or night…call. Is that understood?"

I put the card in my pocket and nodded in agreement. Atwood stood up to leave. "Wait," I said. He sat back down. "What about the police warrant for my arrest?"

He smiled. "Don't worry about it. I'll speak to them and

everything will be fine. In the meantime, let me know if anything develops before next week." Picking up his woolen hat from the table, he left in the same direction he came.

Not to raise any suspicions, my father waited a half an hour before folding up his newspaper and leaving the hotel. I waited another twenty minutes and left by a different exit. I was pleased at how the meeting had gone. Despite Atwood being a patronizing jackass, what he wanted me to do didn't seem all that difficult. I was good with people and made friends easily. All I had to do was keep my nose out of trouble. My father wanted a full re-cap of the meeting on the way home. He didn't say much and we finished the drive in silence, lost in our own thoughts.

As soon as I got home to Townfield, I gave Peter Barrington a call. I wasn't at all nervous about ringing him up, he seemed like a nice enough fellow and for some reason he liked me. He was pleasantly surprised to hear my voice on the other end of the phone. Wallasey was only about a twenty-minute drive from my house, so we agreed to meet later that evening for a drink at a local pub.

I was already sitting at the bar sipping my drink when Peter walked in wearing a mega-sized grin. He was a skinny guy, about six feet tall and always looked like he'd just rolled out of bed and forgotten to shave. He gave me a big friendly wave and pulled up an empty stool.

"Great to see you John! So glad you called. I was wondering what I might do with myself tonight and well…here you are!" He nodded as the bartender filled him a pint of draft and set it on the soggy coaster.

"They know me here." Barrington smiled, tipped the glass back, and drained almost half the contents in a couple gulps. "They got Craig and Andy you know?"

"I know…I heard."

"Poor bastards. I talked to Andy a couple days before the arrest and he was saying things would have been fine if Craig hadn't been a fucking moron and tried the gig on his own. Not sure what he was thinking."

"I've been wondering that myself," I said.

Barrington was laughing, "The man's got shit for brains I think! I mean how fucking stupid can you be? It's like he was asking to be caught and couldn't have cared less that he was taking you and Andy down with him." He took another swig of beer. "How is it that you're still free and the other two are in jail anyway?"

I shook my head. "I don't know. But I'm sure the police are getting close. In the meantime I'll enjoy my freedom." I ordered up another drink and desperately wanted to steer the subject away from my involvement. I wasn't anxious talking to Barrington but I also didn't want him to pick up any signals I may have been inadvertently giving off. I needn't have worried. He was too busy downing his drink and trying to get in the pants of the cute brunette sitting a few stools over. Unfortunately, he wasn't having much luck.

"Let's get the fuck out of here and go to my place," he said throwing some bills on the table from the stash in his pocket. He was staring at the brunette. "The action's a little stale tonight."

I was quite certain Barrington didn't have a job, yet he always seemed to have enough money for food, smokes, drink, and whatever else peaked his fancy. He was generating an income somehow and it wasn't by selling Girl Guide cookies. Halfway out to the car he changed his mind.

"Screw my place, I have a better idea. I want to introduce you to some friends of mine."

That was exactly what I wanted to hear. First meeting with my contact and I'm getting introduced to the circle of friends. This undercover work was a piece of cake. I'll just get the information Atwood wanted and be on my way. Andy and Craig were rotting away in prison and here I was at the local pub having a few pints and shooting the shit. It wasn't such a bad deal.

We pulled the car up to a dilapidated house that desperately needed a bright yellow condemned sign and a date with a wrecking ball. The roof was caving in over the porch and the whole structure reeked of rotten wood. Barrington knocked and pushed open the door. The inside of the house was almost as bad as the out. How could people live in such a disgusting mess? Stained with dampness, the half painted pale blue walls sported long sheets of wallpaper that hung down like they were rolls of toilet paper. It would take more than a coat of paint to freshen up this place.

As I walked in the door, the intense smell of marijuana engulfed my senses and I could feel my lungs searing with each inhale. I followed Barrington down a very narrow and claustrophobic hallway to a dingy sitting room, where a group of about five or six people was hanging out smoking pot, and drinking beer. They gave Barrington a warm hello.

"This is John," he said. "He's a friend of Andy and Craig's. Make him welcome." The group nodded and smiled, seeming to recognize my name. I didn't know if that was a good thing or a bad thing.

Barrington handed me a can of beer from the table and motioned his hand. "Go ahead and mingle." I lit a cigarette and Barrington lit a joint.

"Ahh...that's better," he said taking a big breath in. He held the drag in his lungs for as long as he could, then slowly exhaled, sending the smoke to rest on the dirty, discoloured lampshade. He held the joint out for me.

"Oh no thanks," I said. "I like to stick with cigarettes."

He shrugged his shoulders and turned his attention to one of the girls. I never touched marijuana myself, couldn't stand the smell and I'd never had any desire to experiment with harder drugs. I could drink myself silly but drugs were not my cup of tea. Now Peter Atwood was asking me to dive head first into the drug world and it was up to me whether I was going to sink or swim. I wasn't even sure what kind of drugs Andy's crowd was in to. I'd seen them smoking weed and popping the odd pill or two but I was no expert on the subject. In order to survive and not arouse any suspicions, I'd need to be a fast learner.

I surveyed the room, looking for a place to start. I caught eyes with an attractive brown haired woman and smiled. She smiled back and casually made her way over to where I was standing.

"So you're Andy's friend are you? My name is Jane."

"Hello Jane."

"Seems he got himself in a wee bit of trouble didn't he? Him and Craig…and you for that matter."

I sort of laughed. "I guess you could say that."

"Oh God…you guys are the talk of the bloody town. Didn't cha know that?"

"Actually, I had no idea," I answered. "I've been trying to keep a low profile."

"I bet you have," said Jane. "Well with Craig and Andy already in jail, the police must be hauling up your ass."

"So far so good," I said crossing my fingers. "Let's hope it stays that way."

Jane and I spent the rest of the night talking and getting to know each other. She wanted to keep talking about Andy and Craig and I engaged her for as long as possible without having to backtrack on my story. I took extra caution choosing my words and did my best not to say anything that might tip her off. I didn't get a chance to talk to anyone else in the room; nobody other than Jane seemed to give a shit I was even there. It was only my first visit and I didn't want to push things.

I dropped Barrington off at his place around one am and we made plans to get together again the next week. I was quite happy with the progress I'd made and wondered if Atwood would feel the same. Probably not, but tonight I didn't care. I was glad to be on my way home to Townfield, where the air was fresh and I wasn't afraid of picking up a communicable disease by sitting on the couch. It was a big night for me. I hadn't seen any drugs, except the pot, but I did solidify my friendship with Peter Barrington and met Jane. She had some potential in more ways than one.

As scheduled, I met with Atwood at the Midland Hotel on Saturday. Once again, my father took an inconspicuous seat on the platform and watched the proceedings.

"What did you find out?" said Atwood flatly. He took out a little notepad from his pocket and started writing.

"Well I met Peter Barrington for a drink at a local pub and then he suggested he go to a friend's house."

"Where was the house? What did it look like? And who lived there?"

I answered all his questions, told him about Jane, and said how she was very interested in what was happening with Craig, Andy and I.

"How many people were there?" asked Atwood.

"Oh I don't know…about five or six…not including Barrington and me."

"What was everyone doing specifically?"

"Specifically?" I laughed. "They were drinking beer, smoking weed, and just sitting around. It really wasn't all that interesting."

"This girl Jane…do you think you can get close to her?" he asked. "She seems like she enjoys chatting. Get to know her real well and see what you can find out."

"I'll do my best."

"By the way, I need to know what car you were driving. The colour and the registration number."

"Why does it matter?"

"It's not your concern why it matters, I just need to know."

I shrugged my shoulders and gave him the information about the car, which in fact belonged to my father. It never dawned on me he wanted the information so he could have me followed.

"When are you meeting with Barrington next?"

"We made plans to get together next week," I answered.

"Not until next week?" He sounded disappointed. "Well where are you meeting and what are the plans?"

"Not exactly sure what the plans are," I said. "We didn't make up an itinerary."

"Don't get smart with me John," he answered sharply. "Remember, I'm the one holding all the cards at the moment and keeping your ass out of jail."

"How could I forget," I retorted. "You remind me every time we talk."

He folded up his little black note pad and shoved it into an inner pocket of his sloppy suit coat. "We'll meet again here next week at the same time. It's a good start but try and probe a little deeper. I need something more solid to go on."

"I'll do my best."

"You do that John." He picked up his briefcase from beside the table and walked out.

A few days later, my lawyer called with an update. There was a warrant for my arrest, but the police wouldn't get around to enforcing it for at least a month or two. The judge also agreed to bail. I hung up the phone and breathed a huge sigh of relief. Perhaps Atwood wasn't quite the jackass I thought. I guess he did make a few phone calls on my behalf. At least now, I could walk by a cop on the street and not worry about him slapping on the cuffs and carting me away.

The last few weeks had been torture for my parents and I. Every phone call, every knock on the front door caused a tightening of the muscles and dryness in the throat. With a month or so reprieve, I could concentrate on getting the information Atwood wanted and maybe, just maybe, put myself in a position to make a formal deal with the government that would save my neck. Failing that, I now had enough time to finish cleaning out my bank accounts and prepare for a midnight dash to South Africa.

CHAPTER THREE

"So I can't quite figure out why your sorry ass hasn't been arrested yet," said Barrington as we drove out to Middlesbrough in Yorkshire. He needed to meet some 'business partners' and asked if I wanted to tag along. "Andrew and Craig are being held without bail and you're still free."

"I'm not sure what's going on," I lied. "I guess they don't have enough evidence on me yet."

"Ya…that's probably it." He looked at me and grinned. "You lucky bastard. Wouldn't that be something if they never got hold of you?"

"Ya that would be something wouldn't it?

Middlesbrough was a long drive from Liverpool and I was a bit apprehensive about having to spend the night in a strange house with people I knew nothing about. The journey would take us completely across England, over the Pennines Mountains, through the desolate moors of Yorkshire and then northward toward the Scottish border. The city of Middlesbrough itself was working class and quite run-down with a crime rate almost double that of the rest of the United Kingdom. It was a perfect spot for drug runners to set up shop with its proximity to the River Tees and the North Sea.

The hammering rain did nothing to enhance my first impression of the poor inner city housing estate Barrington had me turn the car into. Children dressed in torn and ragged clothing playing in the streets stopped and watched us with sunken and hungry eyes, while gangs of too-tough teenagers stood around throwing stones at anything they could see. It looked like war zone with broken windows and beaten up cars ditched along the side of the road.

We pulled up to a house that hadn't quite recovered from the German Luftwaffe attacks of the Second World War. The front gate was hanging by a single hinge and an old tire was lying in the front garden, if you could even call it a garden, it was so overgrown with weeds. With much trepidation and concern, I parked the car and got out.

Barrington saw me eyeing the group of teens loitering across the street.

"Don't worry John, they won't touch the car. Not if it's parked in front of this house."

Not convinced, I gave them my best "you'd better not touch my fucking car or I'll fuck you up bad face," glaring at them all the way up the path. They seemed to get the message; at least I hoped they did. The faded and peeling yellow paint on the front door attempted a cheery hello as Barrington knocked and walked in. Tired and hungry from the trip, I really wasn't in the mood to chat or be friendly, but I was also smart enough to know a grumpy disposition wasn't the most inviting personality, and I needed people to start talking. I put on a happy face and followed Barrington into the house.

The front hall was small and congested, made worse by a bicycle pushed up against the wall. Mud from the tires was smeared across the floor making things quite a mess. No matter, I didn't plan on taking off my shoes in this shithole anyway. Bouts of laughter sprang from a room down the hall.

"Peter my boy how the fuck are you?" said a grungy man with a three-day scruff and well-worn, sullied shirt. He was sitting on the couch with his arm around a blond woman.

Like the house in Wallasey, this one reeked of must and marijuana. Girls slouched in chairs drinking beer and smoking pot, not knowing if they were half-alive or half-dead. Barrington shook the man's greasy hand and the assortment of girls gave him hugs and kisses hello. The girls looked young, very young. A couple of them couldn't have been over the age of fifteen.

"This is my friend John," Barrington said.

"Hello John!" was the collective response. One of the girls offered me a can of beer and a drag of her joint. I took the beer but declined the joint. She seemed surprised I didn't want the weed then just shrugged her malnourished shoulders and walked away. A young red headed girl pointed to the couch.

"Have a seat."

"Thanks," I answered. The faux velvet couch was full of cigarette burns and was disgustingly dirty. I smiled to hide my disdain and sat down beside Peter and some girl who was falling asleep with a joint hanging out of her mouth. It certainly wasn't the classiest place I'd ever hung my hat. There wasn't much to do and most of the girls were too stoned or drunk to talk, so I just sat uncomfortably on the couch, drank my warm beer, and tried to blend in.

After a bit, Barrington got up from the couch and made his way over to the other man and the two started talking. He never did give his name and I thought it best not to probe too deep. I tried to listen to what they were talking about but between the blaring television and their hushed whispers, I wasn't having much luck.

A tall man with blond stringy hair down to his neck strutted through the door, "So who's got the flashy car outside?"

Barrington smiled and pointed in my direction, "That's

John's car."

The man held out his hand. "Name's Ian."

I shook his hand and was about to start up a conversation but he wasn't interested. Ian grabbed the hand of the young red headed girl and whispered in her ear.

"Let's you and me go upstairs and have a fuck." The girl shook her head no and laughed. Ian laughed back. "You're all talk…you haven't got the guts to fuck me have you?"

The girl grinned and took a sip from her can of beer. "Okay fine. Let's see what ya can do then!" She pulled Ian out of the room and up the stairs. The room erupted with laughter.

"Ha! Carol's a good fuck anytime," roared the slobby man.

"Ya but she pisses when she cums!" added Barrington. Once again, the room burst into laughter. I was shocked as hell by the inappropriateness of the comment but wasn't in the position to speak out, so joined in to keep appearances.

Barrington lazily got up from his chair and sauntered over to the group of girls. "So who here is a really good fuck," he said with a devilish grin.

A smallish brown haired girl shot her hand in the air like she'd won the damn lottery. "I am!" She was one of the very young ones.

Peter leaned over and whispered in my ear, "Go ahead and choose one for the night. There's no sense in being lonely. They all fuck for free!"

"Nah," I said. "It's fine, I'm all right." First off, none of the girls really interested me and second, Peter was embarrassing me.

"Don't be bashful," he said. "Here…" He grabbed one of the girls by the arm. "Do you like this one?" Not knowing what to say I mumbled a laugh. "Then it's settled, you'll spend the night with her." He put her hand in mine and marched us upstairs to one of the bedrooms.

I'd never felt so awkward in my life. The poor girl couldn't look me in the eye and she clearly wasn't too thrilled at having been picked to be my bed partner for the evening. She started undoing the buttons on her shirt.

I held up my hand. "That's not necessary…please. I'm not going to make you spend the night with me. You can go back downstairs." She seemed relieved to leave and I was more than happy to be left alone. I took off my pants, placed them at the bottom of the bed, and climbed under the covers.

Even though I was dog-tired, I had trouble falling into a deep sleep. A strange house, a strange bed, and definitely some strange people. I was lying there half-awake when I heard a noise in the room, like a mouse or a small crinkling noise. Then it stopped. I shuffled my pillow, rolled over and attempted to get comfortable. I heard the noise again and quickly sat up in bed. I could have sworn I heard someone running down the stairs.

To save my sanity, I got out of bed, turned on the light, and checked the hallway. The house was still.

"My mind is going bloody crazy with all this undercover shit," I thought as I walked back toward the bed. That's when I noticed the five-pound note sticking out of my pants pocket.

"Bloody hell…someone was in here trying to scoff my cash. Jesus…" These last few weeks I'd become accustomed to carrying around a wad of bills, in case of emergencies. I'd stashed the cash deep in my pants pocket before I took them off but apparently, it wasn't deep enough. I counted the remaining bills and found myself several hundred pounds short.

"Son of a bitch!" I said smacking my hand on the

mattress. I was very cross but also unsure. I didn't want to cause a scene or make any trouble that might jeopardize things. I dressed, shoved the money back into my pocket, and tried to fall asleep.

I pulled Barrington aside in the morning and told him what had happened.

"Are you fucking kidding me?" He was furious. "Don't worry…I'll get it all back for you."

"It's not that big of a deal, don't make a fuss," I said.

"No. You're my guest and I didn't invite you to come with me so you could get fucking robbed. Just stay in your room and I'll deal with it."

He closed my door and I heard heavy footsteps going down the stairs. He wasn't wasting any time. There was quite a commotion below and I heard the slobby man swearing and cursing at someone. It wasn't pleasant. A few minutes later, there were footsteps on the stairs and a knock on my door.

The man was holding one of the girls by the hair. "Is this the girl who took your money?"

"To be quite honest, I never saw anyone," I answered. He shook the girl hard and she silently passed me a bunch of bills. He shook her violently again.

"I'm so sorry that she be taking your money," he said. "Trust me, she won't be doin' that again." He pulled her by her long brown hair into another room and slammed the door shut. Barrington apologized once more.

"Don't worry about it," I said. "It's really not that big of a deal." My sentence was interrupted by a loud "whoosh, smack and scream" coming from the other room, turning my blood cold. What the hell was he doing to the poor girl?

Barrington was laughing, "That's how we keep control around here." I didn't even know how to respond.

Thankfully, after a minute or so, the screams ended and I heard the man drag the girl down the stairs.

"I want to show you something," said Barrington. I followed him down the hall to another room. A small soiled cot was pushed up against one wall and the water stained net curtains were ripped and half hanging from the rod. The room was horrendously dirty. Taking up the majority of the space in the middle was a large table.

He pointed to the table and smirked. "He puts them up there to tan their asses." I was appalled but Barrington was looking at me for some sort of response.

"Good!" I lied. "Serve's the bitches right to get a lesson now and again."

Barrington laughed and picked up the cane from behind the door. "It's a right nasty cane too…lots of good whip!" He flicked the cane in the air and I winced. "Sometimes he even fucks them afterward!" Sure enough, there was a sad and dirty pair of girls' knickers lying on the floor by the table. I couldn't stand to look anymore.

"So is there any food in this house? I'm starving."

"Nah…there's a little cafe down the street," said Barrington. "We'll go there."

He shut the bedroom door and headed downstairs. The girl who been whipped was sitting on the couch with her head down. Her back was shaking and it was clear she'd been crying. I wanted to reach out and tell her I was sorry for getting her in trouble but I didn't have an opportunity. Besides, I thought it best to just put the incident behind me and move on. Everyone else had. The other girls gave us a cheerful hello and acted as if nothing had happened.

Barrington took me to the little cafe and we both ordered a big breakfast of bacon, eggs, toast, mushrooms, tomatoes, and the Yorkshire specialty, black pudding. I hadn't really eaten much since before we'd left Liverpool the day before and was starting to get a headache. I lit a smoke and enjoyed the steaming cup of coffee the cute waitress set on the table. She saw me checking her out and smiled.

Barrington leaned across the table, "Now, she looks like she'd be a good fuck doesn't she? What I wouldn't do to gnaw on her bacon for a while."

"You're a sick man Peter," I said laughing. "She is cute though." She brought the bill and I paid for the both of us.

"I have some business back at the house," said Barrington as we left the cafe. "Mind tagging along?"

"That's fine with me."

The house was empty except for the man, who was sitting on the couch scratching his balls beneath his pants. I'd tried to ask Barrington his name but he wouldn't budge. I wondered if he was maybe that "Brian" man Atwood had mentioned.

"I'm sure the girls brewed up some coffee there in the kitchen before they left," said Barrington. "Why don't you go help yourself?"

I took that as a cue he wanted me to leave so they could talk in private. Apparently, I hadn't yet earned the trust to be privy to such conversations. I stepped into the kitchen, purposely leaving the door ajar so I could listen to the exchange. With some difficulty, I found myself a clean mug, poured some coffee and snuck back toward the door.

While I couldn't exactly hear what they were saying, I did pick up some information about a delivery having been made somewhere down south that was now being collected and brought up to the north. They didn't say precisely what the delivery was but I presumed it had to be drugs. I moved closer to the door, taking great care not to be seen or heard. It wouldn't serve the purpose to be caught spying.

They mentioned a few different names I didn't know and talked about some things I didn't understand. I longed for a pencil and paper to write everything down but clearly, that was impossible. My ears perked up when I thought I heard the name Michelle, since that was one of the names Atwood had mentioned, but I wasn't positive. I also wasn't sure about the town or village named Darlish. The voices stopped and I had to jump back into the kitchen area in a hurry as Barrington walked through the door.

"I can't seem to find the damn sugar," I said pretending to scour the countertop.

"Second cupboard to the right of the fridge. At least that's where it usually is but judging by the mess of this kitchen, it could be just about anywhere." He didn't seem to suspect I'd been listening at the door. It was a close call though; in the future, I'd have to be more careful.

We left later that morning to return to Liverpool. It was a quiet ride. Barrington slept off and on, giving me a chance to go over and clarify the events in my head. There was a lot of information to process and I was trying to remember every detail so I could tell Atwood at our next meeting. At least this time I could relay some names and places, he should be pleased with that. But this world of drugs and violence was totally foreign to me and already at this early stage of the game, I knew I was way out of my league.

Atwood was clearly pleased with the information I had for him when we met the next Saturday.

"You say the name of the place is Darlish? Are you sure?" he asked.

"No I'm not sure but that's what it sounded like." He kept asking me over and over again. "Look I said I didn't know for sure okay?"

"Fine…let's move on."

He didn't give a shit when I talked about the girls and the caning incident but almost fell out of his chair when I mentioned hearing the name Michelle.

"Was she there? Did you meet her?"

"No she wasn't there and I didn't meet her," I answered.

"Well what did they say about her?"

"I don't know exactly…I just heard the name, they didn't really talk about her."

"All right, so go over the entire conversation again for me."

Again? I've already told you twice."

"Well humour me John and tell me a third time."

"I was in the kitchen and they were in another room, so I couldn't quite hear their voices clearly. The man…"

"Yes the man…you keep saying the man but you never tell me his name," said Atwood.

"I don't know his name…no one would tell me. I don't know why it was some big secret but I didn't want to raise suspicions by asking too many questions."

"Fair enough but next time, get a name. 'The man' isn't much for us to go on." He sounded pissed and was getting snarky with me.

"Look Atwood, I'm doing the best I can?"

"Just continue."

"Well he was telling Barrington about some delivery being made in the south that was on its way up north. Neither of them mentioned what it was so don't even bother to ask. And then I heard the name Michelle and the town of Darlish."

"I need you to find out more about Darlish and why it seems to be so important. Also…Michelle…I need to know much, much more, and like I said…find out the name of the man at the house you stayed at. What was the address by the way?"

I told him the address and answered all of his other monotonous questions. I was beginning to believe he had a hearing impediment, making me repeat the same shit so many times. I guess that was his way of confirming the accuracy of the information. He could quiz me all he wanted though - my story wasn't changing. It didn't have to; I was telling the truth.

Bad news waited when I arrived home from the Midland Hotel. The solicitor had called to tell my father my arrest would take place tomorrow. Oddly enough, the police weren't coming to Townfield to cart me away, but I was to surrender myself at the Liverpool Court House, using the special entrance for judges and not the main doors. The press would be banned from the proceedings and my identity would be safe from public knowledge. The judge would grant bail if my father could prove to the courts that he could cover the amount. That wasn't even a question and my father didn't hesitate to give them the information they required. I was nervous about the arrest and being formally charged but it did seem like working with the Customs and Excise Department was paying off with some preferred treatment at the courthouse.

The Liverpool Magistrates' Court was an old building in the city center of Liverpool. My father and I swept around the side of the building, pulled onto a side street, parked the car, and entered the building through a small door. My lawyer was there waiting for me.

"You ready?"

"As ready as I'm going to be," I answered fixing the knot on my tie.

"Just keep a straight face and only answer the questions they ask. Don't offer up any other information."

A court clerk led us to a room no bigger than a box of tissues and told us to have a seat at the desk and wait for the police. I was too antsy to sit.

"Calm down John," said my lawyer. "It's going to be okay."

"That's easy for you to say. You're not the one who's about to be arrested and charged with a crime."

"It could be worse."

The door opened and a policeman walked in carrying a folder of papers. He smiled and beckoned toward the empty chair.

"Have a seat," he said. He had bright blue eyes and thinning gray hair. Placing the folder on the desk, he took a seat opposite us. "I just need you to confirm some information for me." He asked my full name, address, and date of birth, all the while making some marks on the papers.

"In the matter of Her Majesty Queen Elizabeth vs. John Coventry," he said reading from one of the documents. "John Coventry, you are charged with Deception in that you attempted to forge documents when applying for government loans for employees that are alleged to be non-existent."

I kept a solemn face and avoided looking the officer in the eye. Hearing the charges made me feel guilty and ashamed for what I'd done. How could I have been so stupid and naïve to get caught up in such a scheme? I was a criminal and would have a criminal record for the rest of my life. No amount of undercover work for the Department of Customs and Excise could change that. This indictment was a permanent stain on my life.

The officer passed a copy of the charge to my lawyer who gave it a quick read over.

"This is just a formality John," said my lawyer. "You'll

be free to leave soon."

"If you say so," I answered. I really had no idea what was going on and just went where the people told me go. I wasn't in a position to ask questions.

The clerk met us outside the door. "Follow me."

She led us through a myriad of corridors flanked by official looking doors that opened into official looking offices. Suddenly I found myself in the court chambers. My knees weakened and the tie around my neck felt like a noose. The main doors to the courtroom remained closed and guarded by two large and husky policemen. The clerk guided me to the dock.

"Just stand here and wait," she said.

Despite the courtroom only having four or five people in it, I was tense. The authorities made my father wait back by the parking entrance so I didn't even have a friendly face for comfort.

The grey haired judge took no notice of me standing there and looked bored as hell, stifling a small yawn attempting an escape from his mouth. The usher handed him the folder of papers and whispered something in his ear. The judge read the documents and turned his head in my direction. He didn't seem bored any longer. The usher whispered in his ear again and the judge motioned for my lawyer and the Prosecution lawyer to come forward. They all started whispering and I was about to lose it. I wanted to scream, "Just tell me what the fuck you're talking about and let's get on with it!"

Finally, they stopped whispering and the judge gave me a stern stare.

"Usher read the charges against the defendant please," he said. The usher read the charges. "How do you plead?"

"Guilty, your honour," I answered.

"This matter will now be passed on to the Crown courts to be dealt with. Bail has been set at the agreed amount." The judge bowed his head and left the courtroom. I was free to go.

I exhaled as if I'd been holding my breath since the Stone Age, feeling such a sense of relief as my lawyer and I left through the side entrance and made our way back to meet my father. Except for a handful of people, no one knew I'd ever set foot in the courthouse. That was a good thing. Had Barrington or any of his cronies been there, or for that matter, any of Andy and Craig's friends, my cover would have been blown. Denied bail by the judge, Andy and Craig were remanded to custody, yet here I was on my way home. That alone would have raised suspicions and put me in a very awkward position.

My situation was extremely volatile and could turn nasty in a hurry if something went awry. For the moment, I was safe, and with this part of the case behind me and the main hearing months and months away, I was feeling much happier. Now all I had to do was continue to give Customs what they wanted and keep myself in one piece.

My father was anxiously waiting by the parking entrance.

"Let's go home," I said holding open the door.

"Sounds good to me," he answered.

On the ride home, I recapped everything that happened in the courtroom. My father had taken a huge leap of faith posting my bail and sharing in my undercover secret. I'd put my parents' lives in danger as well as my own by agreeing to dig up dirt on the drug running operation, and judging by the whipping incident, Barrington and his buddies weren't a crew you wanted to annoy. They were probably just the tip of the iceberg.

"I'm glad this part is over," said my father turning into

the lane at Townfield.

"So am I," I answered. "Thank you for everything."

"There's no need to thank me son. You know the rule, no matter what, family comes first."

I smiled at him and actually felt my eyes well up a little. I wasn't someone who cried easily but this was just one of those moments and I couldn't help if a tear or two dribbled out. I turned my head to look out the car window and pulled myself together. We Coventry's don't cry…we suck it up and get on with it, that's the motto, however, it had been such a stressful day and I was utterly exhausted both physically and emotionally.

"I think Mother asked Helen to cook a roast beef and pudding for dinner," said my father smiling. "Won't that be nice?"

"That sounds delicious. I could use a good hot meal and a relaxing evening with my family."

There was a message from Atwood when I returned to the house. He needed to see me as soon as possible. Can't he leave me alone for one bloody night? I purposely didn't call him back until late in the evening.

"Where have you been?" he said answering the phone.

"I've been out with my Dad. Is that a crime too?" I answered.

"No…of course not. I need to meet with you."

"I hope not this evening," I said. "It's late and I'm worn out."

"Tomorrow at one in the afternoon. We'll meet on the Parade at Parkgate in Wirral. Do you know where that is?"

"I do."

"Good show. I'll see you tomorrow then."

"Tomorrow," I said. "I'll be there."

I hung up the phone, poured myself a tall drink, and lit a

cigarette. Tomorrow I would go back to being an undercover agent. Tonight I just wanted to be John Coventry, son of John and Evelyn. Tonight that was all that mattered.

CHAPTER FOUR

Parkgate, situated on the bank of the river Dee about a half-mile west of Neston, consists of a long row of houses and shops – known as the Parade. All the buildings face the river, and looking out over the marsh you can see the hills of Wales. It's a spectacular view and one I remember well from my early childhood days when I attended the Mostyn House School, a private and exclusive school run by the Grenfell family. At the start of each term, I always tried to get a bed by one of the windows overlooking the river. It was such a beautiful sight, even at night, and somehow made the time away from Townfield and my parents a tad more bearable.

Parkgate used to be a major port in the days of sailing and tall ships, and was a favoured transport area for trade with Ireland. Rumour had it, Lady Hamilton, the mistress of Lord Nelson used to bathe in the local waters because she thought it would cure a skin aliment. She lived in one of the cottages on the Parade and to this day, the name of Nelson is marked in stones outside the cottage. The Parade is full of quaint shops selling wares such as ice cream and the famous Parkgate shrimp. In the middle of the street is the historic Red Lion Pub, still standing and serving fine quality ale after almost three hundred years.

Atwood found me leaning up against the outside of Mostyn House, enjoying the view.

"Coventry. How are you?"

"Fine. And yourself?"

"Good, good." He looked down the Parade. "Let's go grab a beer at the Red Lion." We found a seat at one of the outdoor tables and Atwood ordered a couple of beers. "So how did it go in Court?" Clearly, he knew all about the proceedings.

"It went okay," I answered. "I guess I should thank you."

Atwood just smiled. "I need you to tell me again about this house in Middlesbrough."

"You're serious? I've already told you everything I know a hundred different times now." I was angered at having to answer the same questions repeatedly.

"I'm more interested in the conversation you overheard. Is there anything more you remember now that you've had some extra time to think about it?" I shook my head no. "Okay…well I did some checking, and it turns out there's a small fishing village on the south coast called Darlish, so you probably heard the name correctly. See if you can find out more about what's going on here. And it's very important John, you find out as much as you can about the girl called Michelle."

"I'll try, but it's not like I can come right out and ask, or bring the subject up."

"Of course you can't. I'm just saying, keep your eyes and ears open at all times…and I still need to know the name of the man who owns the house in Middlesbrough. If it's okay with you, I'm going to bring another gentleman to our next meeting."

"Who is he?"

"Don't concern yourself about it right now, just concentrate on getting the information I asked." He pushed his chair back from the table. "Keep up the friendly relations with Peter Barrington as well. You're doing quite well John. At first I wasn't sure you'd be up to the task…so far I'm pleasantly surprised." He smiled and stood up. "Call me immediately if anything develops."

I sat looking out over the marshes and finished my beer. Atwood hadn't touched his, and since it's such a shame to let an English pint go to waste, especially one I didn't pay for, I gulped his down as well. The sun was radiant, making the sky over the Welsh hills a stunning blue. People young and old were milling about the Parade, eating ice cream, laughing and doing the sorts of things that bring families together on a brilliant summer day.

Since the weather was so nice, I spent the rest of the afternoon at Townfield, sitting by the pond in the garden and watching the goldfish. Around four pm, my mother came out of the house carrying a large tray of tea. It's as if she read my mind. A short while later, my father joined us, taking a seat beside me on the bench.

"So how are things going son?" he asked.

"Had a meeting with Atwood today. He says I'm doing a good job, but he needs me to probe deeper."

My father shook his head and a worried frown crept across his brow. "I don't like it John. I don't like it at all. Just how involved do they want you to get? Are there limits as to what you can and can't do? I mean what if the drug people want you to start selling…do you do it?"

"I don't know," I said honestly. "I guess I'll just have to take things as they come." I didn't know what else to tell him.

"I just wish there was some other way to deal with this matter," he said.

"So do I…but I don't see that I have many options at the moment."

He took a deep breath and I could tell the whole affair was weighing heavy on him. "Promise me one thing," he said putting his hand on my thigh.

"Anything," I said.

"Promise me you'll be very, very careful."

"I promise Dad…I promise."

I hated seeing my father so concerned and I wish I could have told him for real that everything was going to be okay, and I would walk away one day soon unscathed, but I couldn't. I didn't have a crystal ball, only a chilling feeling in my bones that things were going to get a lot more dangerous the longer I hung around Barrington. I was going to have to take some risks…risks I'm sure my father wouldn't be happy with, but with Customs and now apparently some other new guy breathing down my neck, I didn't have a choice. But at least I wasn't in jail, and I was grateful for that.

A few days later, I found myself again in Wallasey at Barrington's place. The girls from the other house had come over and there was quite a little party going on. Even in times of fun, I had to be on my guard and watch I didn't say anything stupid or out of the ordinary that might arouse suspicion and get me into trouble. Jane came over with the girls and I was happy to see and chat with her. She was growing on me and I guess right or wrong, I was starting to fancy her a bit. I figured what the hell; I might as well make a move and see what happened. She was attractive, I was a single man, and there was a definite spark between us.

She had thrown a few cushions on the floor for us to sit on, so while we chatted I guided my hand across her shoulders. I half expected her to pull away, and was pleasantly surprised when she moved her hand to touch mine. It gave me confidence, not only that I might soon get laid, but that the group was starting to accept me and treat me as one of their own.

"Want to share a joint?" asked Jane.

"As much as I'd love to, they just don't agree with me," I answered.

She snuggled into the crook of my arm and grinned. "Poor baby."

Out of the corner of my eye, I saw Barrington motioning at me to join him in the kitchen.

"I'll be right back."

Barrington was smirking as I entered the kitchen. "So you fancy Jane do you?"

"I do," I smiled.

"Seems she's taken a liking to you as well."

He nonchalantly walked across the room and stood in front of a piece of wallpaper that was semi-dangling from the wall. Lifting it back to expose the brickwork underneath, he pushed one of the bricks and to my astonishment, it moved, revealing a hole in the wall.

"Ya that Jane is something else let me tell you," he said sticking his arm in the hole and pulling out various plastic bags full of pills, powders, and what not.

I tried to act calm and cool; like it was no big deal he was showing me his stash of drugs, but on the inside, my heart was jumping like a monkey. He sorted through the different bags until he found one full of marijuana, which he slipped into his pocket. Shoving the other bags back into the hole, he replaced the brick, and smoothed out the wallpaper. If I hadn't just witnessed what I witnessed, I'd have never known the hole was there. Being unfamiliar with drugs, I had no idea what exactly was in the little bags, nor did I know how deep the hole in the wall was. I knew Atwood would ask, so I had to find a way to get a look in that space for myself.

Jane appeared in the kitchen and I got the impression by the possessive way she hugged my arm, she expected me to spend the rest of the evening with her. The whole time, my mind was swirling, trying to figure out a way to peek in that hole without getting caught. Jane and I sat on the couch talking and cuddling. We seemed to be the only two that were still awake or not stoned into oblivion. Then it struck me. All I had to do was wait until Jane and a few of the others fell asleep and I would have my opportunity.

I encouraged Jane to have another joint and a beer. The more out of it she was the better. After an hour or so, Jane finally conked and I had my chance, except of course she'd fallen asleep with her arm around me.

"How the hell am I going to get off this couch without waking her?"

I carefully lifted her arm and attempted to slide my body out from behind. Immediately she stirred and repositioned her arm. Shit! I tried again, this time moving a centimeter at a time. She stirred slightly, then hugged the pillow I'd tucked in the spot to replace my body. Success! I stood up, waiting a few more minutes to make sure she was truly asleep.

"Dear God please let her be a sound sleeper," I prayed.

With great concern, I made my way out of the room and tip toed toward the kitchen. I stopped in the hall to have a listen and was rewarded with the sound of utter silence. The pitch-black kitchen made walking difficult. I held my hands out in front of me like a blind man feeling his way, and inadvertently hit the dining table, sending a knife crashing to the floor.

"Stupid fool!" I thought.

In the stillness of the house, the deafening sound was like the smash of a cymbal resonating at the end of a drum solo. I was horrified and thought for sure Barrington would be at the kitchen door wondering what the hell was going on. For the longest time, I didn't move a muscle and just stood in the middle of the kitchen like a granite statue. I listened for even the slightest sound of movement from upstairs or the sitting room, but all was quiet. Breathing a sigh of relief, I slowly edged my way over to the corner of the room.

With my eyes now more accustomed to the dark, I found the spot of wallpaper and gingerly peeled back the corner, stopping every so often to listen for intruders. The wallpaper lifted off the wall with ease, only fastened with some sort of special glue. My fingers trembled when I saw the bricks. I took a quick look over my shoulder at the door, then started probing each brick to see which one moved. The first one didn't budge, so I shifted to the second one. I was just about to tap on it, when some movement in the sitting room stopped me dead in my tracks. Terrified I slapped the wallpaper back on the wall and jumped toward the sink.

"What 'cha doing in here?" said Jane flipping the light switch.

"Oh just trying to get a drink but I can't seem to find a clean cup." I tried to steady my voice but I'm sure the words came out fast and mumbled. I could feel my chest heaving as panic ran through my veins. I wondered how long Jane had been standing there.

"Check in the cupboard to the right of the sink," she said laughing.

"Oh shit…here they are. Thanks Jane."

She watched me make a cup of coffee and didn't seem the least bit suspicious. We chatted as I waited for the coffee to brew and I couldn't help but think how attractive she looked standing there in the shadow of the overhead light. Her hair delicately falling on her shoulders, and a smile that made my senses weak. Normally I would have been delighted to take this girl to bed, but not getting a look at Barrington's hiding spot was distracting me. It was a huge breakthrough in the investigation and I had failed. Atwood was going to be furious.

Jane sauntered over to the sink and took my hand.

"What's the matter? You look like you have the weight of the world on your mind."

"I'm fine Jane," I lied. "Just thinking about some things, that's all."

"Anything I can help with?"

I brushed back her hair. "Nah…but thanks for asking." I gently kissed her on the lips. They were soft and tasted like sweet cherries. I knew she wanted to go further but I just wasn't in the mood.

"Come back into the sitting room," she said putting her arm around me. "I wasn't done snuggling you yet."

"Okay, but just until I finish my coffee, then I've got to get going home."

"Really?" She sounded disappointed. "Are you sure you can't stay longer?"

I couldn't resist her sultry voice. "Okay…well maybe just a bit."

CHAPTER FIVE

Atwood was quite pleased when I met him later the next day at the Midland Hotel. He didn't seem that upset about me not being able to have a look in the hole myself.

"I couldn't help it. Jane walked into the kitchen and I never got another opportunity," I stated.

"I understand," he said. "But you're going to have to find a way to somehow get another crack at it. I need to know what kinds of drugs are in there and the amounts."

"Well there's the other problem," I said. "Besides the marijuana, I have no idea what the drugs look like or how to tell them apart."

"Come with me."

He led me to his car and we drove down to Custom and Excise Head Offices in Manchester. His office was stark and bleak, just like his personality. There was a bookcase full of books, a dying plant in the window and some files sitting on his desk. Atwood closed the door and took a seat behind his desk. He pointed to the empty chair.

"Have a seat." He took a key out of his pocket and placed it in the lock of the bottom desk drawer. I watched him pull out a bunch of small clear plastic bags.

"This powder here is cocaine and this bag is, of course, full of marijuana." He went through the contents of each package, explaining the characteristics of each pill and the best ways to recognize it quickly. "Now you have no excuses. You have to try and look in that hole again. It's imperative I know the specifics of what's in there and the amounts."

"I'll try again as soon as I get the chance," I said. "There's just always so many people lurking around."

"Do your best but try and get it done sooner rather than later." He put the drugs back in the drawer, locked it, and placed the key back in his pocket. "We can finish talking on the way back to the Midland."

He dropped me off near my car and told me to call him if there were any new developments or if I had an opportunity to look under the wallpaper.

A week later, quite surprisingly I got my chance. I'd been hanging out with Barrington at his house in Wallasey when he ran out of smokes.

"I'm just going to dash down to the shop to get some cigs. You need anything?"

"No, I'm good," I answered.

"Well make yourself comfortable. I'll be back in a few minutes." As soon as he shut the front door, I sprinted to the kitchen and found the spot on the wall. I quickly but carefully peeled back the wallpaper and went to work on the bricks. I found the right brick on the third try and was amazed at how smoothly it slid to one side. The hole was much, much larger than I imagined, and I could see various bags of pills and some huge bundles of marijuana. There was so much there, I didn't have time to examine them all. I made some mental notes, pushed the brick back into its spot, and smoothed down the wallpaper. Barrington hadn't yet returned, so I put on the kettle and started to make myself a cup of coffee.

I'd hit the drug jackpot. From what I saw, Barrington had quite the little operation going on. I had no idea how much all those drugs would be worth in street value but now I understood why he didn't have a day job. I was almost giddy with excitement. Barrington was a nice guy, and I felt sort of bad having to squeal on him, but if it was going to save my ass; I was doing it, no questions asked. I waited until Barrington had been home for an hour or so, then made up some excuse about having to get up early the next morning to go out of town with my father. I wanted to get out of there so I could call Atwood and set up a meeting.

"That many?" said Atwood sounding surprised.

"Honestly, there were so many bags with all the different kinds of drugs you showed me. I didn't have time to go through and count them all."

"Well done John!" he said with a smile. "Now tell me exactly where this hole in the wall is."

I gave him a detailed description of the kitchen, and told him precisely where the secret hole was located. I fully expected the Drug Squad to raid Barrington's home, but over the next few days and weeks, nothing happened. I asked Atwood about it at one of our meetings, and he made it quite clear, it was none of my business what he and his department did with my information.

One evening, quite out of the blue, I was hanging out at Barrington's house, when a rather large man walked in without even knocking, silencing the once buoyant atmosphere. At least 6'4" tall, he had to bend over to get in the doorways. Sunglasses with very dark lenses shielded his eyes and I felt Jane's body tense up beside me. I had no idea who this man was but he certainly had a powerful presence about him.

Barrington immediately stopped what he was doing and greeted the man with a grin.

"Good to see ya."

"Let's go in the kitchen where we can talk." The man's voice was hoarse with a strong Irish accent. They stepped into the kitchen and I heard the door shut behind them.

"Who's he?" I whispered to Jane.

"He's one guy you don't want to mess with. His name is Brian and he's one mean motherfucker. Nothing but bad news he is…scares the hell out of me every time."

I tried to hide my excitement. This was the Brian guy that Atwood was talking about! Jane was right. He did look mean. When he first walked in the door, his face snarled in a nasty grimace and his sheer size made him an imposing figure. No wonder Jane was frightened of him.

"So what does Brian do for a living?" I knew it was a loaded question but I wanted to see if I could get any information out of her.

"He owns a scrap yard but he's also got his hands in a bunch of different businesses…if you know what I mean."

"I can only guess," I answered. "But he can't be that bad?"

"Don't kid yourself John." She leaned in real close to my ear. "Rumour has it he once cut off a guy's hand because the guy disobeyed some order he gave…I'm not sure of the details but it was pretty gruesome."

"Did the guy go to the cops?" I said.

"No…if he did that, I'm quite sure he'd be dead. From what I hear, Brian likes to keep all of his business dealings very, very private…and he knows a lot of people…people who wouldn't hesitate to cut off more than just a hand. Whatever you do John…be very careful around that man," said Jane. "I'm serious…"

"Thanks for the warning," I smiled.

Barrington didn't return to the sitting room for well over a half an hour.

"Where's your friend?" I asked. "Doesn't he want to stay for a beer?"

"No," Barrington chuckled. "Hanging out with me and my friends on a social basis isn't really Brian's thing." He looked around the room. "Who's got a joint?" One of the other girls handed him a joint and Barrington lit up. I could tell he was done talking about Brian. I wanted to know more, but I also didn't want to push my luck.

The nightly news came on the television, and once again, the lead story had to do with another IRA bombing. The troubles in Ireland had boiled over and now the Provisional Irish Republican Army was bombing mainland Britain. This time some poor club in Birmingham was the target. There'd been constant bomb alerts in Liverpool but so far, nothing had gone off.

"Good God!" I said. "When is all this bombing going to stop?"

"I know," said Jane shaking her head. "It's a bloody shame…and I don't even quite understand what all the fuss is about? I know the Irish are mad about something but what I'm not sure."

"The English have been having problems with the Irish ever since the days of Oliver Cromwell back in the mid 1600's. In fact, when King William brought his army up from London to try and 'settle' the Irish problem, they used the grounds at Townfield, my family home, as a campsite. Every once and awhile we dig up the odd cannon ball or other interesting artifact."

"It that right?" said Jane. "You seem to know a lot about history…"

"See Jane, in my opinion, the IRA are just killers and have nothing to do with trying to gain Ireland's independence. The real problem is religion. The south of Ireland is Catholic and the north of Ireland is filled with Protestant's and fanatical Royalists. The people living in Northern Ireland want to stay in the United Kingdom and hate the Catholics. Protestants and Catholics haven't gotten along since the beginning of time but that's another matter entirely. I say, if the majority of Northern Ireland wants to stay associated with the rest of the United Kingdom, then you can't just cut them off. They have rights too. In any case, if the British left Northern Ireland right now, there would be a blood bath between the two religions. The British Army is there to keep the peace."

"But don't the IRA want a united Ireland?" asked Jane.

"They say they do," I answered. "But they're just using the situation and the history behind it for their own benefits. It's totally against all those Irish who live in Northern Ireland. The IRA says they do not want to abide by the Southern Irish government either. They just want to create their own rules and laws. Neither the Southern or Northern Irish government's support them, their cause, or the way in which they go about their business. I mean car bombs and sniper attacks? Killing innocent people? Is that really going to accomplish anything? The IRA is filled with nothing but blood thirsty terrorists."

"I see what you mean and certainly don't disagree with you," said Jane. "But you might want to keep your thoughts to yourself, especially around Brian since he's Irish."

"Good point," I answered. "The last thing I want to do is cause any more trouble between the English and Irish!"

I went into the kitchen to make myself another cup of coffee. I guess you could say I'm a bit of a coffee addict. Barrington followed me and closed the door. For a brief moment, I was nervous and thought he might have something to say about my conversation with Jane about Ireland and the IRA.

"So how are things going with you John?" he asked.

"Fine I guess."

"How's the money situation? Are you short? I know you

haven't been working since the whole government thing…"

"I'm doing okay…but of course more is always welcome," I laughed.

"Isn't that the truth," Barrington smiled. "So here's the thing…I have a little business I need to attend to down south for a couple of days and I was wondering if you'd like to come along?"

"That would be nice, but what exactly is involved?" I was hoping he might inadvertently offer up some information. Instead he laughed.

"You'll maybe get to learn that when we get there."

"Oh…no problem," I said covering my tracks. "I was just curious that's all. Just wondering what I needed to pack. Where are we going anyways?"

"I'll let you know. We'll leave in a few days," he answered.

My next meeting with Atwood was a much cheerier affair than the last. We met again at the Red Lion Pub in Parkgate and this time there was another man with him.

"Just call me Nigel," the man said holding out his hand. He was the opposite of Atwood – well dressed in an expensive tailored suit. The way he disregarded Atwood made me think he was a higher up the Government food chain.

"Nice to meet you Nigel," I said. "Do you work in the Custom and Excise Department?"

Nigel totally ignored my question, sat down at the table and motioned to the waitress. "Gin and tonic please." He looked bored and wasn't amused with the conversation.

"A couple of beers," added Barrington. "So John anything new to tell me?"

"Well nothing much…except I finally made contact with the man you call Brian."

Nigel sat up straight in his chair like a jack knife. He was paying attention now. Atwood was delighted and started firing the questions.

"I didn't get to speak to him myself," I said. "He was only in the room for a few minutes. I just got a look at him and then he was off to the kitchen with Barrington."

"There's nothing more you can tell me?" asked Atwood.

"I'm sorry...no. Like I said, they went into the kitchen and closed the door. I couldn't hear a word they said. Although everyone in the room shut up as soon as he walked in. They all seemed pretty scared of him."

"And rightly so," said Nigel under his breath.

"Interesting..." said Atwood itching the bridge of his nose under his glasses. "So you say you're going south with Barrington on a trip? Whereabouts?"

"I don't know yet," I answered. "And I have no idea what we'll be doing so don't even ask."

"Okay...I need you to go through everything again from the top."

I was annoyed. "Look Atwood. Every meeting it's the same damn thing. I tell you what I know, and then you make me go through it again a ridiculous amount of times. Why is that?"

Atwood scowled. "The deal was you answer my questions and I help you. There was never any limit as to how many times I would ask you a question. I think in your predicament, you'd do best to just answer them."

"Fine. I'll start from the beginning." I recounted the events two more times and was quite exhausted by the time I'd finished.

"I wonder if the Irishman will be where you're going?" mused Atwood.

"I really don't know. As soon as I find out more details

I'll let you know."

"Did you hear the name Michelle again?"

"No I didn't. There was no mention of her at all," I answered.

"Well John, I am very pleased with what you've had to tell me today. We've made some great progress. Good job!"

Atwood was earnest in his praise, and it made me feel like all the hassles and troubles were worth it. He was very happy and excited about something I'd told him, but I wasn't sure which part and he clearly didn't intend to let me in on his little secret.

"Very well," he said closing his notebook and putting it back in his suit coat pocket. "I think we're about done here. Remember…as soon as you find out the details of the trip and the destination, you must let me know immediately. Agreed?"

"Agreed," I replied.

Atwood got up from the table and headed to the door. Nigel hung back.

"Listen John," said Nigel. "I need to know everything about Brian and Michelle. I don't care about the drugs – I care about Brian and Michelle." His eyes were bearing down on me like he was trying to read my mind. "You can help me out with that can't you?"

"I'll do my best," I answered.

It'd been a long meeting and I was drained. All I wanted to do was go home and relax. I'd taken an apartment in the city of Chester, mainly so Jane and I could get to know each other a little better, but for some reason I found myself on the road to Townfield. That really was home anyway. Both my mother and father were there when I arrived.

"Good to see you son," said my father. "We were just sitting down for a pre-dinner cocktail. Care to join us?"

I smiled. "I'd like nothing better."

We sat in the drawing room and for the most part kept the chatter light. My father asked me about the undercover work and I filled him in on how things were going. He was concerned about the trip with Barrington, especially since the details seemed so sketchy. I tried to reassure him as much as I could, but it was hard, seeing I was somewhat tentative about the trip myself.

Based on the conversation I'd overheard between Barrington and the slobby man a while back, I could only assume we were headed south to pick up some sort of shipment. I had no idea who might be there. I knew Atwood was hoping Brian and maybe even Michelle would make an appearance, but there were no guarantees.

I ended up staying the night at Townfield. There was just something warm and comforting about the house that made me feel safe and secure. Maybe it was all the happy memories with my family or just the idea that at Townfield, I was part of a clan, "The Coventry's" and that made up for some of the loneliness I felt. I remember once when I was around seven years old complaining to my Grandmother Poldy about my lot in life. She grabbed my wrists, held them very tight, and looked sternly into my eyes.

"John! Remember you are a Coventry! Nothing will ever change that!"

My line of the Coventry family is in fact a very old and established English family, with roots dating back to the 1600's and connections to Lords, Knights and, even the Lord Keeper of the Great Seal of England. I'm sure there were rogues and a few rascals included in the bunch, every family has their black sheep whether they want to admit it or not. But in England your name and title means everything.

Shortly before she died, Grandmother Poldy told me,

"John…at the end of the day…whatever people say…there is only one thing that counts, one thing that makes an English Gentleman…breeding!" Rules of etiquette were important in our family and it fit in with the notion of living life with that "stiff upper lip" the British are famous for. You played the hand you were dealt and nobody needed to know your business except you and perhaps those closest.

A few days later, Barrington rang me up on the telephone and invited me over. He pulled me aside as soon as I got there.

"We'll leave on Friday for Darlish."

"Darlish? Never heard of the place before," I lied.

"It's just a real small fishing village down on the coast, nothing too big or exciting. We'll stay overnight but I think it's best if you don't stay with me. There's a pub in town that rents rooms. It's a great spot." Barrington didn't give a reason why I couldn't stay at the cottage but I figured it had something to do with the fact that this was my first trip and whomever we were meeting at the cottage didn't quite trust me.

"That's fine. As long as I have a bed and a pillow I'm good," I answered cracking open a beer.

There was a small party going on and I was happy just to kick back, relax, and not think about the trip to Darlish. Although I couldn't help but wonder who might be there. Brian? Michelle? Any other players I'd yet to meet in this little charade? I took a long gulp of my drink, then tilted my head back onto the couch, and closed my eyes. Trying to forget this whole sordid mess was easier said than done, especially with the gnawing sense of fear churning in my stomach.

CHAPTER SIX

"Don't worry," said Atwood. "There'll be an unmarked car following you all the way to Darlish." He was ecstatic I'd finally been able to phone him with the concrete plans of my trip. "At some point, I will contact you but I can't tell you exactly when or where. We'll have to see how things play out."

"That's fine," I said. "As long as I know you're around, I'll feel a whole bunch better."

"It's going to be okay John. We won't let you out of our sight. I promise."

The more I thought about the trip to Darlish, the more apprehensive I became, but it was too late to back out. Both Barrington and Atwood were counting on me. Of course, both had very different reasons. I'm not going to lie; I was worried. While traveling to Darlish was the next step in the investigation, it also meant I was getting in deeper with Barrington and his crew. My first impression of Brian wasn't full of sunshine and flowers. He was a menacing character and my gut said it was best to stay out of his path.

I picked Barrington up at his home in Wallasey at nine in the morning. The trip would take around eight hours, all the way to the south coast and the English Channel. As soon as we hit the motorway heading toward Birmingham and London, it began to rain. There's nothing worse than a long car ride in the rain. I kept checking in the rearview mirror for the car Atwood said would be following, but there didn't seem to be anyone trailing.

I gripped the steering wheel a little bit harder and kept on driving. That car was supposed to be my protection, my safety net, and not seeing it made me very anxious. I wanted to turn around and go home but coming up with a logical explanation for Barrington would be impossible. I had to keep going. We stopped for lunch at a place off the highway and I was glad to get out of the car, walk around, and stretch my legs.

Back on the road, Barrington proceeded to fill me in on Brian.

"First off, he's rich…very rich and he's the kind of person who has his hands in many different pies, so to speak." I nodded. "He comes from Belfast in Northern Ireland…has a huge home there and one in Dublin…but he also has a business operation in Darlish."

Barrington didn't tell me what kind of business Brian ran and I couldn't imagine why he would set up shop in a small fishing village like Darlish. Call it naivety on the rookie undercover agent.

"I told Brian you were a cool guy," Barrington continued. "He wants to have a word with you when we get there."

Great. I had no desire to speak to Brian whatsoever; especially after the stories Jane told me. Atwood would be happy but I wasn't amused. Brian scared me. After many hours, we arrived in the picturesque village of Darlish. It was a sleepy, little community with a small harbour, some fishing boats and few pubs.

"Pull over there," said Barrington. "That's the pub where you can rent a room. You go check in and then we'll head up to the cottage."

I left Barrington in the car and entered the pub. The gentleman was very friendly and gave me a great rate for the night.

"Pleased to have ya sir," he said. "We don't get many

guests around here."

"Well I'm happy to stay. The place looks great." He handed me a key and I quickly placed my bags in the room and went to rejoin Barrington. After such a long drive, I was dying to crash on the bed for a nap, but Brian was waiting for us and from both Jane and Barrington's descriptions, Brian didn't like to be kept waiting.

I waved at the gentleman on the way out. "I'll be back in a bit. Don't wait up."

He gave me a hearty laugh. "Right o' then."

"Nice place, very friendly people," I said getting back in the car.

"Yes…I knew you'd like it. And wait till you see what they cook up for breakfast. It'll fill yer belly up full!"

I drove down the main street until Barrington directed me to turn up a narrow road. At the end of the road was a small country cottage with a thatched roof. The front garden was full of the most amazing rose bushes, even my Grandmother Poldy, the rose connoisseur, would have been impressed. Barrington opened the little white gate and we walked up the stone pathway toward the front door. The door was so tiny, I had to bend over to get inside, and I'm only five foot nine. I couldn't imagine how Brian fit.

"Hello all!" said Barrington.

The sitting room was quaint with its wooden beams and country charm. Brian was sitting in an armchair talking to a very attractive woman with long dark hair and tight jeans. A man dressed in a waterproof fishing jumper and Wellington boots was watching from the couch. Brian and the woman were speaking French.

"Hello," said Brian. His tone was pleasant but businesslike. "Please sit down."

The woman just looked at me and smiled. There was

something about her…something beyond her stunning beauty that caught my eye. She had a mysteriousness and intensity I'd never really seen before. It was in the way she tilted her head and held her hands in front of her. She exuded confidence and I was both intrigued and slightly frightened.

Brian turned his attention to me. "So…do you like Darlish? Have ya ever been here before?"

"I do like Darlish," I answered. "It's very charming and pretty…but no this is my first trip here."

"Where are ya staying?"

"At the pub just down the hill."

"Aye…that's a fine place," he nodded. "I know the landlord well. They'll take good care of ya for sure. Do ya mind if I ask ya a few questions?" he said in his thick Irish brogue.

Now I was nervous. Brian leaned back in his chair and smiled. "No problem," I replied. "Be happy to answer whatever you want."

Then the interrogation started. He asked me everything from where I was born, to where I grew up, to where I lived. He wanted to know all about the Department of Industries fraud, exactly why the other two blokes were in jail, and I was free.

"I don't know for certain," I answered trying to stay calm. "I guess maybe the police don't have enough evidence on me yet."

Brian leaned forward and peered straight into my eyes. It was all I could do not to turn away. "Lucky you now, ain't it?"

I mumbled a laugh. "Yes, yes…quite lucky I suppose." Both Barrington and the woman laughed.

Brian took a sip of his drink. "Well John…have you ever

been to Ireland?"

"No, never," I replied.

"Why is that? Don't you like us Irish?"

"Oh no…it isn't that. I've just never had the opportunity. I really don't know any Irish people but I'm sure they're a nice enough bunch."

Brian laughed. "You should be a politician with an answer like that."

The girl said something to me in French and then giggled. I looked at Brian for a translation.

"Oh…this is a good friend of mine…Michelle. She's from Reims in France," said Brian.

I smiled at her and attempted one of the only French phrases I knew, "Bonjour en chanté."

Michelle laughed again and gave me a saucy grin. "Good try."

She spoke perfect English, but her French accent sent the blood rushing to every part of my body. It was so, so sexy. I had to take a minute, catch my breath, and make sure my heart rate went back to normal. In all the excitement, my brain had failed to register that I was sitting here in the same room with both Brian and Michelle – the two people Atwood and Nigel wanted to know the most about. I was literally in shock.

"It's getting quite late," said Brian. "Peter…why don't 'cha take John here back to the pub for the evening."

"Oh I'm quite fine to make it on my own," I answered.

"I'm sure ya are but I'd much rather have Peter take ya. Just in case you get lost or something on the way." Brian didn't let anything slide. He didn't quite trust me, so there was no way he was going to let me get in a car unattended and drive off into the night.

"But it's my car," I said.

"Don't you worry laddie…we'll take good care of it." There was no arguing with him.

I said my goodnights and let Barrington drive me back to the pub. I kept wondering where the hell Atwood and his Customs buddies were hiding. There hadn't been any sign of them all day.

"I'll pick ya up in the morning," said Barrington. "Like I said, make sure you try the breakfast here. You'll love it."

"Will do," I answered. Barrington drove off and I went up to my room. I didn't even have access to a telephone to call Atwood, then I realized if Brian knew the guy at the pub, he probably told him to keep an eye on me. I was just going to have to trust Atwood and pray he kept his word. I didn't have a choice.

Feeling totally alone and abandoned, I stripped down to my underwear and went to bed. Exhaustion gripped my body and it didn't take long for me to fall into a deep sleep. Sometime in the middle of the night, there was a soft rapping at the door. Half asleep and clumsy, I hauled my ass out of bed to answer it.

"Hello John," said Atwood. "Quick inside boys." Three men in dark suits filed into the room. Atwood shut the door behind them. Instantly I was wide-awake.

"Don't worry," said Atwood, "no one knows we're here. We've sorted it all out with the pub owner…so just relax and take a deep breath. You look like you've seen a ghost."

"Where the hell have you guys been?" I said rubbing my eyes.

"We've been around all day John. I can assure you."

"I've been worried you weren't going to show up."

"Nonsense," said Atwood. "I told you we would be here. You have to trust me a little. I do know what I'm doing. Okay, why don't you have a seat on the bed and tell us what's been going on."

I sat on the edge of the bed, half-naked and feeling somewhat uncomfortable. I didn't like feeling so vulnerable.

"Start from the beginning," said Atwood. "Any interesting conversations on the way down in the car with Barrington?"

I told them what Barrington had told me about Brian being rich and being from Belfast, and then gave them directions to get to the cottage.

"Brian was at the cottage along with some fisherman guy…I don't know who he was and he left shortly after we got there. Oh…and there was some woman named Michelle." I'd purposely waited to tell them about Michelle.

The three men turned sharply toward me. "Describe what she looked like," said one of them.

"She had long dark hair and wore skinny jeans. Very attractive lady. She was definitely French. Brian said she came from Reims in France."

The man nodded his head at Atwood. "That certainly sounds like her."

"John," said the man. "I don't work for the Customs and Excise Department but I have been brought in on the operation because Michelle interests us greatly."

"Well what organization do you work for then?" I asked.

"It doesn't matter," he said. "What does matter is what you can tell me about Michelle."

"I honestly don't know that much. I just met her today and we really didn't get a chance to talk. She is pretty though, I can say that."

He laughed. "Do you like her?"

"You mean do I like her looks?" I said. "Of course I like her looks. I can't imagine who wouldn't."

He asked me a few more questions and then Atwood took

over with his regular routine. At least it was shorter than normal.

"Okay John," said Atwood. "Do your best to find out as much as you can. We'll be around and will try to contact you again sometime soon."

"All right."

With that, they silently opened the door and disappeared into the darkness of the night. I climbed back into bed and fell into a very troubled sleep. At least I knew the Customs agents were here. That was some comfort.

As I was finishing my breakfast the next morning, Barrington bounced into the pub dressed in a t-shirt and jeans.

"Morning John," he said.

"Morning Peter."

"I see you found the breakfast menu," he said laughing.

"I sure did," I said shoving the last forkful of eggs into my mouth. "Just give me a minute. I'm almost done."

"No problem mate," he said pulling up a chair.

"So what's on the agenda for today," I asked.

"Rather not say at the moment," Barrington answered looking around the room.

"Oh yes of course," I said. "Sorry 'bout that." I emptied my coffee and threw a few bills on the table to cover the tab. "Okay, let's go."

Barrington drove us back to the cottage where we found Brian sitting alone in the armchair reading the morning news.

"Have a seat John," he said putting down the paper. "So how would you like to earn yourself a little bit of money working with us?"

"I'd love to," I answered.

"Very well then…for starters you'll team up with Peter and he can show you the ropes…get you familiar with the way things work. Then, in a few weeks we'll talk again…see how you're doing and go from there. Sound good?"

"Yes," I answered. "What sorts of things will I be doing?"

"Just running errands and doing some driving and such. Nothing too complicated or intricate. Peter will show you…don't worry. Can you drive a lorry?"

"Yes I can," I replied.

"Good," he smiled.

Just then, Michelle walked into the room with a towel wound around her head. She looked incredible with her hair pushed back off her face, wearing a tight sweater and a short denim skirt with boots.

"Did you have a good night at the pub John?"

For an instant, I thought she was being sarcastic and knew the Customs people had paid me a visit. I could feel my face go red and tried to cover it up with a hearty laugh.

"Oh yes…I had a wonderful night. Nice soft pillow…it's all you can really hope for isn't it?" I knew I sounded stupid, but with Brian and Michelle both staring at me, I felt uneasy and insecure.

"I agree," said Michelle. "Nothing like a good soft pillow." She smiled and started to rub her head with the towel. No one in the room seemed to suspect anything and I breathed a sigh of relief.

Brian left later that afternoon in his blue Jaguar. Whatever kind of work he did, it certainly had to pay well because it was a very nice car. I was impressed.

"So John, let me fill you in a bit on what Brian wants you to do," said Barrington.

"I am a little curious," I answered.

"I hope you don't have plans for next weekend," he asked.

"No…nothing at the moment."

"Splendid. You're to hire an empty van in Liverpool, drive it to Darlish, pick up a few things and then go to the house in Middlesbrough and drop them off."

"What am I picking up?" I asked.

"Just a bunch of crates, nothing special. Once you arrive in Middlesbrough the crates from Darlish will be unloaded and replaced with a different bunch for the return trip to Liverpool."

"Whereabouts am I taking the crates when I get to Liverpool?" I asked.

"The docks. I'll meet you in Liverpool and direct you to the right dock. Do you think you can handle all that on your own?"

"I think I can manage," I smiled. "How much does this job pay?"

"Depends on how well you do…but it won't be for a month or so…Don't worry. If you do a good job and everything runs smoothly, Brian will take care of you."

"All right," I said. "Sounds fair. Bit of a trial run I suppose."

"Something like that," Barrington answered. "But I don't anticipate there being any problems."

"No…neither do I."

"We'll talk later in the week and make final plans and such. I'm not going to worry about it right now. Actually I'm gonna go lie down for an hour or so. Slept like shit last night."

"So what's the plan for today anyway?" I asked.

"We'll head home later this afternoon if that works for you."

"Yes of course, that's fine."

"When are you heading back to France?" Barrington said

to Michelle.

"Sometime this evening."

"Right o'..." answered Barrington. "I'll be back in a bit."

"Have a good nap," Michelle called out to him. Barrington gave a back handed wave and walked out of the room, leaving me alone with Michelle.

"So are you flying back from London then?" I said making conversation.

"No, no," she answered. "I never fly...prefer to take a boat."

"A boat? That seems like a funny way to travel, especially since the ferry to France takes forever. How are you getting to the docks? Do you need a lift?"

Michelle laughed. "No thanks, I have a friend who brings me here in his boat and then picks me up when I need it."

"Oh." I didn't quite know how else to respond. Taking a small personal boat across the English Channel to France was pure madness. Hundreds of large merchant ships filled the Channel on a daily basis. It was a very tricky and dangerous journey. Why Michelle would undertake it on a regular basis was beyond me.

"Have you ever been to France?" she asked.

"I've been there a few times for vacation...Paris, Cannes, and some other places in the south but that's about it."

"You must come one day and let me show you the beautiful countryside. There really isn't anything like it." She twirled a piece of her long hair through her fingers. "I love France...more than you'll ever know..." She had a far off look in her eyes. "I would do anything for my country."

"I love Britain," I said with a laugh, "but I'm not sure how far my patriotism goes."

"What do you mean?" she asked.

"I don't know really...I'm not someone who likes

violence or confrontation. I'm not sure I'd make the best soldier." I lit a cigarette and took a long drag. "But I guess if I had to defend my country I would…in some sort of capacity. I don't know…war and fighting…it's not very romantic."

"There's nothing *more* romantic than fighting for something you believe in John," she answered. "I think that's part of the problem with people today…they just aren't willing to fight for the things they love…you know?"

"I suppose," I said rising from the couch. "Can I get you some more coffee?"

"I'd love a cup. Thank-you."

I filled our mugs from the pot in the kitchen and made my way back to the sitting area.

"Do you come to England often then?" I asked.

"Quite a bit…mainly for business with Brian."

"I see." I didn't dare ask her what kind of business she had with Brian. I figured she wouldn't tell even if I did. Everyone was always so secretive, and the last thing I wanted to do was appear to be digging for information. By the sounds of it, Brian and Michelle weren't newcomers to the "business". I was going to have to be extra careful with my words and actions.

We chatted off and on during the afternoon and Michelle was very friendly and nice. Much like Brian, she asked me a slew of questions, which I tried to answer the best that I could. For some reason though, I felt much more comfortable and relaxed with her, than I did with the Irish brute. Maybe it was her sexy French accent, lulling me into a false sense of security, or just the way she smiled and slanted her head when she laughed.

"Aye," said Barrington plopping himself on the chair. "That was a wonderful nap. Feel much better now."

"That's good," I answered. "You actually look refreshed."

"I am…refreshed enough to get in the car for the long haul home," he laughed. "You just about ready to hit the road? We can stop and get a bite to eat on the way…break up the trip a little."

"That sounds like a good idea," I said draining the last sip of coffee from my cup. "Well Michelle…it was very nice to meet you. I've enjoyed our conversation."

She smiled, "I have too."

I held out my hand, "Have a safe trip home and I hope we meet again soon."

"You never know John," she grinned. "It may be sooner than you think."

"Michelle," said Barrington. "Always a pleasure."

"You two drive safely now…and good luck next weekend John…I know you'll do just fine."

I couldn't stop thinking about Michelle the whole way home. There were so many questions I wanted to ask Barrington but couldn't. I didn't want him to think I was interested in her. I didn't even know if I was interested in her. There was no denying she was one intriguing woman. Beautiful, sexy and mysterious – a lethal combination. I had to be careful and not let this woman become a distraction. The sooner I completed the task, paid my dues to society, and got on with my life, the better.

CHAPTER SEVEN

Atwood wanted to see me that Monday afternoon at the Red Lion Pub. I walked in to find both him and Nigel sitting at a table.

"Good afternoon John," said Atwood with a smile. "Have a good weekend?"

I sort of laughed. "It was all right I guess. Nothing out of the ordinary."

"Have a seat," said Atwood taking out his notepad. "Let's go through everything from the top. I know you told me some things the other night but I want you to go over everything again."

"After I checked into the pub on Friday night, Barrington and I drove out to the cottage and Brian was there with Michelle and another man…he looked like a local fisherman. He didn't stay all that long. Brian asked me a bunch of questions…drilled me quite hard for information actually. I answered everything as best I could, and he seemed satisfied. After that, Barrington took me back to the pub. Brian didn't want me driving by myself…"

"Doesn't quite trust you yet I suppose," said Atwood.

"I guess not. Anyway, you guys showed up in the middle of the night and scared the living hell out of me. Barrington picked me up in the morning and we went back out to the cottage. This is where things get a bit more interesting." Immediately Nigel perked up and leaned forward in his chair. "Brian asked if I wanted to make some extra money, so I said sure."

"What does he want you to do?" said Atwood.

"I have to rent a van in Liverpool, drive it to Darlish, pick up some crates, drive them to Middlesbrough, drop them off, pick up some new crates and then take them to a specific dock in Liverpool. I don't know which dock…Brian didn't tell me…Barrington is meeting me in Liverpool on the way back to show me."

"Any idea what you're picking up?" asked Atwood.

"No…sorry…I don't have a clue. Nobody mentioned it and I was too afraid to ask."

"I highly doubt they would have told you anyway," said Atwood. "When are you supposed to make the trip?"

"As far as I know, next weekend."

"Here's what I want you to do. Do exactly what Brian wants in delivering the goods. Don't deviate from the scheduled plan one bit…but you must make a note of any sort of shipping marks on the crates. Whatever you do, don't try to open the crates…that would raise serious alarm bells, and put you and the operation at risk. Also try and find out which boat you're making the delivery to in Liverpool."

"I already said I have no idea, they didn't tell me." I swear to God Atwood didn't hear a word I said half the time.

"Yes, yes right…but if you can, that'd be a big help."

"I'll do my best, but I can't make you any promises there," I answered.

"I realize that John," said Atwood. "And when you're checking the crates over for the shipping labels, do see if there's any other sort of distinguishable marks and such. Anything that might set them apart from other crates."

I nodded, "Will do."

"I think I'm finished," Atwood said putting away his notepad. "Oh wait! You said you have to rent a van?"

"Yes, I have to rent one in Liverpool," I answered.

"Does it matter where you rent it from?" Atwood asked.

"I don't think so. Barrington just told me I had to rent the van, he didn't specify where."

"Okay then, see if you can't rent the van from a company called Hertz in Liverpool."

"Okay," I answered.

"Nigel I believe you had some questions for John?" said Atwood.

"Did you find out anything more about Michelle?" said Nigel.

"Actually yes I did. We talked off and on for a couple of hours in the afternoon while Barrington had a nap."

"About what?"

"At first it was just small talk…she asked me a number of questions about myself, much like Brian had done. Again, I answered them as best I could. Barrington asked her if she was leaving to go back to France that day and she said yes. But this part I found quite strange. When I asked her if she was flying out of London, she said no, her friend was coming over in a boat to pick her up. That's how she travels I guess."

I could see Nigel's eyes flicker but he kept his excitement under wrap. "Any idea what kind of boat?"

"From what I gathered, it was some sort of smaller personal boat…but I'm not positive."

"Where was the boat picking her up and where in France was she going?"

"That I don't know, but Brian did say she was from Reims in France. It seems that she stays with friends. I also got the impression she spends a lot of time in England doing business with Brian…whatever sort of business that is…"

"What about Brian? Anything more you can tell me?" asked Nigel.

"Nothing much. He drove off in a blue Jaguar when he left, but I don't have a clue as to where he was going."

"Please tell me you got the license plate number Coventry."

"No…I'm sorry…I didn't."

"For God sakes John…how do you forget something as important as that?" Nigel was clearly pissed at me. Getting the license plate number hadn't even occurred to me. Apparently, I sucked at finding out details. I would have to make a note and do better the next time.

"I need a coffee," said Nigel getting up from the table. "Anyone else?"

"Yes please," I said.

"Make that two," added Atwood.

"Sorry about the license plate," I said to Atwood.

"It's all right. Just remember John…the details are important. You might not think so, but it's the details, that lead to the arrests.

"I fully understand that…I do. It just slipped my mind at the time, that's all."

Nigel was still up at the bar getting the coffee. "So Nigel doesn't work for you at the Customs and Excise?"

"No…Nigel definitely doesn't work for me," said Atwood laughing. "Can't say much more about it though I'm afraid."

If Nigel didn't work for the Custom and Excise Department, then who the hell did he work for? It had to be some branch of the British Government, but I didn't have a clue as to which one, and it was apparent neither man was going to tell me. Once again, I was at the mercy of the unknown.

"Here we go," said Nigel setting a tray of coffee on the table. "By the time the waitress got round to bringing it by, the damn stuff would have been cold. I hate cold coffee." He poured himself a cup and started to drink. "Well I'm not going to serve you as well," he mocked.

"Of course not," I said hastily. I filled the remaining two mugs and handed one to Atwood. He nodded thanks.

"Okay John," said Nigel. "Let's go over the information about Michelle again."

"You two do like to torture me don't you? I'm not sure what else I can tell you! Good God."

"Just go over the events again please."

"Fine." I started from the beginning and went through everything at least three more times. It was ridiculous and the whole ordeal was making me cross.

"What was she wearing the first day you saw her on the weekend?" asked Nigel.

"Jeans and a T-shirt."

"And the second day?"

"A tight sweater and a short denim skirt with boots."

Nigel looked at me and gave a sarcastic laugh. "Well I see it's easy for you to remember certain details if you want to."

I couldn't help but laugh. It was true. I knew exactly what Michelle was wearing both days and could still smell the lingering aroma of her perfume…a lavender scent.

Nigel became more causal in his attitude and handed me a cigarette. "I would love to learn as much about Michelle as I could John. Do you think she fancies you?"

"I have no idea. We didn't get to spend that much time together and now she's back in France. I don't even know if I'll ever see her again." Secretly, I hoped Michelle did like me or at the very least wanted to get to know me better.

"Oh I'm sure you'll see her again John," said Nigel. "I wouldn't worry about that."

"We'd also like you to get close to Brian," added Atwood. "Do you think you can do that?"

"I can try, but I have no idea when or if I'll ever see him

again either." I must have sounded a bit too aloof in my response because Nigel jumped all over me.

"Look John," said Nigel sounding quite annoyed. "Yes, you are doing us a favour, but don't think you can get all smug about it. We have done you a huge favour have we not? Are you in jail?"

"No," I replied.

"That's correct…but don't think for a moment we wouldn't make a phone call. That's all it would take. We can make things easy on you, but only if you help us."

"I am helping you," I pleaded. "I'm doing the best I can. I'm sorry if it's not up to your expectations but I've told you everything I know. I've gotten quite close to Barrington, which has led us to Brian and Michelle. I'll try to get close to Brian, but I don't think he lets anybody get too close to him. You don't understand the way he looks at you…with these eyes that make you feel he can see what you're thinking. I don't want to raise any suspicions that might blow the whole operation. It's not like I do this sort of thing for a living you know."

"Yes, I know," said Nigel. "Just do your best."

The tension in the air eased but the foul taste in my mouth for both Atwood and Nigel lingered. I took a deep drag of my cigarette and peered out the window of the pub.

"So am I allowed to ask you people any questions at all?" I said.

"Depends what they are," answered Atwood.

"Who are Brian and Michelle? You must have some idea or at least have a hunch as to what they're up to."

"We really have no idea what they're up to," Atwood responded.

"That's bullshit and you know it," I answered. "You just don't want to tell me. If I'm going to snuggle up and get close to someone, I'd at least like to have some sort of idea who that person is. Why are they so important? You know about the drugs. I told you where to find them at Barrington's house, but so far, the house hasn't been raided. Now I'm delivering God knows what…I'd really appreciate knowing what I'm walking into. Yes, you're keeping me out of jail…but I'm the one who has to worry about keeping myself alive…or maybe that part doesn't concern you at all. Is my life that dispensable?

"Calm down John," said Atwood. "You're getting yourself all worked up over nothing."

"Nothing? You call this nothing?"

Nigel leaned across the table. "John…we will only help you, if you help us."

"Thank-you for reminding me once again. Did you ever think I might be able to help you more, if you'd just tell me who they are?"

"Knowing anything more is not going to help you," said Nigel.

"Why?"

"Listen to me Coventry," said Nigel sternly. "Don't fuck with us. I'm warning you. We can make your life easy, or we can make it so fucking hard you'll wish you'd have listened. Do you understand me? Prison would be a piece of cake compared to what we could do to you."

"Well maybe that's what I should do then," I answered. "Take my punishment and go to jail. But don't think for a second I won't hold a nice little press conference beforehand. I think a lot of people would be quite interested in what I have to say."

Both Atwood and Nigel looked like were ready to leap across the table and pound the living shit out of me. I don't know why I was being so confrontational today. I guess I was just tired of being the puppet – the ventriloquist's dummy. They had all the information, yet I was the one putting my bloody neck on the line. I knew Brian was a bad seed. I didn't know exactly what he was into, but he had the look of a seasoned thug. Obviously, Atwood and Nigel didn't give a damn about my well-being. As long as they got their bloody information – that's all they cared about.

"No one would believe a word from your mouth Coventry," said Atwood. "They would see you for who you really are…an arrogant idiot who thought he could defraud the government and get away with it. Besides, you don't think we have contacts in the press? Don't kid yourself John. The story would be discounted, and you'd be left looking like a fool…a fool who now had to spend a good chunk of his adult life locked up in prison. I don't think I need to tell you how nasty prison can be. Think of your family. Make the right decision John. Don't do something so stupid and utterly foolish because you seem to be having a bad day."

I was done arguing. I wasn't going to win anyway, so there really wasn't much point continuing.

"I never said I wasn't going to keep helping you. I just stated it might be nice to be kept in the loop a little more than I am. I haven't heard the most encouraging stories about Brian and quite frankly the man terrifies me. I just want to know what I'm up against. Does he sell drugs? Is he IRA?"

"Unfortunately John," said Atwood. "We're telling you as much as we can."

I shrugged my shoulders. "Whatever you say."

"You've made a wise and sensible decision John," said Nigel. "I understand this is hard for you but you have to trust us. A lot is riding on you and the information you're providing. Atwood here assures me you've been quite a big help on the drug end of things. I'm just asking for more on the personnel involved…mainly Brian and Michelle."

"Like I said, I'll do what I can. Are we done here because I'd really like to get going home?"

"Yes," said Atwood. "I'm done."

"Go ahead and go home," added Nigel. "But we'll both want to see you again as soon as you get back from the Darlish run. Call Atwood to set it up. Make us proud John…Make us proud."

"Fuck you," I said under my breath. I couldn't wait to get the hell out of there. It'd been one of the most stressful meetings yet. Who were they to threaten me like that? I'm sure they had connections but damn…if I was their only link to Brian, their investigation was seriously flawed. I hoped to God they had a back-up plan, because there was no way in hell, I was going to befriend Brian. The man scared me to death. Was I just supposed to walk up to him and go, "Hey Brian…how about you and I head down to the local pub for a couple of brews. So how's the family? By the way…what do you really do for a living…I mean seriously…I'm your new best friend…you can tell me."

Nigel and Atwood must have thought I was the stupidest bloke on earth. I didn't trust anyone - Brian or the government. In fact, I was having trouble discerning the good guys from the bad. They could all go to hell as far as I was concerned. Except for Michelle. I'm not sure why Nigel was so interested in her. I'm sure she was only a bit player in the whole game. Maybe sold a few drugs or whatever. I couldn't image her being heavily involved in anything. Shit…she could have been shagging Brian on the side for all I knew. Nigel was wrong about her; I could feel it.

Later that week I received a surprising call from my brother Max. Since my exit as Managing Director from Sim and Coventry, the family business, we hadn't exactly been on the best of terms.

"Do you know of any reason why one of Sim and Coventry's containers would be stopped on the docks?" said the voice on the other end of the phone.

"Well hello to you to Max," I answered sarcastically. "How are you doing? How's the family?"

"Everyone is fine," said Max. The annoyed tone of his voice made me chuckle.

"What can I do for you?" I tried to sound as cheery as I could, just to piss him off.

"Customs Agents stopped one of the containers on the docks, pulled, and searched all the contents. It delayed things quite a bit and cost the company a fair amount of money."

"I have no idea why they would do that," I lied. I knew immediately Atwood and his friends were sending me a message by flexing their muscles. Stupid arrogant jerks.

"I can't for the life of me figure it out either," said Max sounding rather perplexed. "I was just wondering if you had any insight from past experience."

"Sorry Max, but I'm at a loss as well. Maybe they were just doing some random checks…cracking down to see if everyone was following the rules and regulations. You know what the government is like. If they have a chance to make your life hell or cost you a few extra bucks, they will."

"I think they must take great pleasure in it," said Max. "They took forever and went through every last item. Wouldn't give an explanation or answer any questions. Anyway, I was just wondering if you knew anything."

"Sorry Max…can't help you." I hung up the phone and smiled.

Sure, I was pissed Atwood was being a prick, but I loved seeing Max confounded by things, especially since I was the cause. If he only knew why Customs stopped the container. He'd have shit his drawers for a month of Sundays thinking I was getting Sim and Coventry involved in something below the board. I wasn't of course, but Max would never see it that way. He had made up his mind about me, and nothing I could ever do or say would change it.

The situation was sad really. We'd gotten along so well as children and even into our early twenties. So many times in the past, I'd run to his rescue and bailed him out of trouble with friends, girlfriends, the police, but those instances seemed to be conveniently forgotten. I didn't want to fight with him, and I know it broke my parent's heart that we were no longer on good terms.

Sim and Coventry had nothing to do with the drugs, Brian, or the government. Atwood was just trying to make a point and I received the memo loud and clear. I guess he didn't appreciate me speaking out at the last meeting. I didn't care, I had some things to say, and for once in my life, I actually stood up and said them. I'd have to be careful and keep my outbursts to a minimum. But my dealings with the government were my concern; Atwood had no right to use the family business to make his statement.

A few days after Max's call, I received an urgent telephone call from my father asking me to come out to Townfield.

"Is everything all right with you and Mother?" I asked in a panic.

"Yes we're fine John," answered my father. "I just don't want to speak of the matter over the phone since I believe it might concern you. Why don't you come for cocktails and dinner? It's about time we caught up on a few things. Since you got the apartment, we don't get to see you as much."

"I know…I'm sorry Dad. Things have been a bit crazy lately. I'd be more than happy to join you for dinner."

"And cocktails…" he added.

"Yes of course," I laughed. "I'd never forget about the cocktails."

I hung up the phone and took a quick look at my watch. It was only one thirty. I still had a few hours to kill before heading out to my parents, so I decided to straighten and clean up the apartment. Not that I was expecting company, but I could only stand dirty clothes on the floor and dishes in the sink for so long. I tackled the kitchen first and spent forever trying to get a spot of dried spaghetti sauce off the cupboard door. How in the hell it got there was beyond me. Same for the strawberry jam on the underside of the refrigerator door. The splattered egg on the stovetop was from breakfast that morning. I'd just been too concerned with eating my eggs before they got cold, to wipe up the spill. Breaking an egg into the frying pan with one hand was definitely harder than it looked on television.

"That's much better," I said taking a look around the kitchen. "Best tackle the bedroom now."

I was one of those people who didn't mind having a conversation with themselves every once and awhile. Living alone could get boring and lonely. Sometimes you just needed the sound of a voice, even if it's your own, to break the silence. By the time I finished cleaning I was tired and frankly, in need of a shower. Who knew cleaning was such a workout? I let the hot, steamy water pound on my back and release the tension in my neck. These past few months had been very stressful and my body was showing signs of rebelling. Headaches, stiff neck, and fatigue. No amount of sleep could restore that fresh faced feeling. Hopefully, that would come once this whole ordeal was over.

My father and mother were already seated in the drawing room when I arrived.

"Hello all!" I said.

"John! Hello!" said my mother. "It's so good to see you. You've been a stranger lately." She kissed me on the cheek and beckoned me to the chair. "Let me pour you a drink. The usual?"

"That'd be great mother, thank-you."

She handed me the glass. "You look tired son…is everything okay?"

"Just a busy last couple of weeks that's all," I answered. "So what was it you wanted to tell me Dad?"

"Well we had the oddest thing happen at Sim and Coventry…"

"If it's about the shipping crates being blocked and searched, I already know, Max telephoned me a few days ago."

"No it was something different," said my father. "A couple of men stopped by the office…"

"What did they look like?" I interrupted.

"I didn't recognize them if that's what you're wondering. Atwood wasn't one of them. I'm sure of that. They said they were with some Special Branch of the Government. They flashed a couple of security cards. I gave them a look over and they seemed legit."

"What did they want?"

"I'm not sure. They just sort of poked around, having a look here and there, not saying why they'd come or what they wanted. It was more of a nuisance really…but they did hang around for quite a while."

"Nigel," I said under my breath.

"Who's Nigel," asked my father.

"I'm not really sure. He's been coming to my meetings with Atwood lately. He works for the government, although I don't know what branch."

"He's not with Customs?"

"No, he's not," I answered.

"John, I don't like this one bit."

"I know Dad…but I don't think you have anything to worry about with those men. I think Nigel was just making a point…see I'd gotten into somewhat of a row with both of them the other day. I think Nigel and Atwood are just trying to scare me. It's fine Dad, nothing to worry about. I can handle it."

"Are they harassing you?"

"No, no," I said taking a drink. "They like to remind me they have a certain amount of power over my life at the moment." I laughed. "Feeds their egos I suppose."

"If that's all it is John, then okay."

"I promise Dad, it's nothing more than that."

"How are things going otherwise?" he asked.

"Not bad," I answered. "Things are progressing and generally the government is very happy with the information I'm giving them. But let's not talk about it anymore. How are you and mother doing?"

I was happy to change the subject. I hated lying to my father or putting on a happy face when really I was worried. Having a Customs agent search a shipping crate was easy to cover up, having to explain why two government agents mysteriously showed up to search the Sim and Coventry offices was trickier. I wasn't concerned about my parents asking questions, they were in on the secret, it was Max and the others at Sim and Coventry.

Atwood and Nigel's little power trip had only furthered my desire to hasten the operation - get them what they needed and then get the hell out of there. I despised living my life always looking over my shoulder. Now it seemed the government wouldn't hesitate throwing my family into the fire if need be. How nice of them. Glad to know my tax money went to support such fear-mongering tactics. I already had the upcoming delivery run for Brian weighing heavy on my mind, I didn't need to add unexpected government agent visits to my family.

I wanted to call Atwood and Nigel and tell them to lay off, except I didn't want to give them the satisfaction of knowing how much their actions bothered me. If they asked, I'd just pretend I didn't know anything about it. Two can play at that game. I might have made a dumb mistake getting wrapped up in the fraud mess in the first place, but I wasn't a complete idiot. I could be selective in the information I passed on about Brian, Michelle and the drugs if I wanted to. They wouldn't know the difference. If they wanted to fuck with my family and me, go right ahead, I knew how to fuck them right back. The government boys thought they held all the cards, and while it was true they had a pretty good hand, I still had an ace or two up my sleeve.

CHAPTER EIGHT

Barrington gave me a call Thursday morning wanting me to stop by his place to go over the final plans for the delivery. I was somewhat apprehensive about the trip as a whole, but didn't mind that I'd be travelling alone. The long drive would give me a chance to think and ample opportunity to check out the crates and see if I could tell what might be in them. I knew Atwood told me not to look, but I was determined to give it a shot.

"Did you rent the van yet mate?" said Barrington.

"Not yet…was actually just about to go and do it after I left here."

"Where are you going?"

"I was thinking about the Hertz place in Liverpool," I answered.

"What about using Avis."

"Doesn't matter much to me," I said. "A rental van is a rental van."

Barrington laughed, "Then use Avis if you don't mind."

"Sure that's fine."

"Okay here's the plan. You need to meet Bob, the fisherman, at the cottage in Darlish at nine Saturday morning. When are you leaving?"

"I'm going to head out Friday morning and stay overnight at the Pub in Darlish again."

"Okay good. Once you leave Darlish, head straight for Martin's house in Middlesbrough."

"Martin?" I asked. "Who's Martin?"

"He's the fellow who owns the house in Middlesbrough.

You know, you've met him before."

I played stupid, "Martin…Martin…oh yes of course…Martin! Sorry had a bit of a brain freeze for a moment there." At least now, I'd be able to tell Atwood the man's name instead of just referring to him as 'the man in Middlesbrough'.

"The next leg of the journey is from Middlesbrough back to Liverpool. Meet me in car park before the docks in Liverpool when you get back on Sunday. I'll be waiting. Any questions?"

"No, I think I'm good," I answered.

"Perfect. Good luck. It's a piece of cake and you'll do just fine."

I stopped by Avis on my way home, set up the rental van then went to my apartment in Chester to rest and get ready. I packed a small bag with a change of clothes and some toiletry items. I'd only be staying over the one night, so I didn't need much.

The next morning, I was up with the first ring of the alarm and raring to go. I couldn't help but feel a tiny bit excited. After all, this was my first solo mission in the operation, and not everyone gets to "legally" participate in an "illegal" activity, a bit of a thrilling sense of adventure. I'm sure if something went wrong and I ended up with a gun to the side of my head, I'd quickly change my tune, but for now in the safety of my apartment, I could have a little fun with it.

The drive to Darlish was long, boring, and uneventful. Besides stopping for fuel and lunch at a horrible roadside service station, I drove straight through and arrived at the Darlish pub by early evening. The pub owner was glad to see me, and I think he appreciated the repeat overnight business. I checked into my room, got myself settled, and then headed back down to the pub for an excellent meal of ham and eggs.

After the garbage I ate for lunch, my stomach welcomed this meal with open arms.

I hung out for a bit in the pub having a few drinks and talking to the owner. He was a real nice fellow, down to earth and genuine. One of those people who woke up at the crack of dawn, worked their ass off all day, went to bed exhausted, only to get up the next morning and repeat the cycle all over. He seemed to enjoy it though, always had a smile on his face, and ran a clean and tidy establishment. The world ran on people like him, hard-workers with an industrious attitude. I felt kind of bad knowing that the government money I stole probably came from this poor guy's wallet in taxes. I made sure I left him a substantial tip for the dinner, drinks, and conversation.

This time I was prepared for a midnight visit from Atwood and the Customs agents, but when my alarm sounded at eight the next morning, it was clear no one was coming. After a quick hop in the shower, a coffee, and a cigarette, I was out the door and on the way to the cottage, reaching my destination at eight fifty-five, a full five minutes to spare. Leaning up against the cottage smoking a pipe, Bob the fisherman greeted me with a nod, then ambled off toward a small hut just beyond the cottage.

He motioned for me to back the van in and pull as close to the barn like doors of the hut as I could. As he swung the doors open, I could see seven or eight fair-sized wooden crates sitting in a pile. We each grabbed a side of the first crate and lifted it into the van. Whatever was inside was bloody heavy. I could hardly keep my end up. After about 20 minutes, all the crates were loaded and secure in the back of the van. I closed the rear doors and gave Bob a wave goodbye. He was already leaning up against the cottage, smoking his pipe. Stage one of the trip was over, now it was on to Middlesbrough.

The whole time we were loading the crates, I was dying to know what was inside. I didn't dare ask Bob and I had to be conscious of keeping my enthusiasm to a minimum. I waited until I was way out of Darlish and back on the motorway before I pulled over at a roadside service station to have a peek. I sat in the driver's seat for a moment puffing away on a cigarette, watching the traffic coming in and out of the station. I wanted to be sure Brian hadn't placed a tail on me.

About ten minutes later, I finally got the nerve to crawl to the back and check out the crates. Each crate had several different shipping marks, and it looked as though fresh marks had been plastered over older marks. I made note of all the marks on each crate, down to the last detail and wrote them on a piece of paper. I took off my shoe and placed the paper under the insole. It would be safe there.

There was no way in hell I was getting a look inside the crates though, every lid secured in place with a bevy of nails and pieces of steel wrapped around the crate two or three times. I would have to break the steel without ruining it and then remove each nail without making a mark or scratch. The feat was impossible.

"Bugger!" I said tugging on a sheath of steel. "Whatever's in here must be pretty damn important to lock it down this tight." Could it have been drugs? Guns? From the weight and size of the crates, it was hard to tell, and I wasn't exactly schooled in the weight of drugs or guns. I returned to the front seat and lit another smoke. Well at least I could give Atwood the shipping marks. That should help.

I turned the van back onto the freeway and continued the journey north to Middlesbrough. Again, it was boring and run of the mill. The radio in the van was having some serious personal issues, continually fading in and out and in out, so in frustration I finally just shut it off and drove in silence. I had a bit of trouble finding the house in Middlesbrough, as the streets were a complete maze. Normally Barrington was my guide.

Martin must have been watching for me, because as soon as I drove in front of the house, he was out the door. I would have never guessed he could move that fast.

"John…how are you?"

"Fine thanks, you?"

"Good, good. Back the van into that garage over there will ya."

"Sure thing." I backed the van into the garage, turned off the key and went around the back to help him unload.

"Oh that's all right mate," said Martin. "I got it."

"You sure?"

"Oh ya…I'll be fine. Listen, why don't you go into the house, grab yourself a coffee and a bite to eat. Put your feet up for a bit and relax. I'll let you know when the van's ready to go again."

"Well I would love a coffee," I answered.

Nothing had changed in the house since my last visit. The girls were still all there lying around drinking beer and doing drugs. The place was a disgusting pigsty with empty beer cans, dirty dishes, and take-out food packages strewn about the floor.

"Ladies," I said.

The girls who still had the wherewithal, lifted their stoned heads and gave me a nod. I fixed myself a snack, made a cup of coffee, and found an empty spot on the couch to wait for Martin. Despite the stench and unforgivable grime in the room, I must have fallen asleep. I guess pure exhaustion clouds your senses.

"John," said Martin tapping on my shoulder. "The van's all ready to go."

"Okay great," I said wiping my eyes. The hands on my watch read two in the morning. If I left now, I would be in Liverpool by noon and hopefully home and fast asleep in my own bed shortly after that. I didn't even dare glance in the back at the crates while Martin was standing by the side of the van.

"Have a good run back to Liverpool," he said.

"Will do."

Since it was the middle of the night, the roads were empty of traffic and the driving was quick and easy. When I stopped for fuel, I took the opportunity to have a look at the crates up close. They were wrapped exactly like the other ones, and again, there was no way I could open them. I wrote down the shipping marks on a separate sheet of paper and placed them in my other shoe.

The service station only offered junk snacks that didn't suit my tastes, so I drove a bit more before pulling into a restaurant for an early morning breakfast. I was ahead of schedule and would make Liverpool way before noon, so I took my time, enjoyed my meal, and had a second cup of coffee. I could use the caffeine. Dog-tired and stiff from driving, my body ached in places I didn't think it could ache. I went into the restroom to have a pee and splash some cold water on my face and eyes. I looked like a piece of dirt. My eyes were blood shot red and the bags underneath were dark and droopy.

"Geez John," I said peering in the cracked mirror. "This certainly isn't your finest hour on the looks front. Holy Christ." I brushed my hair back with my fingers in an attempt to look somewhat presentable but I'm not sure it had much affect. Who the hell cares? It's not as if I'm going to be bumping into the Queen or anything.

I paid my breakfast bill, got a coffee for the road, and continued on the last leg of my illicit adventure, which honestly hadn't turned out to be much of an adventure at all. The trip had been quite boring – just a bunch of driving, waiting around and then more driving. Oh well, if this was as exciting as my undercover work got, then that was okay with me. It meant I was keeping my ass out of trouble and that was a good thing.

True to his word, Barrington was waiting for me at the carport by the Liverpool docks. He hopped in the passenger side of the van, and out of the corner of my eye, I saw him sneak a peek at the crates in the back.

"Glad to see you John. You made great time."

"Ya, the roads were quite bare of traffic, especially this morning. Where am I heading now?"

He led me through the docks, which were a hive of activity, with multiple ships being loaded and containers being moved and stacked, eventually coming to an old warehouse. Barrington jumped out of the van and ran to open the large sliding front doors.

"Drive it all the way in," he yelled. I followed his instructions and drove the van in. It was a tight squeeze. "Good job. Now we'll just leave the van here and be on our way. I'm starving. Let's head down the street and grab something to eat. Grab your overnight bag."

The Holiday Inn was a few blocks down the street and Barrington and I entered the small onsite pub and restaurant. We found a table, sat down and ordered some lunch.

"So that's it?" I said. "The job's over?"

"That's it John," Barrington laughed. "I told you it'd be a piece of cake didn't I?"

"You did…I guess I didn't quite think it would be that

easy though. I could get used to it."

"Sure beats having a day job doesn't it," he snickered.

Just then, I felt a hand on my shoulder and a warm pat. I turned around and almost fell out of my chair when I saw Michelle standing there. She laughed and took a seat in one of the empty chairs. The woman looked incredible dressed in a very short denim skirt, high black boots, and a tight white T-shirt that framed her ample bosom. I knew I was staring but I just couldn't help myself. She was beautiful and gave off this vibe of animal magnetism. I could feel the blood rush as my cheeks blushed a crimson red.

"What are you doing here in Liverpool?" I asked quickly, trying to cover my embarrassment.

Michelle smiled at me in her beguiling way and my heart melted. She was so confident and self-assured – the way she talked, the way she dressed, even the way she walked.

"I had some business in the area," she answered. "How'd you get along on your little trip?"

"Oh quite fine…dull and boring actually."

"That's a good thing John," she chuckled. "It means it went well."

"I don't know about you two," said Barrington, "but I'm beat. I'm going to head on home. You need a lift John?"

"What about the van?" I asked. "It's in my name and it has to be back at the rental place by a certain time."

"Don't worry about it mate," said Barrington. "The van will be returned later in the day and the account will be squared away."

"If you say so…"

Michelle started laughing, "Oh John! You are my little virgin boy!"

"I am not a virgin!" I replied hastily. "I can assure you I've…"

"No, no, no," she said laughing. "I didn't mean it that way. I meant you are so new to what you're doing."

"Yes, I certainly am new here," I said. "In fact, I really have no idea *what* I'm doing."

She was laughing hysterically, almost to the point of tears. I wasn't quite sure what the big joke was and I didn't like being laughed at. She managed to calm down enough to take my hand in her own.

"Oh my little virgin boy…I think that's what I'll call you from now on…My little virgin boy."

I didn't like the title one bit and thought it was rude and demeaning. Of course, rather than speak up and voice my opinion, I laughed right along with her and Barrington.

"Are you coming or what?" said Barrington still laughing.

"No," I answered. "It's easier for me to just pick up my car from the car lot. It's actually quite close to the hotel."

"No problem…talk to you later then," he said giving a wave and walking out of the restaurant.

"I should get going too," I said.

"Oh…you have to leave so soon?" Her voice actually had a hint of disappointment in it.

"Well it's been a really long couple of days…a lot of driving…it gets exhausting."

"Can you at least stay for another minute? I'm staying here at the hotel and it's just too early to go up to my room yet for the night. It's still afternoon! Keep me company won't you?"

No man in his right mind would refuse that offer. "I guess I could stay for another coffee or so." I waved my hand to the waitress and she filled my mug. "Would you like a coffee Michelle?"

"No I'm good thank-you though," she said.

We chit chatted for a bit about trivial things and shared a

laugh or two. I would have loved to stay all night, but I was truly exhausted and I'd promised my parents I'd drive out to Townfield for a visit.

"It's been great talking to you Michelle, but I'm afraid I have to cut it short and get going."

"You do look rather tired." She looked right into my eyes and smiled.

I drank the last of my coffee and stood up to leave. I thought about shaking her hand but that seemed too formal, so I gave her a peck on each cheek, nothing serious. It was sort of a French thing to do. A sexy grin crept over her face and to my ultimate surprise; she returned with a gentle kiss on my mouth. It was all over in a second, but for that brief moment, I felt as if I'd died and was floating on a white cloud somewhere up in heaven. I couldn't even find the breath to say goodbye and just walked away.

"Goodnight my virgin boy," she yelled naughtily across the room.

After that kiss, she could call me whatever the hell she wanted - I didn't care. Did Michelle have feelings for me or was it all in my imagination? Now I was utterly confused and probably just blowing things out of proportion. I mean what man doesn't want to be kissed on the lips by a gorgeous, sexy woman. Maybe I was just flattered by the whole thing and the flattery had gone to my head. Still…I didn't see her kissing Barrington on the lips.

"Ah…she's French," I said to myself while driving out to Townfield. "They do things like that with kissing and hugging." I wasn't going to read anything more into it. Michelle was just a very friendly girl.

I joined my father for a drink in the morning room, me with a very large glass of "Famous Grouse" whisky, and he with a Dubonnet. He pulled out his notepad and readied his pen.

"Okay John…tell me about the trip," he said.

I told him in detail about the last couple of days and even showed him the papers I still had hidden in my shoes.

"Very interesting," he mused. "You say there were fresh marks over older marks?"

"Yes."

"Hmmm, that's very unusual." His pen was flying in a fast and furious manner. "Continue."

"Well the trip was ordinary for the most part." I didn't tell him about Michelle kissing me on the lips. He didn't have to know everything.

He set down his pen and took a sip of his drink. "John, I am very worried about you making these deliveries. You have no idea what's in those crates."

"I'm sure it's just drugs," I said.

"Oh…just drugs," he said. "You say that so nonchalantly."

"I didn't mean it that way Dad. If it weren't drugs then why would Atwood and the Customs people be so interested? I'm just trying to think things through rationally."

"John I don't think there's anything rational about what you're doing. I have to be honest, I don't like the sound of this Irishman Brian…Good God son, he could be IRA."

The thought of Brian being IRA wasn't new to me; I just didn't want to acknowledge the possibility. It made sense though, selling drugs to fund their terrorist activities against Britain. If that was the case, then I was in deep shit.

"I'm sure it's just about drugs," I said trying to ease his concerns. "Atwood wouldn't get me wrapped up in IRA and terrorist stuff. He's knows I'm not qualified for work like that."

"I wouldn't be so sure John. I wouldn't be so sure."

I left Townfield later that evening with a real sense of dread. If Brian was IRA then those heavy steel encased crates were probably full of guns or explosives. Great…just what I needed. What the hell was Atwood thinking? I was okay with relaying the whereabouts of a drug stash or tattling on a few dealers but I wasn't cut out for this IRA garbage. And if Brian was IRA, who the hell was Michelle? She couldn't be IRA…she was French…yet she did a lot of business with Brian? After the meeting with my father, I had more questions than answers.

By the time I arrived back at the apartment, I could hardly keep my eyes open. I quickly whipped off my clothes and collapsed onto my bed. Atwood and Nigel had wanted me to call as soon as I got back from the run, but those bastards could wait. I was too tired to breathe, let alone think. They could wait until I was ready to talk. That might be tomorrow or it might be the next day, I didn't really give a shit. Tonight I was going to sleep, and if my subconscious wanted to re-live the kiss with Michelle, then who was I to stop it.

Sure enough, my phone was ringing bright and early the next morning.

"You said you'd call as soon as you got back."

"Look Atwood, I didn't get home until late and I was bloody exhausted. I was up for over twenty-four hours straight, so just lay off okay?"

"We need to meet today sometime. How about in an hour or so?"

"How about not," I answered. "I can do later this afternoon around three."

"Fine we'll make it three then…at the Red Lion Pub in Parkgate?"

"Ya wherever, you're the boss."

"Very well, I'll let Nigel know."

"You do that," I hung up the phone and pulled the covers over my head. The bright morning sun was beating through the curtains and stinging my still weary eyes. I just wanted darkness and silence for a few hours longer.

Nigel and Atwood were already sitting at a table when I walked into the pub. Atwood was quite animated in his conversation but Nigel looked like he didn't give two pennies about whatever Atwood was blabbering on about.

"Gentleman," I said sitting down.

"You're late," said Atwood looking at his watch.

"Arrest me," I answered snidely.

"So how did it go?" asked Nigel.

"Went well…the trip was boring. Barrington told me to rent the van from Avis instead of Hertz, not sure why, but I did. Then I drove from Liverpool to Darlish and stayed overnight at the pub. I had to meet Bob…he's the guy who's always dressed in the fisherman's garb…at the cottage at nine in the morning. He had me back the van up to a little hut off to one side. I'd never noticed it before. Anyway, there were seven or so wooden crates stacked in the hut. I helped Bob load the van…the crates were heavy, that's for sure."

"Did you get a chance to look inside them?" asked an excited Atwood.

"Well I waited until I was on the motorway before I pulled off at a service station to have a look. Unfortunately they were nailed shut and had steel wire wrapped around them. There was no way I could open them without anyone finding out."

"Bloody hell John. So you're sitting with a van full of crates and you can't even tell me what's in them?" he said sarcastically.

"Are you kidding me Atwood? Before I left, you told me not to even try to open them…I'm just following your goddamn orders."

"Did you at least get the shipping information?"

I threw the two pieces of paper on the table. "Yes. The first one is for the crates I carted from Darlish to Middlesbrough and the second is for the crates from Middlesbrough to Liverpool."

Atwood looked them over as I explained about the two sets of shipping marks on each crate.

"Splendid job John. So who took the delivery in Middlesbrough?"

"The man who owns the house," I said. "His first name is Martin. I have no idea what his last name is or Bob the fisherman's last name. Martin told me to go in the house and he would take care of the unloading and re-loading of the van. There may have been someone else with him in the garage, but I didn't see anybody."

"There's a garage?" said Atwood.

"Yes…off to the side of the house. It's not attached and doesn't really look like it's even part of the property."

"Now where did you take the Middlesbrough shipment?"

"Barrington was waiting for me in the car park like he said he would…then he led me through the docks to an old warehouse. I drove the van in there and that was it."

"Was the warehouse large?"

"No, not all at. Fit the van, but I can't imagine much more."

"If I needed you to, would you be able to show me where the warehouse is located?"

"Ya sure. It's actually just down the road and within walking distance of the Holiday Inn. That's where we went for something to eat…and much to my surprise saw Michelle."

"Michelle was there?" said Nigel.

"Yes, she was staying at the Holiday Inn overnight…although she could have been staying there longer, I'm not really sure."

"Did you get a chance to talk to her?"

"Well after Barrington went home, she and I talked for a bit over coffee. Nothing serious. She asked me how the run went, so I told her. Then she asked me some more questions about myself…not in an inquisition kind of way like before, or the way Brian did…it was more like just talking and getting to know you types of questions."

"Did she tell you anything about herself?" asked Nigel.

"No…from what I gather…she doesn't like talking about herself. Not even the slightest details like family or friends. I didn't want to push things and spoil the good conversation we had going."

"You did the right thing John…well done," said Nigel. "You seem to be getting on well with Brian and Michelle…keep it up."

"Yes John," Atwood interrupted, "Keep it up and keep telling us what you're doing."

"Any plans for another run?" said Nigel.

"I don't know yet," I answered truthfully. "I'm going to catch up with Barrington later in the week. I don't see why there wouldn't be…both he and Michelle said I did an excellent job."

"And you said there was no sign of Brian on your trip?" said Nigel.

"No, didn't see him at all. In fact his name didn't even come up in any conversation."

"Well that's all right John. Just remember to keep your eyes and ears open, especially when it comes to Brian and Michelle. Can you do that?"

"Yes of course," I replied. I purposely didn't mention

Michelle's kiss. I wasn't sure how either of them would react and really, it was none of their goddamn business.

"Until next time then John," said Atwood rising from the table. "Give me a call as soon as you know something more, especially if you have another delivery."

"Goodbye Coventry," said Nigel with a doff of his hand.

I ordered myself a beer, downed it in a couple of swallows and left. On the way home, I stopped at the market for some groceries, since the refrigerator at the apartment was currently housing a soured jug of milk and rapidly decaying piece of cheese. I made myself a great dinner, and then settled on the couch with a book. It felt good just to relax for a night and read about someone else's struggles for a change. Sometimes I felt my own life was an unbelievable work of fiction – I just didn't know how the hell it was going to end.

CHAPTER NINE

A week or so later, I was on the way to Darlish for my second run. This time Barrington came with me. I had mixed feelings about having a sidekick for this trip. On one hand, I was glad to have the company, driving that distance with no one to talk to but the dead bugs on my windshield was a bit mind numbing. On the other hand, there wouldn't be any opportunity to check out the crates and copy down the shipping information. Atwood was going to be mightily peeved. Oh well, it wouldn't be the first time and it probably wasn't going to be the last.

We left early in the morning and arrived in Darlish late that afternoon. Once again, I'd being staying at the pub while Barrington bunked at the cabin. I really didn't mind lodging at the pub. It gave me a chance to be alone and meet with Atwood if need be. I pulled the van into laneway at the cottage and immediately noticed Brian's jaguar.

"Shit," I thought. I was hoping it would have just been Bob again. I knew Nigel wanted me to get closer and spend more time with Brian, but the thought of it made my stomach churn.

"Park it up by the side there John," said Barrington pointing to an empty spot by a rather large and imposing oak tree. The tree reminded me of Brian, tall, strong, and powerful.

Brian was sitting in his usual armchair having a drink.

"Barrington, Coventry…did ya have good trip?"

"Not bad, traffic was light…so that made things easier," answered Barrington.

When I returned from the bathroom, a welcome and familiar voice greeted me.

"There you are my little virgin boy!" laughed Michelle. Of course, Barrington started laughing and I was slightly embarrassed. Brian had a look of puzzlement on his face but said nothing.

"Come and sit down beside me John," said Michelle taking my hand. "Let me pour you a drink."

"You don't have to do that Michelle, I can get it myself."

"Nonsense," she smiled. "You've had a long trip." She handed me a glass of whisky and got comfortable on the couch. "How have you been?"

"Good…yourself?" I answered. It felt awkward talking to Michelle with Brian there. I wanted to take her away from all of this and just spend some time together. All I could think about was her lips on mine, and the way it made my heart pound and my knees buckle.

"I've been well. You look more refreshed since the last time I saw you."

"Well the last time I saw you, I was severely lacking in sleep," I laughed.

"Speaking of last time," said Brian. "You did a good job. I'm told everything went smoothly."

"Yes, I didn't encounter any problems on my end."

We all sat and chatted for an hour or so before settling in for some dinner. Barrington was a horrible cook but we managed to eat the chicken he grilled. After dinner, it was back to more chatter in the sitting room. The chicken must have soured Brian's mood, because it had definitely changed from earlier in the afternoon. Once again, I was on the hot seat, the recipient of a multitude of questions. I kept my cool and answered everything, but I was getting the distinct feeling Brian either didn't like me much or trust me at all.

More than once, I caught Michelle watching me, almost willing me with her expressions to give the right answers. That gave me some comfort.

"Well laddie, there's something I need you to do for me," said Brian.

"Okay. If I can, I'll do it." I answered.

"Oh I know you'll be able to do this my boy."

I didn't like the sound of his voice and I was almost afraid to hear what he wanted me to do.

"I need to hire a few new bodyguards…as you know…you can never be too careful in Ireland these days."

I nodded and hoped to hell, he didn't want me to be one of his bodyguards. That was one job I'd knew I'd fail at immediately.

"Now I have half a dozen boys or so in mind, but I want you to interview them, give them a medical, and see if they're fit enough for the task."

"You want me to give them a medical? You do realize I'm not a doctor don't you?"

Brian laughed. "Okay this is what you're going to do." He put great emphasis on the word "do". "I will give you some printed forms, the boys will complete them…I need their names, addresses…things like that. As far as the medicals go, it's very straightforward. Just ask them the questions on the form, then tell them they need to strip naked."

I almost shit my drawers. No way was I asking anyone to strip naked. What the hell was Brian getting me into?

"Once they're naked, you need to take their exact weights and heights. I need their measurements for a uniform."

"I'm just wondering why they need to strip naked. Can't I take the measurements with their clothes on? Will it really make that much difference?"

Brian gave me a cold, hard stare. "Listen John, the first thing you need to understand is that no one questions my orders. Do you hear me?" His voice boomed a little louder. "No one questions my orders. No one." He paused long enough to make a point and then continued. "Second, I need to know their precise weight. The only way to get that is to weigh them naked."

"Okay…whatever you say," I answered. I knew better than to challenge his word. "Where are the interviews to take place?"

"You will be at the Posthouse Hotel, outside the city of Chester at two pm on the Tuesday a fortnight from now. You will go to the reception desk and register for a private conference room, using the single day rate. It has all been arranged and is already in your name."

I nodded my head like a good puppet does and kept my mouth shut.

"There's one other thing laddie…you will be telling no one about this will you?"

"Absolutely not," I said. "Wouldn't dream of it."

I didn't like Brian's menacing tones and was more than happy to get my ass out of the cottage and back to the pub for the evening. Not even Michelle's sexy blue top could keep me there. I ordered up a steak and kidney pie, and ate it in bed while I watched television. Around ten pm I switched off the light and fell asleep.

Just after one am, I heard a tapping on my door.

"Must be Atwood," I thought. "I certainly have some things to tell him."

I hopped out of bed and opened the door. Michelle walked in. I was in complete and utter shock. First off, I was standing there in front of this woman wearing only my underwear, and second, Atwood could come knocking on my door at any moment. She put a hand to her lips and whispered for me not to make a noise until she shut the door behind her.

"I'm so sorry if you were asleep," she said. "I brought a bottle of wine for us...if you're interested."

I was interested but couldn't find the words to speak. It would seem very odd to turn her away. I mean...how often does a beautiful woman show up on your doorstep in the middle of the night with a bottle of wine? I'd be a daft fool. She might wonder why and start to ask questions, which might jeopardize everything. Besides, I didn't want to turn her away.

"Can I sit down?" she smiled.

"Of course, of course," I said, my mind snapping out its trance. I pointed to the bed. "Sorry but I don't have a chair."

She laughed and sat on the edge of the bed. "That's all right. I don't mind sitting here. Come sit beside me."

I felt like a nervous schoolboy. My heart was jumping inside my chest, and no matter how many deep breaths I took, it wouldn't settle down. I managed to find a couple of plastic glasses and handed them to her. I needed a drink, and I needed it fast, before my hormones got the best of me and did something foolish. She opened the bottle and filled the glasses.

"I hope you're not angry I've come to your room so late at night?"

"Oh God no," I answered. "Why would I be angry?"

"I don't know...some people like their sleep," she laughed.

"Is everything okay?" I asked. "I'm just a little surprised to see you here, that's all."

"Everything is fine. I was bored and a little lonely, so I thought I'd come and see my little virgin boy."

I laughed. "There you go with the little virgin boy name."
"You don't like it?"
"It's just a little embarrassing."
She touched my bare arm and ignited shocks throughout my body. "You have nothing to be embarrassed about." She finished her glass of wine and poured both of us another. "So John Coventry…tell me about yourself. I want to know everything there is to know about you."

"I'm sure if I told you everything about me, you'd run the other way as fast as you could. I think we've already covered most of it anyways."

"Oh I don't know about that," she grinned. "We all have our secrets."

"I guess you're right," I answered.

We talked and talked and I told her almost everything. I left out a few childhood experiences I wasn't yet ready to face myself and of course, I didn't mention a word about Atwood and the Customs people. She wanted to know all about the Department of Trade fraud, and how I'd managed to get myself mixed up with a couple of dolts like Andy and Craig.

"I don't know honestly," I said. "Sometimes you just get yourself involved in shit…and before you know it…you're in so deep, it's almost impossible to get out. I don't blame Andy or Craig for my mistake. I could have said no… should have said no…but I didn't."

"But you didn't get caught, so that's a good thing right?"

"True…but I have this feeling one day the police are going to figure out I was involved and come knocking on my door."

"Ooooo…you're such a bad ass my little virgin boy," she laughed. "I like it."

Throughout the entire conversation, she'd been gently stroking my arm and running her fingers over my own. My insides were about to burst.

"So now you know all about me," I said. "Tell me something about you? Who are you? What do you do?"

She had a mysterious twinkle in her eye, "Oh I do lots of things."

Then she looked at me in such a way – a curious vulnerability, that I threw inhibition to the wind and kissed her on the lips. She responded immediately and with great determination, saying hello to my mouth with her tongue, as I ran my hands under her shirt. Her skin was warm and soft, like the silk spun on ancient looms. It took everything in my power not to rip her shirt right off and expose her flesh to my wondering eyes.

She must have read my mind, for she backed away from our kiss, and slowly undid the buttons on her blouse. I tried to reach out and pull her into my arms, but she held up her finger and grinned, forcing me to wait in agony as she removed her top and undid the button on her jeans. Standing there naked in the silhouette of the window, she was stunning, the moonlight illuminating every curve and arch of her well-toned figure. I couldn't stand it any longer. I reached out for her arm and swept her down on top of me as she giggled.

"Oh my God, you are so beautiful," I said letting my hands run freely up and down her back.

"Make love to me my little virgin boy," she whispered in my ear.

We spent the whole night in frantic lovemaking, every ounce of my passion received with enthusiasm, and returned with animalistic fervor. As if our spirits were one, we found endless ways to satisfy the insatiable appetite we had for each other. I'd never quite experienced something so powerful on both a physical and emotional level. It didn't feel like two people just getting together for a good shag…it felt more like a connection, a bond only the two of us would share. Whether it went past this night and this room, I didn't know, but for that moment, it was everything.

As morning dawned through the window, I opened my eyes to see Michelle standing naked making us some coffee. She looked as though she didn't have a care in the world.

"Morning," she said with a smile.

"Good morning to you," I said.

"I'm just making you some coffee…I know how much you like it."

"You actually expect me to drink coffee while you're standing there naked?" I laughed.

"That was the idea," she said with a smirk.

"I'm sorry but that's just not going to happen. I think you need to come back over here for a minute so I can explain to you exactly why I can't drink the coffee you're making."

She glided over and sat on the edge of the bed. "Now tell me why you can't drink the coffee I'm making."

"For starters, this bit of hair that's falling over your face is distracting me. Let me move it out of the way." I took my hand and gently brushed the hair back. "That's better…but wait…now it's on your neck."

I nuzzled my face into her neck and showered her with kisses. She moaned and tilted back her head to give me a better angle. I followed the line of her collarbone with my mouth and I could feel her chest heaving as I explored her breasts with my open mouth.

"Oh God," she groaned. "Yes…this is much better than coffee…" Her response made me laugh and I had to stop for a second to re-group. "Do not stop…please…do not stop."

I continued my kisses and navigated every inch of her body with my hands. I wanted to know this woman more intimately than any other woman I'd ever been with. I wanted to sear the memory of every wrinkle and every freckle into my brain, so I could read her like a blind man reads Braille. We made love in the morning sun with even more enthusiasm than in the mist of the moonlight.

"I think the coffee is cold," Michelle laughed kissing my ear.

"I don't give a flying fuck about the coffee," I replied. We kissed for a few minutes before Michelle pulled away.

"I have to get going."

"No…please stay," I said.

"I can't."

"Just for another day or so."

She laughed. "Another day or so…I think they would come looking for you by then. Doesn't Peter need a ride home?"

"There you go breaking the mood with work."

"I'm sorry. I'll kiss you once more to make it all better." She kissed me hard on the mouth and got out of bed. Watching her quickly get dressed was far less interesting than her seductive removal of clothes the night before.

"Goodbye my virgin boy," she grinned.

"Will we see each other soon?" I asked.

"Maybe," she said. "Who knows…wherever the wind takes us." She closed the door behind her, then quickly opened it and ran back to the bed. "One more kiss." She placed her lips on mine and we kissed goodbye. As our lips parted, our eyes locked in a lingering trance.

"You be careful. Look after yourself," she said in a kind but stern voice. Then she was out the door and gone.

I really couldn't believe last night hadn't been a figment

of my imagination. Michelle, "the" Michelle, showed up on my doorstep, because she wanted to be with me. That was one detail, I might not tell Nigel and Atwood. It was none of their business who I slept with, or what happened in my personal life. They might think it is, but I had a differing opinion. Stupid bastards would shit if they knew. I'd have to be careful and not let them find out.

I pitched the coffee Michelle had made and prepared myself a new batch. A quick check of my watch told me I still had some time before I had to be at the cottage for the drive home. I wondered if Michelle would be there. In a way, I hoped she wouldn't. I preferred to remember our goodbye with the passionate kiss, instead of an awkward hug or wave in front of Barrington or Brian. I sat on the bed, enjoying my coffee and lost in my thoughts. It'd been a fantastic night and I was exhausted.

"Holy hell," I said laughing to myself. "That night came out of nowhere."

I could still picture Michelle's naked body lying next to mine and could smell the scent of her perfume on my skin. I could never, ever think of her in the same light as before. I was smitten, and was fairly confident she felt the same way. I hated not knowing when I would see her again.

"Wherever the wind takes us…what the hell did that mean?" I had no way of contacting her, no address, no phone number, no nothing. She was like a phantom, coming in the night, stirring up the fires and then leaving without a trace. I knew almost nothing about her, yet my heart felt as if I'd known her forever.

"Did ya sleep well last night John," said Barrington as I stepped in the front door of the cottage. He had a funny look on his face, like he knew about Michelle, but I wasn't about to offer up any information.

"Slept fine, thank you," I answered.

"The van's all ready to go," said Barrington. "Let me just grab me stuff and we can get out of here."

"Sounds good to me." I peeked around the cottage but didn't see any signs of Brian or Michelle. It was just as well.

Besides a short stop in Birmingham to drop off a single crate, the drive was smooth sailing all the way home to Liverpool. Barrington must have thought I was being a total ass for not wanting to talk much, but I couldn't concentrate on simple conversation when my mind was consumed with Michelle. I replayed the events over and over in my brain, and I prayed to God Barrington didn't look over and see the goofy smile on my face.

Over the next couple of weeks, I continued to make several runs back and forth to Darlish and was disappointed at not seeing Michelle. The trips were routine and even though I'd yet to be paid, it was easy money. I met regularly with Atwood and kept him abreast of what was going on, except for my rendezvous with Michelle. That was a secret. He didn't ask and I didn't offer. Maybe the Customs agents weren't keeping quite as close an eye on me as I thought. If they were, they surely would have recognized Michelle entering the pub that night and not leaving until early in the morning.

I didn't tell Atwood about interviewing the potential bodyguards for Brian either. I probably should have, but the intimidating tone of Brian's voice and the way he made me promise not to tell anyone, really frightened me. If he found out I was ratting on him, I was a dead man. Brian was a hard nut to crack – rich, powerful, and intelligent. I clearly hadn't gained his full trust and always felt like he was testing me, with the questions he asked, and the jobs he made me do. Just waiting for me to change my story, leave out a detail, or worse, say something stupid that would blow my cover.

The Posthouse Hotel in Chester was easy to find. I went up to the reception desk, gave the lady my name, and registered for the room. She handed me a sealed manila envelope, which I assumed had all the questionnaires and other instructions.

"Send the gentlemen up to the conference room when they arrive will you?"

"Yes sir, Mr. Coventry," answered the receptionist.

By the time the clock struck two, there were around six or seven young men gathered in the room. They all looked around eighteen or nineteen years old. While I was waiting for everyone to arrive, I'd opened the envelope and looked at the papers. Brian left me a note asking that I take each man's temperature after I complete the "medical." I had no idea why he would need to know their temperatures, but I wasn't going to argue with him.

I passed out the forms and each guy filled in his name, address, telephone number, and pertinent medical information. Then I took them one by one into an adjacent room for their personal interview, and the required height and weight measurements, along with their temperature. I was thoroughly embarrassed asking the men to strip naked. If Brian was trying to put me in an uncomfortable position, he was doing a damn fine job of it.

"I'm so sorry," I repeated, "but I'm going to have to ask you to take off all your clothes."

"Everything?" said one of the men. "Even me knickers?"

"Yes everything…those are my instructions. Again, I'm terribly sorry."

I did my best not to touch any of the men while I measured their height, and I purposely made them stand face first against the wall, so I'd only have to look at their ass. I figured that had to be less discomforting for both of us, then to have them staring at me with their willies dangling about. I still didn't understand why Brian needed them to strip. It was all quite bizarre. The whole thing was over in a couple of hours, and as per Brian's instructions I put all the papers back into the envelope (along with the thermometer and tape measure) and dropped them off at Barrington's house in Wallasey.

"How'd it go," he asked.

"All right I guess."

"Seemed to be a little over the top with the stripping and temperature taking," I laughed. "Any idea what that's all about?"

"No idea…but I learned a long time ago not to question or go against anything Brian says. I just do what I'm told and keep my ass out of trouble," he said handing me a beer. "Some of those boys are a raw and rough bunch. Take Martin in Middlesbrough…you know how he likes to cane the girls when they fuck up…well one of the girls…Suzy…she stayed out all night and Martin hates that. When she came home in the morning, she had a huge bruise below her right eye. Some bastard beat her up…anyway, Martin was pissed and wanted to know who she'd been out with and what happened. Suzy wasn't going to talk, but Martin marched her up the stairs and tanned her hide with the cane for almost thirty minutes until she gave the guy up. He even made all the other girls watch to teach them a lesson. Martin had the guy…I guess it was some young punk…picked up and brought over to the house one night. Four big bastards held him up against the wall, while Martin took out a long knife and taunted the kid. Then he stuffed a rag in the poor lad's mouth, ripped open his shirt and pants and squeezed his balls so tight, the kid vomited. Martin laughed and then cut the kid's balls clean off."

"Are you kidding me?"

"I wish I was," answered Barrington shaking his head. "Now I'm all for a little spanking when you done wrong, but cutting off a guy's balls…now that's just sick and cruel."

"You can say that again," I said. Good God these people were insane.

"Ya, Martin's a bit of a character. He's always been okay with me; then again, I always steer clear of him when he has a knife. I like my balls thank you very much." Barrington cracked open another beer and lit a joint. "Speaking of Martin and the girls…do you remember Kelly?"

"The one with the short blond hair?"

"Ya that's her," said Barrington. "Someone sliced up her face with a beer bottle the other day."

"What?"

"I guess she got to drinking too much one night at the club and started yaking her mouth off about the drugs and shit at the house. Next thing she knew, there's a broken beer glass flying across her face. Her cheek was cut wide open and right through…she's scarred for life now…really is a shame…she was such a pretty girl."

"That's crazy!" I said.

"That's what happens when people don't keep their mouth shut and follow the rules. People like Martin and Brian won't think twice about messing you up if they think you're fucking with them."

A nervous laugh slipped from my throat. "Thanks for the heads up. I'll keep that in mind."

Barrington laughed, "I wasn't talking about you. You're a cool shit Coventry. I like you and so does Martin."

"What about Brian?"

"Ah fuck John," Barrington laughed. "Brian doesn't like

anyone. I think he only pretends to like me."

I laughed along to hide my own discomfort. These people were crazy bastards – whether it was the drink, the drugs, or just a plain malfunction of the brain, they were all mad. And here I was, plopped right smack dab in the middle of it all. I'd be lucky to come out of this thing unscathed, I knew that, I just didn't want to admit it.

The phone rang and Barrington got up to take it in the other room. He was gone for around twenty minutes.

"Speak of the devil," he said with a chuckle. "That was Brian. He wants you to travel to the cottage this weekend. Has some business he wants to discuss with you."

Here we go…the shit was about to fly.

CHAPTER TEN

Brian thrust a couple thousand pounds into my hand. "That's for the work you been doing." He looked so smug and condescending, like he was doing me a huge favour.

"Thank you," I said politely. Brian couldn't have cared in the least.

"Tomorrow you will fly to Paris with Barrington," he said.

"Tomorrow? That's awfully short notice," I answered.

Brian stared me down and continued talking. "You'll fly out of Heathrow and be met in Paris by another contact. They will tell you what the task will be."

"How do I know who to meet? Is there a name?"

"They'll know you and meet you when you get off the flight. It's already set up."

I wanted to ask Brian some more questions but from the surly face, it was clear I wasn't going to get any answers.

"Well I look forward to the trip," I lied. "I guess I should head down to the pub and check in."

"That won't be necessary," said Brian. "You'll stay at the cottage tonight. There's plenty of room."

"I really don't mind the pub," I said. I didn't want to stay at the cottage and was doing my best to weasel my way out. "The bed is great and I love the food." I smiled but Brian wasn't sharing my enthusiasm.

"You'll stay here at the cottage John. That's final."

Brian seemed uneasy and even more abrupt than usual. That scared me somewhat. What scared me more was having no idea why I was going to Paris in the first place. Atwood was going to fly the coop when he discovered I'd left England without telling him. I wanted to let him know but there was no way for me to get a hold of him. I couldn't risk using the cottage phone and the pub was out. He'd just have to understand. I knew he wasn't going to like it, but seriously, what the hell was I supposed to do?

The night at cottage was boring and dull. Brian kept to himself in another room and I think Barrington was a bit peeved at having to escort me to Paris. He didn't say anything but his sour disposition told me all I needed to know.

"Any idea why we're going to Paris?"

Barrington shook his head, "This is your party in Paris mate, not mine."

His response only fueled my curiosity. "What's that supposed to mean? My party?"

"Just that this one is your gig…I'm only tagging along because Brian wants me to." He reached into his shirt pocket and took out a joint. "I'm going to go for a little walk. Want to join me?"

"Nah…I'm fine. You go ahead," I answered. I wasn't in the mood for a second hand smoke high, my mind was already cloudy enough.

"If Brian asks, tell him I'll be back in a bit."

I followed Barrington out the front door and took a seat on the old wooden chair by the side of the cottage. According to the newspaper, it had rained like crazy a few nights ago in Darlish, and I could still see the faint imprint of tire marks leading up to the storage shed. I wondered if they'd just received a fresh delivery of goods. I would have loved to spend some time in that shed with a crowbar, finding out exactly what was in those crates.

If Brian was IRA as I suspected, there could be guns,

explosives and all sorts of very nasty and illegal wares. Maybe that was the reason Atwood hadn't bothered to raid Barrington's home in Wallasey, even though he knew all about the drug stash. Maybe the drugs were just a small part of the operation, and Customs was looking for a much bigger haul. I lit a cigarette and took a long deep drag. Then who was Nigel? He only appeared onto the scene once I told Atwood that I had indeed made contact with Brian. Come to think of it, Nigel never gave a shit when I'd talk to Atwood about the drugs. All he cared about was Brian and Michelle.

But why Michelle? What was her part in this whole thing? The question drove me nuts as I turned what little information I had, over in my head. I felt such a strong connection to her and wanted to protect her from people like Martin and Brian, but I had no idea how. I had enough trouble trying to protect myself.

The flight from Heathrow to Paris only took about an hour. Barrington was in a bit of a better mood, chatting on about football, although I had other things on my mind, and would have preferred sitting there in peace. The French Border Control Guard glanced at my British Passport.

"Welcome to France."

"Thank-you," I answered.

Brian said someone would be there to pick us up, but as I scanned the crowded terminal, I didn't recognize a soul. We found our luggage and walked outside. Out of nowhere, a young man strode up and tapped me on the shoulder.

"John Coventry?"

"Yes," I replied.

"Follow me please." He led us to his car, popped the trunk for our luggage, and helped toss the couple of bags inside. Since it was such short notice, I only had a single change of clothes. I kept the cash Brian gave me securely tucked in the inside pocket of my coat. I could always buy some more clothes if I needed them.

The young Frenchman started the car and we took off into the countryside at a hell of a rate. The French countryside is a beautiful place, with all the farmers' fields, wild flowers, and forests. We traveled on the main road for about an hour and then the Frenchman turned off onto a country lane and we travelled for another hour or so, coming to the edge of a dense forest. He steered the vehicle down a very narrow, bumpy path, running through the trees and brush. In a small clearing sat a small broken down farmhouse.

The Frenchman, who hadn't spoken a word the entire journey parked the car and beckoned us toward the front door. The farmhouse was old and leaned slightly to the left, like a drunken man after too many hours in the local pub. I couldn't imagine living in a place like this, then again all these drug houses like Barrington's, Martin's and even the cottage at Darlish seemed to have that "nobody gives a shit" appearance. He kicked at the stiff front door a couple of times to release it from its rusty hold and walked in.

The door opened into a single room with a sitting area and a small kitchen at the far end. Two huge horizontal wooden beams held up the low ceiling, and someone had haphazardly secured diagonal wooden pieces in between for extra support. The coldness of the concrete floor matched the air in the room. A single log burning in the fireplace was trying to ward off the chill but failing miserably. The whole place had a look of doom and gloom.

Five men jabbering away in French were all huddled by the fireplace. My cheery smile hello was greeted with nasty "what the fuck are you doing here" glares and my eyes were drawn to the revolver tucked into the belt of the large dark haired man. A shiver flew up my spine and I wanted to turn and run as far away from the house as I could.

"You okay mate?" said Barrington. "You look a little pale and sickly."

"I'm fine. Just a little tired from the long trip I guess."

"Well…go stand by the fire and warm up. It's so cold in here a fellow might freeze his nuts off." Barrington walked toward the fire and the men. "Bonjour Simone."

The man muttered something back in French and suspiciously looked my way. Barrington smiled and the two of them conversed back in forth in French. Then they started laughing and the man looked at me and smiled. I had no idea what they were saying, but by their expressions and body language, I knew they were talking about me. I felt so stupid.

A noise coming from upstairs diverted my attention to the small winding staircase. Like a vision, Michelle swept down the stairs and ignited the room.

"Welcome to France my little virgin boy!" she yelled.

I was surprised to see her but delighted when she came right over and kissed me passionately in front of Barrington and the other men. One of the guys mumbled something in French, and then laughed. Michelle snapped around, and with fire in her eyes replied in a very stern and angry tone. The man shrunk away and laughed no more.

"Pay no attention to these clowns," she said taking my hand and leading me outside. "Let's go for a walk."

I was much happier now that Michelle was by my side, but I still felt a real sense of uneasiness about the men and being in France.

"I'm so happy to see you John."

"I'm happy to see you too Michelle. It was quite a shock when you came down the stairs there."

Michelle laughed and leaned in close to my body. "You should have seen your face! You were white...like a ghost or something."

We ambled along old worn pathways through the beautiful forest, where in spots the denseness of the trees would block the sunlight from shining through. It was an enchanted setting, two lovers walking hand in hand, talking, and laughing their way through the gorgeous French countryside. I was full of questions but Michelle was very skilled at answering none of them. She just kept grinning, giggling, and saying how happy she was that we were together again.

"Don't you see John," she said. "This is the way things should always be...beautiful and free...it makes me sad to think moments like these are so fleeting."

"They don't have to be," I answered.

She smiled at me and shook her head. "You have no idea do you?"

"How can I have an idea if you refuse to tell me anything?"

"Let's just walk and enjoy the time we have okay? I will tell you more tomorrow. Right now...no more talking...just walking and laughing."

I wasn't going to press the situation, I was just happy to be able to spend this precious time with her. We walked a bit more and Michelle shared her love of France. She was very knowledgeable and had some strong opinions on what was right and what was wrong with her country. At the time, I didn't pay much attention to her political ramblings. Maybe I should have.

"Let's go back to the house and I'll cook you a nice dinner," she said.

"That sounds like a plan," I answered. "I didn't realize

until now, just how hungry I was."

Back at the farmhouse, Michelle cooked up a plate of trout and fresh vegetables for each of us. Of course, there was wonderful French wine to go with the dinner. I glanced out the front window and noticed the man with the gun was standing alone, presumably keeping guard. The behavior of the people in the farmhouse was much different from the houses in Wallasey and Middlesbrough. There was no bad language, or garbage or beer cans strewn about the floor, and absolutely no one touched any drugs. The place just had a different, more civilized vibe to it, which I liked, but there was also an intense seriousness, which scared the bloody hell out of me. I had no idea where Barrington was and frankly didn't care. My business right now was to enjoy my dinner with Michelle.

"How's the fish?" she asked.

"It's fantastic," I answered. "Might be the best I've ever had."

Michelle smiled seductively, "You're just saying that to butter me up for later."

"For later?" I smirked. "What's going to happen later?"

She leaned over and whispered in my ear. "I'm going to fuck your brains out."

"Oh," I said cheekily. "Is that all?"

She playfully slapped my arm, "You're bad my little virgin boy…very, very bad."

I helped her clean up the kitchen, and then we enjoyed a coffee on the front porch as the sun set over the trees.

"What a beautiful evening," said Michelle.

"I think you're the one who's beautiful," I answered.

She looked over at me and smiled. "I think it's time for bed."

She took my hand, led me back into the house and up the

small winding staircase. It only took a moment for us to throw off our clothes and rekindle the passion. The two weeks we'd been apart melted away. We laughed, we loved, we talked and we loved some more, falling asleep in each other's arms. Being together just felt so right and so natural, as if we were an extension of each other.

I never thought I could ever experience the kind of intense emotion or feeling of belonging, the way I did when I was with Michelle. It was almost overwhelming and caught me off guard. In the throes of our love, we moved as one. A singular motion of ecstasy. I know she felt it too, the way she kissed me, the way she touched me, and the way she made love to me. In that moment, nothing else mattered. I felt alive.

The next morning I was awakened with a gentle kiss to my lips.

"Good morning my sweet, sleepy John." Michelle had been up for a while and was already dressed. I took hold of her arms and tried to pull her back to bed. "Not this morning my love," she said laughing. "We have things to do."

"Like what?" I said.

"Oh I don't know," she grinned. "How about just relaxing in France for the day?"

"As long as you're with me, I'm content to do anything."

"Anything?" she giggled.

"Anything." She let me pull her down on top of me and we kissed passionately.

"Get dressed and come down and have some breakfast. I'm making crepes and I've just brewed a fresh pot of coffee."

"All right, all right," I said releasing her from my loving hold. "I'll get up. I don't want to, but for you, I will."

She laughed and blew me a kiss as she walked out the

door. The more time I spent with this woman, the more I lost control of my heart. In a normal relationship, that would be a good thing, but this wasn't a normal relationship. There were so many secrets between us, and I feared one day, if the truth came out, it would end this wonderfully romantic fairy tale we shared. Nevertheless, we couldn't go on the way we were either. At least Michelle knew the basics about me, my background, my family and such. I knew absolutely nothing about her except she lived in France and had business dealings with Brian.

After breakfast, we went for another walk in the countryside and sat down to rest by a small thicket of trees.

"Michelle…I need you to be straight with me. I need to know what's going on…at the cottage in Darlish, here in France. Why does that man have a gun? Are we in danger?"

She kissed my mouth, held my hand, and looked deep into my eyes. "How can I trust you?" she whispered. "There are so many people wanting so many things…it's hard to know."

"You can trust me darling. I would never do anything to hurt you." I could see her hesitate, so I grabbed her close and kissed her passionately.

"John, my virgin boy," she said breaking away from the embrace. "You are such a fool."

"Well that's not a very nice thing to say," I replied.

"You should *never* have gotten yourself mixed up in all of this stuff. You're going to get yourself in such trouble…and I fear for you John…I fear for you because I love you…I think." She sort of laughed.

I smiled back, "I love you too." I paused and took her hand. "I'm a big boy Michelle. I can take care of myself."

"I don't think you can John. I don't think you have any idea just how dangerous these people are…like Brian.

You're mad to get involved with him."

"He doesn't seem so bad," I lied.

She let out a sarcastic snort. "I wouldn't be so sure." She tore at the limbs of a dead twig for a minute, then turned her attention back to me. "What passes between us today John must never be spoken about to anyone else. Do I have your word?"

"Of course you do."

"Promise me."

"I promise," I said.

"Promise me again."

"Michelle, I promise you. I won't tell a soul…even on my deathbed…your secret is safe."

"Don't even joke about death like that John. It's always around the corner…hiding and waiting for just the right moment to strike. Then it's boom! And it's all over."

"I think you've been watching too much television Michelle," I said with a laugh. "You're sounding awfully dramatic."

"This is life John. That's why I fear for you…you don't see it…you don't see the danger." She brushed her hand against the side of my cheek and held it on my chin. "Tell me the truth. What are you really up to?"

She said it in such a way, I wondered if she knew. "I'm not up to anything. I got myself in some trouble with the Department of Trade…I've already explained all that to you…I met Barrington through Andy and Craig, the two guys I partnered with for the scam…we started hanging out and he saw that I needed a bit of money so he offered to hook me up with some work. I've been picking up and delivering different crates from Darlish to Middlesbrough and to Liverpool…you know the drill…you were there."

"Do you have any idea what's in those crates?" she asked.

"I presume it's drugs," I answered.

Michelle shook her head and muttered, "You're such a fool…such a fool."

"I wish you'd stop calling me a fool," I said angrily. "I'm only doing what I can to survive."

"I just don't want to see you get hurt," she answered softly. "Even the deliveries can be dangerous."

"Well can you at least tell me why I'm here in France? I still haven't received any instructions and Barrington seems to have disappeared…so am I going to be picking something up or what?"

"You're here because I asked Brian to send you here," she answered.

"Any special reason?"

"Is missing you reason enough?" Her brilliant eyes twinkled like a schoolgirl when I leaned over to kiss her.

"You don't know how happy that makes me," I whispered.

"I just worry about you so much. I don't ever want anything bad to happen to you."

"I know…and I don't want anything bad to happen to you either…but I feel powerless over so many things."

"That's because you are darling, you are." She stood and pulled me up by the arms. "But I am going to look after you John Coventry…I am going to look after you. You still need to be very careful and stay out of trouble whenever you can. Do you understand me?"

"Believe me Michelle, I don't go out my way for trouble…it just seems to find me on its own." We walked a bit further down the path.

"Are you wanted by the police?" asked Michelle.

"No," I said. "They've already arrested and charged me for the Department of Trade and Industry fraud. I'm just waiting for a court date."

"I see…so you're not a fugitive on the run then?" she laughed.

"No," I replied with a smile. "How about you? Are you wanted by the police?"

She smiled and kissed the tip of my nose, "Of course."

"What for?"

She didn't answer. "We'll talk more later okay? I have some things to do this afternoon away from the house but will you stay and wait for me?"

"Yes I'll stay. I don't have a ride out of here anyway and I have no idea where Barrington has gotten to."

"Oh he's gone back to England. Left yesterday."

"Oh, well I'm glad he let me know. How long did you want me to stay for?" I asked.

I was becoming worried about being out of touch with Atwood for so long. He had no idea where I was or what I was doing. What if he thought I'd become a runner and left the country for good? All hell would break loose. I couldn't let that happen. I hope that he trusted me enough to give me some slack on this one. After all, it wasn't my fault.

"What's wrong John," asked Michelle. "Your eyes look so far away."

"They do?" I said.

"Yes…and your brow is crinkled and you look lost in thought. Are you not enjoying yourself?"

"No…no…of course I'm enjoying myself. I get to spend time with you."

"Okay…as long as there's nothing wrong."

"I think I might just be a little tired," I lied. "You wore me out last night!"

"Maybe while I'm gone, you should lie down and have a nap."

"That actually sounds like a good idea."

"It's selfish really…I need you re-energized for tonight!"

We arrived back at the house and I watched Michelle get into the car with one of the men and drive away. As soon as she was out of sight, fear encompassed my body. Here I was stuck in the middle of the French countryside – no Michelle, no Barrington – just a strange man with a gun and his brusque friends who apparently didn't speak a lick of English.

"Good job John," I muttered to myself as I flopped onto the bed. "You've really gotten yourself into a bloody mess this time. Nobody knows where the hell you are or what the hell you're doing in France." Was this going to be my ultimate punishment? Shot dead in the French countryside? I'd never been so sorry for the stupid crimes I'd committed. I desperately wanted to take it all back and start again but I couldn't.

My only hope was to trust Michelle. If she said she'd be back in a few hours, then she'd be back in a few hours. I closed my eyes and tried to fall asleep, but details of our conversation kept running through my head. Why was Brian so dangerous? I figured he wasn't an angel, but what could he possibly be involved in that made Michelle so afraid for me. Maybe he was IRA? Maybe I was being naïve and not seeing the whole picture. But what did the IRA have to do with armed Frenchmen in France? Barrington seemed to know the men, and obviously Michelle did. So what was the connection? Where did the pieces of the puzzle go? And why the hell was Michelle wanted by the police? Which police? The French? The British? What had she done?

Nigel knew. I wasn't sure what government department he worked for, but I was positive he could shed some light on the situation. Too bad, I couldn't get a word out of him.

It was so frustrating to be playing a game where the players were a mystery, and the rules kept changing as the game progressed. My growing love for Michelle only made matters worse.

The slamming of a car door woke me out of a troubled sleep and thinking it was Michelle, I jumped out of bed, rushed to the window, and pulled back the curtain to take a peek. A white van had pulled up alongside one of the narrow paths on the north side of the farmhouse and two men were standing talking to the large dark haired man with the revolver. Michelle was nowhere in sight. Not wanting to be noticed, I let the curtain drop, leaving just enough space for me to watch what was going on.

One of the men opened the back of the van and I could see at least two wooden crates. They didn't seem to be as big as the ones I'd been delivering but from my viewpoint, it was hard to tell. The men took the first crate out of the van and followed the dark haired man to a small shed hidden amongst the bushes about ten meters away. Despite walking around the grounds with Michelle, I hadn't noticed the shed before. The dark haired man pulled back some branches and unlocked the chain strung through the shed doors. All three men disappeared into the shed with the crate.

I watched them unload four more crates. The crates must have been heavy because I noticed by the fourth crate the men were struggling with the weight and had to set it down numerous times on the way to the shed. The men were very quiet while they worked and what words they did speak were in French and I didn't understand.

After unloading the final crate, they all disappeared into the shed again. I heard some banging but couldn't tell what they were doing. Ten minutes or so passed before one of the men from the van emerged carrying some sort of a gun. I wasn't all that familiar with weapons but judging by the long barrel and the scope attached to the top, it appeared to be some sort of a sniper gun or high-powered rifle.

"Jesus Christ," I whispered under my breath. "That thing's not meant to shoot rabbits."

The man cocked the gun and pointed it towards a tree branch in the distance.

"Bang!" The branch exploded, sending leaves and bits of wood flying. The other two guys rushed out of the shed and they were all pointing at the tree and laughing. The dark haired man took the gun, set aim, and fired. Once again, the men applauded the shot. They fired off a few more shots, nailing a bird and some more branches. The dark haired man was definitely an expert marksman.

Just as he was getting ready to fire again, a car drove up the laneway at a furious pace. Michelle practically jumped out of the car while it was still moving and ran over the men. She grabbed the gun from the dark haired guy and started yelling and screaming in French. While I couldn't make out the complete sentences, the torrid flow of swear words were easy to translate. I'd never seen her so angry. She put the gun in the shed and shut the doors. Every once and a while I'd see her glance nervously towards the farmhouse. I ducked out of the window and didn't move a muscle. It was obvious from her actions that she was afraid I might have seen the guns or hear the shots.

Michelle stood with her arms crossed waiting as the dark haired man locked the shed. The other two men got back into the van and drove slowly down the lane and out of sight. She gave the chain a rough tug and said something more to the dark haired man. He shrugged his shoulders and walked off to chat with the man who'd been driving Michelle. As Michelle turned and headed for the farmhouse, I quickly dove back into bed and pretended to sleep. Out of the corner of my eye, I noticed the curtain hadn't quite fallen back into place.

"Shit!" There was nothing I could do. Michelle was already on the stairs.

"Are you still sleeping John?" she said opening the door with a smile. She seemed somewhat out of sorts, her voice slightly unsteady.

I purposely took my time pretending to wake up. "Oh my God!" I said yawning. "I must have been tired. I slept the entire time you were gone." I rubbed my eyes and stretched my arms and legs.

"You look like a cat stretching like that," she said climbing onto the bed. "Let me give you a kiss."

"It must be all the fresh air of the French countryside," I said. "I slept like a baby…just such a peaceful and tranquil place. I should come here more often."

Michelle just smiled, then tussled my hair. "Well I'm glad you had a good sleep. Enough with lying around for now, let's go outside and enjoy the rest of the day."

She pulled me up by the arms and led me out of the room. Thank God she hadn't noticed the curtain. We had a wonderful afternoon just walking through the fields, picking flowers and talking. She didn't bring up the guns and I didn't ask. I tried to scope out the shed but Michelle was intent on steering us away from the side of the property.

I didn't want to believe that Michelle was involved in trafficking guns yet I couldn't deny what I'd witnessed that afternoon. Maybe she helped ship guns to Brian? That was it. She just helped set up the deliveries. Maybe the crates came from somewhere else in Europe, were delivered to the farmhouse, then Michelle sent them on to Brian. He was the sick violent bastard, not her. She was kind, sweet, and loving.

Still I was curious. Not for the sake of Atwood and Nigel, but for my own. I needed some answers.

"So what sort of things did you have to do this afternoon?" I asked her later that night in bed.

"Just things John…I really don't want to talk about it."

"What's going on Michelle?"

"It's supposed to be another beautiful day tomorrow. How about we go for another walk?" she answered totally ignoring my question.

"Whatever you say."

The next morning we walked again to the clearing in the woods and sat down in the soft grass. We kissed and cuddled for a bit and I was completely engrossed by her presence. Then out of nowhere, she sat up and got serious.

"You must leave tomorrow," she said.

"Why?"

"Because you must."

"Michelle please tell me what you're muddled up in. Is it drugs? What?"

She shook her head. "I can't…this is not the time."

"Michelle…I love you. This is the right time. I need to know. Please trust me."

"I love you too." Her mind seemed far away now, lost in the life she wouldn't share with me. "Let's just enjoy this last day together."

"I just don't want to leave you Michelle," I said holding her tight.

"You must John…I'm afraid you must."

We spent hours lying around in the clearing, talking, laughing, and being at one with each other. The conversation steered clear of work, Brian, drugs and guns, and instead we focused on the moment. Michelle didn't like to talk about the future or make plans. She said the only future that mattered was the here and now. Sometimes she talked in words and phrases I didn't quite understand.

"What politics do you have in England?" she asked abruptly.

"I'm a Conservative."

"Why are you against the poor people?" she asked. Her mood changed instantly.

"I'm not against poor people."

"Yes you are," she argued. "All these governments are controlled by capitalists. They are manipulators of the people. How can you not see that?"

I was stunned by her fervid response and her strong political views. "Are you a Communist?" I asked.

"God no," she sneered. "They are just as bad."

"Then who do you support?"

I could see the words forming on her lips, then she stopped. "Enough my virgin boy. Do not let us have a row over our different politics."

I nodded in agreement, but I couldn't help but wonder what she was going to say. It was right there, then she pulled back. What the hell kind of politics did she follow that she was afraid to tell me? She wasn't a Communist, she wasn't a Conservative, yet it was obvious she felt strongly about the issues, and the state of the world. I loved this woman, but all the mystery was beginning to drive me crazy, I didn't know how much longer I could take it.

That night was rather sad and subdued as I was leaving in the morning. I didn't want to go, and to make matters worse, I had no idea when I might see Michelle again. I hated that.

"Can't we just set a day for our next visit," I asked.

"That's impossible," answered Michelle. We were lying in bed drinking wine. "Things change every minute and I never know."

"That's crazy Michelle. What about a telephone number so I can call and at least talk to you."

"That's impossible as well. I'm sorry John but things are the way they are because that's the way they have to be."

She was talking in riddles again. "Well I don't think I'll ever understand."

She stroked my hair and kissed my cheek. "You don't have to understand…that's part of the adventure…you just do…go where…"

"The wind takes you," I said completing her sentence.

"That's right," she laughed. "Now you're getting it. At least I will come to the airport tomorrow morning and see you off. Would you like that?"

"I'd like it better if you just came with me," I smiled.

"Oh my little virgin boy…you are persistent aren't you?"

"I figure one of these times you'll have to say yes!"

We made love and fell asleep snuggled in each other's arms. It was a beautiful time, and I felt safe and secure, like that was the only place in the world I needed to be at that very moment. If only I could capture it in a bottle and take it back to England with me. Then I would have something concrete to hold on to and not just a fading memory.

CHAPTER ELEVEN

The same French fellow who'd picked me up at the airport, drove me back and I was disappointed Michelle didn't come along for the ride, even though she said she would. She just handed me my ticket, kissed me hard on the lips, and watched us drive away. I didn't want to go but I had no choice. My plane landed in Manchester and I was able to call Atwood straight away from a phone booth just outside the airport terminal.

"Where the hell have you been?" he yelled.

"I can explain," I answered.

"You'd better." He was furious.

"It wasn't my fault. I didn't have the opportunity to call you and let you know what was going on. Brian wouldn't let me go out on my own for even a minute."

"Where have you been then?"

"In France."

"In France? What were you doing in France?"

"Michelle sent for me."

"Michelle sent for you? What the bloody hell? Where are you now?"

"I'm standing in a phone booth outside the Manchester Airport."

"Get in a cab and come to my office right away. I don't want to talk about this over the phone."

"Fine. I'll be there as soon as I can," I answered.

I hailed a taxi and was seated in Atwood's office within thirty minutes. Saying he was in a foul mood would be an understatement.

"I thought I made it quite clear Coventry that you were to remain in contact with me at all times?"

"I couldn't help it. Barrington called and told me Brian wanted to see me at the cottage on the weekend. I called and told you that."

"Yes…yes you did."

"When I got to Darlish, Brian said that I'd be leaving for Paris in the morning. He insisted I stay at the cottage. I tried to tell him I didn't mind staying at the pub but he wouldn't have it. Barrington drove me to Heathrow in the morning and accompanied me to Paris. They didn't let me alone for one second…I wanted to call…I swear I did…but I couldn't."

"Do you think they suspect something?" Atwood asked.

"Honestly I don't know. Barrington is cool but I don't think Brian likes me or trusts me. Barrington said that Brian doesn't trust anyone though."

"That's not surprising." Atwood had calmed down considerably and his normal shade of red returned to his cheeks. "Why Paris?"

"He didn't tell me. He just said that someone would pick us up at the airport."

"And did they?"

"Yes, a young Frenchman picked up Barrington and I and we drove out into the French Countryside. A couple of hours at least."

"Whereabouts?"

"I couldn't really tell. He was driving like a bat out of hell and all the signs were in French. But we turned off a side road and drove up this little path through a forest, coming out to a clearing where there was an old farmhouse."

"Continue," he said.

"I didn't recognize anyone in the farmhouse at

first…there were about five Frenchmen there. Barrington knew at least one of them and he went up and spoke in perfect French."

"So what was the mission?"

"There was no mission," I answered. "I was summoned to the farmhouse by Michelle. She wanted to see me. I guess we've sort of become friends."

"Friends?" said Atwood. I shrugged my shoulders. I wanted to tell him as little about Michelle as I could and I definitely didn't want to mention the crates full of guns. I had to protect her. "So what did you and your new best friend Michelle, do for all the days you were gone?"

"We mainly just went for walks and talked. I tried to get her to talk about Brian and the drugs and such but she wouldn't."

"So that was it then?" said Atwood. "You spent all that time just walking and talking in the French countryside. I'm supposed to believe that horseshit?"

"Believe what you want," I said. "It's the truth."

"I'm sure Michelle has plenty of friends…why all of a sudden are you so important she has Brian flying you over to see her?"

"I don't know. If I did I'd tell you."

Atwood laughed sarcastically. "I'm not so sure about that."

"Look," I said trying to cover my tracks. "What benefit is there for me to withhold information about Michelle from you. You and Nigel told me to get close to her, so I am. I'm trying to get her to talk, but like I said, she's very careful and chooses her words wisely."

"Fine, fine," he said. "Tell me more about the other Frenchmen then."

"Well I know for certain that one of them carried a

revolver tucked in his belt and there was always someone outside watching…standing guard. I didn't see any drugs in the house at all, except for Barrington and his joints and even then, they made him go outside. They always spoke in French, so I had no idea what they were saying."

"Okay," said Atwood, "Let's go through things one more time from the top."

As always, I went through everything at least three times, answering his stupid questions and filling in the gaps. I had to be extremely careful this time, so that he didn't catch me in a lie about Michelle. He tried. God he tried. Asking me the same questions four different ways, mixing up times and the sequence of events. But I kept my cool, took my time, and methodically recalled all the details I wanted him to know. To be honest, I quite enjoyed myself.

"Okay Coventry, I think we're done here."

"Finally," I answered.

"Listen to me though." His voice got all stern and fatherly. "Never lose contact with me again. Is that clear? You're beginning to challenge my trust in you."

"You have no reason to lose your trust in me. I would have called you if I could, and you were the first person I contacted the minute I set foot off the plane. I'm not sure what more you want. It's not like I could whisper to the birds and tell them to fly to Manchester, find Peter Atwood and tell him I'm in France. This isn't the movies, I'm afraid. I did the best I could."

"All right, I understand," he said. "But try not to let it happen again."

I took a taxi from Atwood's office to the train station and caught the first train home to Liverpool. I wanted to see my parents because like Atwood, I'd been out of touch with them for a while and I'm sure they were starting to worry.

By the time I arrived home at the apartment in Chester, I was beat. Townfield was going to have to wait until the morning.

I threw a frozen pie in the oven for dinner, then took a nice long hot shower. I hated to wash the scent of Michelle off my skin. Besides the pictures in my head, that scent was the only thing of hers I had. Maybe I was a fool…getting myself wrapped up in all of this…with her. But sometimes the heart has a mind of its own and leads you to places your head wouldn't dare tread.

Early the next morning I made the trip out to Townfield to see my parents. After some breakfast, my father and I sat around the table and I brought him up to date about what had been going on lately. I left out the part about Michelle and me falling in love and seeing the guns. I think that would have just freaked him out knowing that I was "sleeping with the enemy." Of course, he wrote everything down and made me go over the parts he didn't understand or needed more clarification.

"So John, I must tell you the funniest thing happened the other day," said my father. "We received a visit at the house here from a couple of men. One from the Department of Trade and the other from the Customs and Excise."

"Was it Atwood?" I asked.

"No it was someone different. Anyway, they were asking a bunch of questions about you, where you were, what you were doing and such. Well you know the little computer gizmo I have that tells me the time because I have trouble seeing the hands on the clock?"

"Yes," I nodded. His sight was going, so he'd purchased a piece of electronics that would speak the time out loud whenever he pressed the button. It was about the size of a calculator.

"It was sitting on the television in the drawing room, so I

went over, picked it up and said to the gentlemen, 'do you know what this is?' You should have seen their faces when they thought I'd been recording the whole conversation. It was priceless. The funniest part was I really *had* been recording the conversation, but on a different machine in the room. They went on and on about me recording them with my time device, and how I should have told them. I pretended to erase it on my little computer, and that seemed to calm them down, but I have it on the tape recorder if you want a listen."

"How did you know enough to set up the recording? You didn't know they were coming did you?" I asked.

"No didn't have a clue, but I figured that in light of what's going on, it wouldn't hurt to have the recorder ready just in case. I just walked over to the machine, pretended I was getting something from the table, and turned it on. They didn't know any different."

"That's brilliant Dad," I laughed. "Just brilliant. I must say though, I don't like the idea of people coming out to the house and bothering you and mother."

"It's fine John," said my father. "It really wasn't that big of a deal and I had a good laugh from it." He went over to the bar area and poured himself a drink. "What does concern me is the enormity of your legal bill I received the other day. I will pay it of course, but in my opinion those lawyers are nothing but dishonest crooks themselves. They'll suck you dry. It's a crying shame."

I felt horrible. "Dad I'm so sorry about all of this…the bill…those men visiting…"

"John…don't worry about it. I'm not angry with you. It's the lawyers who ought to go to prison, not you! I just don't like how they take advantage of those in need. Your mother is right – lawyers are the piranhas of society."

I couldn't disagree with his assessment, but without a lawyer, there was no way to navigate the court system. You were buggered no matter which way you turned. I stayed for some late lunch and then headed back to Chester. I felt like I hadn't been home forever and looked forward to spending a few days hanging out by myself watching some television and reading some books.

The following week Barrington called with another message from Brian. He sounded a bit standoffish on the phone and wasn't his usual chipper self.

"Brian wants you to run an errand for him."

"Sure, no problem. What am I to do?"

"Just pick up some more applications for the bodyguard vacancy from a place in Wirral."

"That seems easy enough, no real travelling involved," I answered.

"Ya just go to the office, walk in, and ask for your mail. It's in your name."

"When does he want me to go?" I asked.

"Right away."

Without hesitation, I set off on my simple little errand. I found the office, walked up to the reception desk, and asked the man at the desk for my mail.

"Just a minute please," he said with a smile. The man disappeared down the hall for a few minutes and returned carrying a large brown envelope. "There you go sir."

No sooner had I touched the envelope, than two men flashing police badges, exploded from the closed doors behind me. They grabbed my arms and held them behind my back. I was in shock.

"John Coventry you are under arrest," said one of the men.

"For what?" I yelled.

"Please come with us."

I had no choice but to follow them down the stairs and into the waiting police car. They drove me to the Chester police station and made me wait in the interview room. I had no idea what was going on and I was terrified. I'd already been charged in the fraud case, and Customs knew about the deliveries I'd been making, so for the life of me I couldn't figure out what the problem was.

The door opened and two new men walked in and sat down.

"Your name please," said one of the men.

"John Coventry," I answered. "Can you please tell me what this is all about?"

The tall policeman with the reddish blond hair looked amused. "You don't know?"

"I have no idea," I responded.

"You've been arrested for sexual assault."

I almost collapsed in the chair. "For what?"

"For sexual assault."

I took a deep breath and tried to gather my composure. "I think you have the wrong person. I've never assaulted anyone in my life."

"No, we have the right person," said the other police officer. "A complaint was filed against you by some boys who were applying for a bodyguard position."

"You're kidding me?" I answered. I was stunned and horrified. Not only was the sexual assault charge absurd, it meant that the police knew about the interviews – the ones Brian had forbade me to talk about. I was in some deep shit.

"The men say you impersonated a doctor and gave them medicals while they were naked."

"In no way were those men assaulted by me, and furthermore, I never told them I was a doctor."

"Did you in fact have the men strip naked?" said the tall cop.

"Yes but I was only following instructions from a superior."

"And who might that superior be?"

I was trapped. I couldn't tell them about Brian and jeopardize the entire operation, yet I couldn't let myself get railroaded for a crime I didn't commit.

"You need to call Peter Atwood of the Customs and Excise Department. I've been working undercover for them. I can't tell you anything more because the information is privileged and top-secret."

The two men laughed. "That's a good tale. Really couldn't you have come up with something a little more believable?"

"Call him and ask him for yourself." I gave them his number. "He'll back me up. I'm telling you the truth."

"Sure you are. We'll see how the night in a jail cell with some other 'undercover agents' changes your story."

They carted me off to a cell, pushed me inside, and slammed the door shut. What the hell was going on? Brian was going to pull my intestines out through my ass, when he found out his papers were now in police custody, and Atwood was going to pull my balls through my throat when he realized I'd failed to tell him about the interviews in the first place. I was screwed either way. But that didn't bother me as much as the actual charge itself. Sexual assault? Were they fucking crazy? They obviously had no idea I'd been a victim of sexual assault myself while at school when I was younger. The repeated incidents have haunted me my entire life and left scars that to this day have still not healed.

I was in my teens and boarding at a school called Brickwall in village of Northiam in Sussex. Late one afternoon I was hanging out with a school chum named Raleigh Lofting, a tall, slim fellow with blue eyes and brownish hair. He was from the London area and was a bit of a snob. I guess we weren't so much friends as casual acquaintances. Another rather large boy was in the room as well. We were chatting away about this and that when Raleigh hopped on his bed and sort of spread his legs open a bit.

"Feel me Coventry," he said with a smirk.

I was dumbfounded and stuttered my reply. "I don't know what you mean." My face was beat red and I wanted to run but the other guy came around my back and held both my arms. He was much bigger than I was and I couldn't move. Raleigh pressed his hand against the outside of my pant leg and cusped my penis. His face wore a devious grin.

"Do you like that?"

"No!" I said shrinking away.

"Well maybe you'll like this even better." He undid my pants, took my penis in his hands, and began to rub and masturbate me. I started screaming and yelling as loud as I could until the larger boy whacked me on the chin.

"Shut up you little fucker!"

I was terrified. Raleigh just kept rubbing and rubbing and as he rubbed, he'd look at me and smile.

"See," he said pointing to my now erect penis, "I told you, you'd enjoy it." The two boys laughed and yipped with glee as my erection exploded. Raleigh calmly put my penis back in my shorts and pulled up my pants. "There that wasn't so bad, was it?"

The larger boy loosened his grip and I pushed him away and ran out of the room. The next day Raleigh acted as if nothing had happened at all.

"Don't make a big deal out of it Coventry. Most of the boys do it. The school Masters know all about it and sometimes they join in."

I didn't know how to react or even how I was supposed to feel. My body and mind were numb. I tried to forget the incident and just get on with the school year but it was extremely difficult. Every time Raleigh smiled at me, I wanted to throw up. And then there was his other friend, a kid named Stevens, Raleigh must have told him as well because the little bastard thought it would be funny to tell the entire school. I was humiliated but Raleigh didn't seem bothered by what he'd done at all.

A short while after Raleigh assaulted me; I noticed one of schoolmasters, a greasy looking chap named Williams, kept popping up in the oddest places. He was tall and lanky with dark hair and heavy glasses. He was more a handyman than a teacher and had free run of the school. I first spotted him hovering about the school lavatories, just standing there watching. He smiled at me and not really knowing what to do, I smiled back and then ran on my way.

These episodes continued for some time and I was unnerved how Williams always seemed to be "around" when I was alone, heading to my room or going to the toilets. I remember talking about Williams to my good friend Oliver and we both agreed the man was creepy. Raleigh Lofting didn't share our opinion, and went red in the face when I casually mentioned to him that Williams kept showing up places.

"You're full of shit Coventry," said Raleigh with a nervous laugh.

At the time, I didn't think much of his response. I was still furious with Raleigh but did my best to hide my anger. I figured the best way to deal with the incident was to forget about it. Stevens happened to overhear my conversation with Raleigh.

"Williams is a kind man," Stevens grinned. "He gives you lots of goodies like cakes and chocolates if you want them."

"Really?" I said sounding disinterested. "That's nice."

One late afternoon, I was lying on the grass with Oliver and some other chaps watching our school beat the daylights out of another school in a cricket match.

"Well boys," I said. "I'm going to head back to my room. Got a bit of studying to do for tomorrow."

The route back from the cricket pitch led me past the many tennis courts and along a little path. I saw Stevens approach.

John," he said excitedly, "I'm so glad to have finally found you. Williams would like to see you in his study right away."

"What the hell for?" I asked.

"I'm not really sure, but he had me come and find you straight away."

Like a naïve fool, I followed Stevens into the school buildings, up the main flight of stairs and then a side flight, which brought us to the teachers' room. Stevens knocked on the door and entered without even waiting for the reply.

"Here he is sir," said Stevens. "Don't just stand by the door Coventry, come in."

I sheepishly walked into the room and instantly felt Williams' slimy gaze upon my face. A single red bulb hanging from the middle of the ceiling lighted the room and cast an eerie shadow on the sparse apartment. A desk and chair stood against one wall while his bed was pushed against the other. Half-drawn red curtains only partially covered the setting sun, which illuminated the posters of tennis players and swimmers he had tacked to the wall. Churning out The Beatles song, "All You Need Is Love", was a record player that sat on a small table by the bed. The room stunk of tobacco, weed and Williams own horrific body odor.

He smiled at me with a sly grin before turning his attention to Stevens. "Thank-you son," he said handing him a huge box of chocolates. "You can go now."

My face lit up when I saw the chocolates for they were a rare treat at school but Stevens walked right past without even offering me a single one.

"I see you like chocolates," said Williams. "Don't worry. I have some here for you too."

He pulled out another box and handed them to me. I tore into the package, immediately shoving a couple in my mouth at once. In the meantime, Williams sat on the bed and motioned for me to come and sit beside him. He was wearing a pair of messy looking grass stained trousers and his shirt was hanging open at the top, exposing his very hairy chest. For some reason, his glasses kept steaming up and he was constantly removing and cleaning them. With his glasses off, his eyes seemed to have sunk right back into their sockets. It was a queer and eerie sight.

"It's hot in here don't you think?" he asked.

I shrugged my shoulders and pounded back some more chocolates. It didn't seem particularly hot to me.

"So how have you been doing?" he asked. "Do you like cricket? Did you watch the match? I see you like the chocolates…that's good." He just kept mumbling on and on and I was beginning to wonder if he was ever going to tell me why he wanted to see me.

"Yes, it is hot in here…so hot," he continued.

He started to undo the remaining buttons on his shirt. I was surprised but really didn't pay that much attention; I was more focused on the chocolates. Now bare-chested he turned his attention back to me.

"Are you hot John? You look so hot. Let me help you take off your shirt." Before I knew it, he started unbuttoning my shirt.

"Hey…what are you doing?" I protested.

"It's just so hot in here. I think you'll be much more comfortable without a shirt, that's all."

He started caressing his crotch area over his trousers and to my horror, I saw that he was erect. I suddenly didn't give a shit about the chocolates anymore and wanted to get the hell out of there but I was frozen unable to move or think. He put his arm around my bare shoulder and whispered in my ear.

"Wanna see it?" Williams was grinning like a sadistic cat. Like lightening, he unzipped his pants and pulled out his penis. It sprang out of there like a fucking jack-in-the-box. "It's okay if you want to touch it…don't be frightened…it's all a part of growing up."

To this day, I don't know why I just didn't get up and run away as fast as I could but I think I was in such a state of shock and panic, I didn't say or do a thing. He started breathing heavily and I noticed a small line of saliva dripping from the side of his mouth. His eyes kept rolling back into his head as he stroked his penis and groaned with sickening pleasure. With his free hand, he reached for the front of my trousers and fumbled with the zipper but couldn't get it opened.

His eyes turned yellow and flashed with rage. "Take off your fucking pants!" he screamed.

To my constant shame, I did as I was told. He thrust his hand into my crotch and began stroking my penis. Thankfully, he was more interested in his own penis and increased the tempo of his hand. Suddenly he moaned and a horrible white liquid spurted out and onto his half undone trousers. I felt sick to my stomach and was terrified about what was going to happen next.

He took a deep breath and smiled at me, his limp penis still protruding from his pants. He reached over and I thought for sure he was going for my penis but he grabbed the box of chocolates instead.

"Have another chocolate John." His voice sounded heavy and laboured, like he was drunk and out of breath. I still couldn't speak. He smiled at me again. "You can put your pants back on if you'd like."

I didn't waste a second. I whipped up my pants and threw on my shirt just as Stevens magically appeared in the room and pulled at my arm. I kept trying to do up my zipper but the fucking thing was stuck. I just wanted to cry. Stevens shut the door behind us and led me back to the dormitory.

Stevens glared at me. "You keep your fucking mouth shut...do you understand? You don't want to know what will happen if you don't."

I nodded and he left me alone. I sank onto my bed in utter despair and shock. I told no one and fell into a very disturbed sleep. The same scenario played itself out eight or nine times over the course of the school year before I finally got up enough courage to fight back.

One afternoon I found Stevens alone in a quiet area of the schoolyard.

"What do you want Coventry?" he sneered. "Some more chocolate?" The way he looked at me and laughed made something inside my head snap. I grabbed him and threw him to the ground as hard as I could. I picked up a broken tree branch off the ground and began smacking him on the rear and torso as hard as I could. I just remember tears streaming down my face the entire time. Stevens was screaming like a baby.

"How do you like that you fucking little weasel," I yelled, rearing back the branch for another hit. "You fucking, no good piece of weasely shit!"

"John stop!" he screamed. "I'm sorry…he made me do it! I swear!"

"I don't fucking believe you, you fucking two-faced coward!"

The rage exploded in me like a volcano, and I couldn't control myself or stop hitting him with the branch. On one final stroke, the limb broke. Stevens was lucky, I might have killed him otherwise. I threw the stick away and left Stevens cowering on the ground. As fast as I could, I ran to the Headmaster's study. I had to tell him what happened before Stevens got there and fed him a bunch of lies. Sir John Richie was sitting behind his desk, his freckled face and blue eyes hidden behind a pair of half-moon glasses.

"May I talk to you a minute sir?" I asked politely. My chest was still heaving from the beating I laid on Stevens, so I took a few deep breaths to calm myself down.

"Of course John, come in and shut the door behind you."

"I was nervous about being alone with the Headmaster, even though I knew he wasn't Williams and I had no reason to fear him.

"You seem out of breath," he said gently. "Have a glass of water." He filled a glass from the stainless steel water jug and handed it to me. "Have a seat Hugo and tell me what's going on."

Through tears and anger, my story flooded out. I told him everything, including beating the shit out of Stevens. He was bound to find out anyway.

"Have you told anyone else about this?" he asked.

"No one," I answered.

"Not even your parents?"

"No sir, no one. I've been too embarrassed."

"There's no need to be embarrassed John. Go back to your room and I will deal with this straight away."

I left his study and for the first time in a very long time had a peaceful night's sleep. The next day I was called back to Sir Richie's study and to my surprise saw my parents sitting there.

My father took me aside. "You are coming home with us today John. You can come back for exams but that is it." He leaned in close and whispered in my ear. "As to that other matter with that man, you can forget about it. It is being dealt with and you'll never have to see him again."

That was it. The subject was never spoken about again and to this day, I don't think my mother even knows what really happened. I remember asking her about it a few years ago and she told me the reason I had to leave the school was because I'd been expelled for beating up and bullying that boy. I was shocked and angered by her reply. How could something so horrific be swept under the rug like that? But the more I thought about, the more I put the blame on Sir Richie and the school.

I concluded the Headmaster used the incident of me beating Stevens up as an easy excuse to get rid of me, and keep the whole Williams issue quiet. He obviously told my father about the sexual assaults but downplayed what happened. I guess that's just what happened in those days. It was over and done with, never to be mentioned again. They may have forgotten about it, but I never did. It's haunted me my entire life, affected the choices I've made, and the man I've become.

That's why these boys claiming I sexually assaulted them during the interviews was so outrageous and absurd. If they only knew how uncomfortable I'd been, seeing them naked like that. By the end of the interviews, I was feeling sick to my stomach. I could never ever inflict the same torture and agony on those boys that the man at school inflicted on me. It just wasn't possible.

I'd been sitting in the jail cell for less than fifteen minutes when one of the officers came back.

"Looks like this might be your lucky day." He led me back upstairs to the interview room. "It seems you're free to go, but you must return in the morning and appear before a judge on the charges. We're not letting you off on this one."

The other policeman escorted me out. "I believed your story," he said with a smile.

"Fuck you," I thought.

I hailed a cab and had him drop me off outside the office building so I could pick up my car. I had no idea what just happened and couldn't for the life of me, understand why the police in Chester wanted to charge me for a crime I didn't commit. And if they were so sure I did it, why the hell did they let me go so easily?

As soon as I got back to my apartment, I called Atwood. He was pissed at me for not telling him about the interviews in the first place.

"How can we protect you if you don't tell us everything?" he said.

He did have a point this time. "You didn't see the look in Brian's eyes though," I pleaded. "He made me swear not to tell a soul. He's truly a scary man. I thought maybe he was using this as a test, and I didn't want to blow it and put the whole operation in jeopardy."

"You need to keep me updated at all times," he said. "I can't keep having these surprises. By the way, did you do it?"

"Do what?" I said.

"Sexually assault those men."

"Unbelievable! I never touched those men. I swear to you on my life. The charges are fake." I was furious. "I don't know why they said it, or if someone put them up to it, but I can tell you with one hundred per cent certainty that they are false."

"Calm down John. I believe you. I honestly do."

"Well thank you," I replied. "What do you think is going on?"

"I have no idea but we'll sort everything out tomorrow in court."

I hung up the phone and was worried, really worried. I dreaded telling my parents about this little bump in the road, but I had to. I drove out to Townfield, sat them down at the table, and told them about the charges. They were appalled both by the charges and by the fact I'd spent the day at the police station. I can only imagine what they must have been thinking as I was trying to explain about the boys having to strip in the first place. I was embarrassed myself, and had to admit it sounded quite odd. Needless to say, it wasn't a pleasant evening at the family estate.

The following day I arrived at Chester Magistrates Court, a new building opposite the Chester police station. My lawyer said very little, and by the frown on his face, it appeared as though I was going to be charged and sent to prison for something I didn't do. Wouldn't that just be the kicker?

The hearing started and the first thing I noticed was the emptiness of the courtroom. Once again, it had been cleared of any press or visitors. Obviously, Atwood made a phone call. The clerk called me to the dock and read the charges, "Sexual Assault". Hearing the words again made my heart sink to my toes. I couldn't believe it and I definitely couldn't understand it.

The judge reviewed the papers in front of him for a few minutes, then asked both the Prosecution lawyer and my lawyer to step forward. The three of them chatted, before the judge looked up and told the rest of the court they would continue the conversation in chambers. After a half an hour or so of waiting, the group came back and resumed their seats.

The judge looked at me and smiled, "From the evidence I have here, this is at best a very minor infraction of the offence under which you are charged." He turned his gaze toward the police officers. "Nor am I sure, there is even any evidence for this charge." The officers lowered their heads and avoided his eyes. The judge turned back to me. "I see you are already charged with deception, though no trial date has been set. I will send the papers to that court. You are free to go Mr. Coventry."

I was free to go. After all that, I was free to go. Clearly, the police didn't have enough evidence on me, so why did they even charge me in the first place? Was someone sending me a message? Was it Atwood? Was he still angry with me for not letting him know about my last minute trip to Paris? Or was it Brian? Did he set the whole thing up? Michelle warned me about him being a dangerous man, but why would he take a chance on me squealing to the police? Maybe that was the whole idea. Maybe it was his way of testing me. I had no clue and no way of discovering the truth. I would just have to play along, be cool and let things unfold. Maybe Michelle was right in calling me her little virgin boy because like a virgin, I didn't have any idea what I was doing.

CHAPTER TWELVE

I could hear the phone ringing inside the apartment as I fumbled at the lock.

"I'm coming, I'm coming," I muttered. One last quick turn freed the lock and I pushed the door open. "Hello?"

"John…it's Peter Barrington. How are you?"

"Not bad. Just give me a sec here. I just walked in the door from getting a few groceries." I set down the phone, went back, and closed the front door. I didn't need any hallway stragglers listening to my conversation. "Okay, I'm back. Sorry 'bout that."

"No problem mate," he answered.

"Listen, I have to tell you something," I said. "I had a bit of trouble on my errand yesterday."

"What are you talking about?" his voice was full of concern.

"The police were waiting for me at the office. They took the papers, hauled me down to the station, and grilled me about what they were for."

"What did you tell them?" he asked.

"Nothing," I said. "I kept my mouth shut. Eventually they let me go, but they wouldn't give me back the papers." I knew my story sounded weak but it was the best I could do on such short notice. I didn't want to tell him about the charges because he might wonder why I got off so easily, just like in the deception case.

Barrington was silent for a long time. "Well I'll speak to Brian about it and see what he says. In the meantime, Brian wants us to travel to Dublin, Ireland this weekend."

"To Ireland? What for?"

"Don't know for sure…but he wants to see both of us. Is that doable for you?"

"Of course, that's fine," I answered.

"I'll be in touch later this week with more details."

I hung up the phone and immediately called Atwood. I wasn't taking any chances this time, not like with Paris.

"Dublin eh? Going to one of his houses I presume?" said Atwood.

"Don't know for sure. Barrington is calling me back later this week with more details."

"Okay, well make sure you let me know all the flight details and plans. Keep me informed about what's going on. Try and remember as much as possible from the trip, like landmarks or things that might help us track you and Brian."

"Will do and I soon as I know more details, I'll give you a ring."

I set the phone on the receiver and plopped on the couch. Ireland? I truly had no interest in going to Ireland, especially to visit someone who I now suspected was a member of the bloody IRA. What did Brian want? My mind was swimming with scenarios. He couldn't be angry about the papers because he didn't even know yet, besides that wasn't my fault. I did everything he asked me to.

The ring of the phone startled me. "Hello," I answered.

"It's me, Atwood. Can you meet me at the Red Lion Pub in Parkgate in two hours?"

"I'll be there."

I was sitting at the bar drinking a pint of beer when I saw Atwood and Nigel walk in the door. Atwood motioned for me to join them at a remote table in the corner of the pub.

"Gentlemen," I said nodding hello.

"Coventry. How are you?" said Nigel.

"Doing okay I guess."

"I hear you have a big trip planned for this weekend?" said Nigel.

"Apparently so," I answered.

"Tell Nigel everything from the start," said Atwood.

I re-counted all the details I knew and Nigel seemed very pleased.

"You are becoming very useful to us John," said Nigel. "I need you to get all the information you can about Brian, his friends, places you go, cars, boats, things like that. But don't write anything down, in case they find it. Remember everything."

"That's an awful lot to remember," I laughed.

He looked at Atwood and the two nodded their heads. Then Nigel turned back to me. "I want you to come to London tomorrow at two in the afternoon. There's some information I want to show you, and I want you to look through some picture books."

"Where in London should I go?" I asked.

"I'll pick you up at the London Euston Railway station at one thirty."

The train from Chester to London was monotonous, boring, and of course late. Nigel was waiting for me on the platform, and showed me to his car. His driver got out and held the back door open for us. I couldn't help but feel a bit privileged, getting picked up from the train like this. He asked me again about Brian and I repeated everything I knew for the twentieth bloody time. It really was ridiculous the number of times I had to go over the details.

Glancing out the window, I noticed the car had driven down past Marble Arch, down Hyde Park and Whitehall, over the Thames River and along the embankment, almost on the opposite side of the House of Parliament. The car finally stopped in front of Century House, a modern tower block on Westminster Bridge Road, Lambeth, London. Nigel waited for the driver to come around and open the door before stepping out.

Guarding the entrance to the building were two rather large men who gave me a suspicious look as I passed.

"He's with me," said Nigel pulling a security pass from the inside of his well-tailored suit jacket and waving it before the men.

The main lobby of the building had pale green walls and marble floors. A commissioner's desk sat in the middle. Again, Nigel flashed his credentials to the gentleman sitting at the desk, and we breezed on by to the bank of three elevators. Nigel pressed the up arrow and we stood in silence as one of the lifts returned to the Lobby floor and opened its doors. He hit the number four button and we were on our way.

"Just down the hall here a bit," he said stepping out of the elevator. We walked about thirty paces before he opened the door to an expansive room filled with various chairs, tables and a projector. It looked somewhat like a movie theatre, without the spilled popcorn on the floor or chewing gum stuck to the back of the seats.

"Make yourself comfortable John. Would you like a coffee?"

"Yes please, that would be great."

He nodded his head to another man in the room and within seconds, a fresh coffee found its way into my hand. The lights dimmed and a picture of Brian flashed up onto the screen.

"This here is our friend Brian," said Nigel. "I'm going to put up a bunch of different pictures and I want you to tell me if you recognize anyone. Take your time. This is really important."

The various pictures of different men and women appeared on the screen but I didn't recognize any of them.

"I'm so sorry Nigel, I seem to be of no use to you," I said.

"Nonsense John," he answered. "Just keep looking."

He flipped up a couple more and I was getting very bored and tired.

"Wait! I recognize that fellow," I said. "His name is Bob. He's the fisherman in Darlish. Sorry but I don't know his last name."

Nigel made some notes on a piece of paper and continued with the slide show. About thirty pictures later, I recognized one of the men from the farmhouse in France.

"He was in France at the farmhouse," I said. "He's the one who had the revolver shoved in his belt." I made no mention that he was also the one shooting off the rifle. That would only lead to more questions about Michelle and I wasn't prepared to put her in an uncompromising position.

"Are you sure?" asked Nigel. "Take a closer look."

"Yes, yes, that's him."

Nigel made some more notes on his paper, then flipped up some more pictures.

"Wait! That woman," I said pointing to the picture of a woman with short dark hair framing her petite face. "Who is she?"

"You recognize her?" said a surprised Nigel.

"Not recently…but her face looks so familiar. I'm sure I've met her before."

"Perhaps you've seen her on the television or in the newspapers."

"Perhaps," said John. "But I'm quite sure I know her. I remember those dark eyes."

"I do think you might be mistaken," said Nigel. "I can't quite imagine you two crossing paths. She's a German woman. She belongs to a dangerous and unpredictable faction. Not someone you want to get messed up with."

"What's her name?"

"Verena Becker."

"Hmm…" The name sounded so familiar but I just couldn't place where we met.

"How about we stop and take a break. Give your head a rest. I'm a bit hungry, how about you John?"

"I could eat."

A younger man set a tray of sandwiches on the table and refilled our cups of coffee. Nigel and I didn't talk much during the break; we seemed more focused on our eating. The man showed me where the toilets were and waited outside until I was finished. I guess he didn't want me snooping around in any of the rooms down the hall. I had no idea what government department this was, but I knew it had to be high up. There was just this official and serious feeling in the air.

Except for a clerk sitting at the back, the room was empty when I returned. I took the opportunity to close my eyes for a few minutes and go over some of the photos in my head. There had been so many pictures yet I only recognized three. How many players were there in this operation? I heard the door open and Nigel walked back into the room.

"Keeping you awake are we?" he laughed.

"No, no…I'm just trying to run through some of the pictures in my head again. Seeing if I missed anyone."

"Well don't worry about that because we're going to run through them all again on the screen anyway."

The lights dimmed and the pictures started all over. They didn't appear to be in the same order, as I saw the picture of Bob before the one of Brian. I think Nigel was testing me to see if I really did recognize the people in the photos or if I was just making it up. Then the pictures changed from people to places and things. I pointed out Barrington's house and Martin's house in Middlesbrough, but I didn't see one of the cottage at Darlish or the farmhouse in France.

Much to my surprise a picture of Michelle flashed up on the screen. It was a gorgeous picture of her sitting outside a cafe smoking. Nigel stopped the slide show and turned to me.

"What do you know about this girl," he asked.

"Not much…except she knows Brian and was at the farmhouse. She's a lot of fun to be with." I could feel the blood filling every vessel in my cheeks.

"Are you fucking her?" asked Nigel with unnerving frankness.

"I most certainly am not," I replied. "I have no interest in her whatsoever. Besides, I think she's just a minor player in the whole thing."

Nigel smirked, "I think you're fucking her John." I shook my head no. "No matter, I really don't give a shit who you fuck." He took a sip of his coffee and then stared directly into my eyes. "You are wrong John. She is not a minor player at all. This woman is a big fish. You'd be best to watch yourself. When it all shakes down, the cause is always more important. Just remember that."

I had no idea what he was talking about. What cause? He didn't know Michelle like I knew Michelle. We had a connection, a bond. It had to be stronger than any cause. Didn't it?

Nigel shut off the projector. "Let's go up to my office and have a chat."

Nigel's office was quite large with a huge desk and one of those expensive leather executive swivel chairs. It was very organized and tidy, much like Nigel himself. The only blemish was an overflowing ashtray sitting on the corner of his desk alongside a vase of yellow roses and a family photo. I was impressed. His office was way better than Atwood's little drabby pit hole.

"This is nice," I said taking a seat. "Three telephones? What the hell do you need three telephones for?"

Nigel smirked. "Well one is the office line, another is the line I pretend to be on when my wife calls, and the third is none of your business." He started laughing. "Okay let's just go over a few more things before you go." We talked a bit more about Brian, the trip and if I had any idea what it might be about.

"No I don't," I answered. "Like I've said, I've only been doing the deliveries and then those blasted bodyguard interviews…so I have no idea."

He lit a cigarette and motioned for me to do the same if I pleased. "You understand John that Peter Atwood and I work for different government departments don't you?" I nodded. "I have no interest in drugs, that's Peter's domain, my interest is in…" He paused for a second. "My interest is in Brian and your friend Michelle."

"Michelle is not my friend," I said.

He smiled at my response. "Now my government department has much greater powers than Peter Atwood does. Not only could I get this whole troublesome mess you've gotten yourself into with the Department of Trade and Industry to vanish, I think you could really help some people." I had no idea what he meant by me helping people but I liked the part about the fraud disappearing. "You know, we could even pay…quite handsomely I might add…for this. I think you might be a great asset to this department."

"And what department would that be?" I asked

sarcastically.

"Let's just say we deal in intelligence matters...particularly people like Brian. The real bothersome types. We contact other agencies, say French Intelligence and share certain information about certain people." I did like the idea of being paid well. "Just think about it okay?" He opened up his desk drawer, pulled out a file folder and placed in on the desk. "Before I run you back for your train, I just have a few papers I need you to sign if you don't mind." He thrust the papers in front of me and handed me a pen. "Just at the bottom of each page. Hurry up or you'll miss the train."

I didn't have a clue what I was signing and Nigel was flipping the pages so fast I was only able to catch a few words here and a few headings there; "Home Office", "Secretary of State", "Her Majesty's Government", and "H.M. the Queen".

"All right, that's the last one," he said. He took a quick look at his watch. "We'd better get you out of here." He shoved the papers back into the folder and returned them to the desk drawer. "Come along now John, let's get going."

He escorted me downstairs to his car and watched me get in.

"Try and remember everything from the trip. Do your best," he said. "I'm counting on you!" He slammed the car door shut and his driver sped off to the train station.

What an exhausting day. From the train ride, to the slide show, to the office chat, and now the train ride home. I was beat. I took the opportunity to close my eyes, and try and shut off my mind. The closed eyes I could manage, the shutting off of the mind wasn't happening. So Nigel admitted he worked for British Intelligence but at what level? He couldn't be Military of Defense (MOD) and it didn't seem plausible that he was with the Government Communications Head Quarters (G.C.H.Q.). That meant he had to be MI5 or MI6 but I wasn't exactly sure. MI5 was the United Kingdom's Security Service, dealing with counter-intelligence and internal defense. Closely linked with MI5, MI6 had more to do with security threats against the United Kingdom from outside sources, such as counter-terrorism, counter-narcotics, and international affairs – more of the James Bond type. Either way both departments dealt with Military Intelligence and top-secret security. That was heavy stuff and not something I wanted to do for a career...despite Nigel's offer of a decent paycheck.

I didn't understand why Nigel kept insisting Michelle was a major player or a big fish – like she was some sort of vermin he needed to reel in. I tried to put all the pieces together. Nigel didn't care about drugs, but he cared about Brian and he cared about Michelle. Did that mean that Brian and Michelle weren't involved in the trafficking? And if Brian was IRA, then what was Michelle, and why did he mention French Intelligence? What the hell did they have to do with anything? And where did Verena Becker fit in? I had met her before, I was positive. I wracked my brain trying to remember. Was it at a party? Dinner? A Bar? Where the hell was it?

Amsterdam. It was Amsterdam. Richard Dunhill, one of my close friends at the time, asked if I wanted to join him and two friends, Paul Young (a singer but not "the" famous "Paul Young") and Malcolm Singer and fly to Amsterdam for the weekend to party. In my mid 20's and always looking for some fun and adventure, I was excited about flying in the private Lear jet Paul chartered, and spending three nights in Amsterdam, a city with a raucous reputation. I'd heard many stories about Amsterdam's notorious "Red Light District", where prostitutes legally parade their wares in red-fringed window parlors and you could openly purchase some marijuana-filled "Magic Cakes" from coffee shops.

I'd known Richard for some time as a friend and business associate. Owner of RDR Travel in Wilmslow, a city in Northern England Cheshire, near Manchester, Richard looked older than his thirty years, with a rotund shape and badly decaying teeth. Malcolm, also around thirty, worked at the Foreign Office in London doing very "hush, hush" business as Richard put it.

Paul had arranged for the jet to take off from Manchester airport and fly directly to Amsterdam. Ducking my head to enter the doorway of the sleek, narrow plane, I was amazed at the plush seats, and gold-plated furnishings, no detail overlooked. The flight crew of three, two pilots and a stewardess welcomed us aboard with champagne and a mid-flight cold buffet. I couldn't believe the speed the little plane generated for take-off. We were down the runway, then soaring into the sky before I even had a chance to get comfortable.

Arriving around six pm at the airport in Amsterdam, we hailed a taxi and checked into the Holiday Inn to drop our bags, grab a quick shower, and get ready for a night on the town. Paul went off on his own to meet up with some girl, leaving Richard, Malcolm, and I to find the action on our own. Knowing the city well, Richard took us on a tour of the Red Light District, and I have to admit, I'd never seen anything quite like it. Small narrow cobblestone streets filled with shops, restaurants, cinemas, and of course women of all shapes and sizes sitting on chairs behind large windows, illuminated with fluorescent red lights. As the brothel doors opened and closed, the pungent scent of cheap perfume mingled with the city smells creating a unique odor of money, sex, and indiscretion.

Looking for a specific bar, Richard led us over the canal and down a side street adjacent to the Amstelkring Museum, also known as Our Lord in the Attic because of the clandestine church in the attic used by Roman Catholics who were not allowed to worship publicly after 1578. Wading past the outdoor tables filled with young people drinking, laughing, and smoking pot, we entered the pub and found a spot near the back. The raging music pounded at my ears, while the haze from the cigarette and marijuana smoke seeped its way into my lungs.

"Hey John," said Richard nudging me with his elbow. "That dark-haired chick over there is eyeing you up."

"Really?" I said looking over his pointed finger. "The petite one with the sad eyes?"

"Ya," said Richard, "that's the one."

Cropped short with bangs, her hair barely covered her protruding ears, allowing full view of her dark, almost black eyes, and slender somewhat pointed nose. She was laughing with another young woman and gentleman, but sensing my own eyes staring, glanced back at me and smiled.

"Go talk to her," said Richard.

"I believe they're speaking German," I answered. "Not one of my specialties."

"Good thing you have me!" said Richard getting up from the table.

He said something in German, making the group laugh, then the woman answered, smiled in my direction, then ever so briefly locked eyes with Malcolm.

"Do you know her?" I asked Malcolm.

"Nope," he answered shaking his head. "Never seen her before in my life."

"That's odd," I said. "The way she looked at you…then

turned away…like she didn't want anyone to notice."

Malcolm laughed. "Maybe she just thinks I'm dashingly handsome! C'mon mate! Richard is waving us over."

We picked up our drinks and joined our new German friends at their table.

"My name is Verena," she said in broken English.

"John Coventry," I answered. "So nice to meet you."

"This is my good friend Knut Folkerts," she said pointing to the blond haired, bearded man. I nodded and shook the young German man's outstretched hand.

Verena told me she and her friends kept a small "vacation" apartment in Amsterdam for the times they wanted to get away, since it was an easy, albeit long almost fourteen hour drive from Berlin. We talked about Amsterdam, the clubs, and the Red Light District, keeping the conversation light and friendly, just small talk between a group of strangers brought together by chance.

"Lads! Let's take a picture," said Richard. "To capture our time in Amsterdam." He retrieved a camera from his coat pocket and handed it to the waitress. "You don't mind do you?"

The waitress smiled and clicked, capturing us three English boys, and our new German friends. After a lot of beers (and a few Magic Cakes), we left the club as dawn broke on the horizon, giving the hard-working street cleaners some much needed light. Knut Folkerts and the other young woman hopped on a pair of scooters and disappeared into the damp misty morning, headed back to Germany for work. Since she was all alone and wanted some company, Verena invited the three of us back to her apartment for some breakfast and a nap. It was the morning of April 7, 1977.

We followed Verena's elfin like figure back up the street towards the Museum, veering off on another side street to the right. About halfway down the street, she opened an indistinguishable black door, leading us up two flights of stairs. The tiny one-bedroom apartment consisted of a small living room, a galley kitchen, and an apparent "I don't give a fuck what it looks like" attitude of the occupants. Overflowing ashtrays, dishes, strewn about clothes, and the lingering stink of marijuana threatened to consume the space.

Richard and I went into the kitchen to see about fixing some breakfast or at least a pot of coffee. When I came out, I was a little surprised to see Verena sitting on the broken armchair and Malcolm on the dingy army cot, deep in conversation. Their faces wore serious expressions but because they were speaking in hushed voices and in German, I had no idea what they were saying. As soon as they spotted me the conversation stopped, and Verena smiled and laughed as if Malcolm had been telling a joke.

We had some breakfast, then spent the day just lounging around, chatting, sleeping, drinking, and smoking. Around noon, Malcolm excused himself to go buy some cigarettes, and I don't know whether he got lost or sidetracked, but he didn't return until mid-afternoon. Verena said she had to catch a flight to Baghdad in a few hours so we said our goodbyes and set off to find something to eat. I remember passing a newsstand and seeing the headlines of the late edition paper:

"German Chief Prosecutor Assassinated".

Malcolm quickly threw some money at the vendor, snatched a paper, and began reading furiously, shaking his head and muttering. I glanced at Richard but he just shrugged his shoulders. Nearly nine months later, I asked Richard about Malcolm and the newspaper incident. He said Malcolm was a "secret sort of man" and wouldn't explain. Not satisfied with the answer, I pressed him further. Richard told me that Malcolm had joined the British Foreign Office right out of University and now worked with British Intelligence services. He also told me our friend Verena was arrested and in jail for belonging to the Baader-Meinhof Gang (Red Army Faction), and for seriously injuring a policeman who tried to arrest her. I remember having trouble believing what Richard told me. The woman looked like she couldn't hurt a fly.

I hadn't seen Richard Dunhill or Malcolm Singer in years, losing touch with the passing of time and changing of priorities, and had totally forgotten about our chance meeting with Verena Becker until her picture flashed up on Nigel's screen. I knew it was the same woman, I never forgot a face. Even though I was bushed from the day, the minute I arrived home to Townfield, I dug out my box of old photos, rifling through shots of my trip to Moscow, New York City, and various holiday destinations.

"I knew I was right!" I said pulling out a 5 by 7 photograph from the middle of the pile. There, pure as sunlight was the picture of me sitting in the Amsterdam bar with Richard Dunhill, Malcolm Singer, and our new German friend Verena Becker, dated April 7, 1977.

Finding the photograph of Verena eased my mind in the sense that I knew I wasn't going crazy and seeing things. But it also brought up a few more questions. Like what was a confirmed member of the Baader Meinhof Gang doing in the same set of pictures as Michelle? What was the connection? If only Michelle would open up and just tell me what was going on. Maybe I could help her and Nigel at the same time. People have played both sides before, why couldn't I?

CHAPTER THIRTEEN

Barrington called me later in the week, with details about our trip to Ireland. I wasn't looking forward to going but didn't have a choice in the matter. I'd already called both Atwood and Nigel to inform them of the flight plans. I wondered if any other government agents would secretly be making the trip with us.

Arriving at the airport in Dublin, we were met by a young Irishman who drove us the hour or so out to Brian's house. I tried to make note of the landscape so I could at least give Nigel an idea where we were going, but it was raining and everything looked the same. This was my first visit to Ireland and my first visit to Brian's place. The sound of the rain pounding against the roof of the car was almost as loud as the sound of my heart beating inside my chest. I was scared. I tried not to show it, but inside my guts were churning and I felt nauseous.

The winding country lane led the car to a big, white beautiful house with steps leading up to the porch area. A large, commanding oak door guarded the entryway like a sentinel, keeping out the unwanted and keeping in the unsuspecting. We exited the car and headed up the stairs. There was no need to knock. A big burly man opened the great door and beckoned us inside. He was one person I never wanted to meet in a dark alley. In the large foyer, Brian greeted us with an outstretched hand and I could tell by the wry grin he gave me, he'd felt my sweaty palm and sensed my apprehension. He pointed ahead and guided us into his office.

Brian's study was striking. With oak panels and a huge stately desk, it was a testament to his power and prestige. A bottle of fine whiskey sat on the corner of the desk and I was hoping for a small glass to calm my nerves but the offer never came. Brian was dressed casually in a grey woolen polo neck jumper and a pair of beige corduroy pants. I had met him several times before in England, but seeing him standing in his lair made me wish I'd never gotten on the plane. He dismissed Barrington from the room and we were left alone. Brian didn't waste any time.

"I have a job for you," he said with a menacing grin. "You know all about the import business right?"

I nodded. "My family owns a company in Liverpool but I have nothing to do with it anymore."

"That really wasn't my question," he said looking me so straight in the eye a quiver shot up my back. "Do you know the import business…like how to import large containers from overseas, CIF, Letters of Credit, and customs clearance?"

"Of course," I answered. "I have years of experience in that regard and still have many contacts in the industry."

"Now that's the answer I wanted to hear," he said with a nod. "So if I told you to arrange a shipment…let's say…a container of goods from overseas to Cork or Dublin via Southampton in England…you could do that? And make sure all the paperwork is complete…so that everything goes off without a hitch? Because I don't like hitches when I do business. You understand right?"

I nodded in agreement. I definitely didn't want to be around Brian if there happened to be a hitch. In fact, I didn't want to be around him if things went smoothly. There was just something sinister about him that gave me the creeps.

"So this is what I want you to do," he continued. "I want

you to arrange for a container to be shipped from Hong Kong to Southampton and then have the goods delivered by road to Middlesbrough, Liverpool, and Cork in Ireland."

"I can do that," I answered. "It's somewhat unusual to spilt the goods and send them in three different directions, but it can be done."

"Easily?"

"Fairly. I'd just need to know who specifically you're shipping the goods from…then I'd have to set up a letter of credit for the shipping and payment costs and of course I'd need to know what the goods were," I said with a laugh.

"No Laddie, you will not be knowin' what's in the container."

"But I can't ship the container without knowing what I'm shipping," I protested.

A brief smile snaked out of the corner of Brian's mouth. "You will ship the container because I'm goin' to tell ya what the goods might be called." I didn't like the smile or the Machiavellian laugh that followed. He took a few strides towards me and rested his hand on my shoulder. I wanted to back away but was caught in the shadow of his presence. He leaned in close and I could smell the power on his heated breath.

"Listen here…there are two things you should know right here and right now." He tightened his grip on my shoulder. "First, you always do what I say…without question…Got that?" I nodded. "Second," he said pointing to the ceiling, "see those big beautiful oak beams up there?" I nodded again. "If you open your sweet mouth to anyone at all about me or what we're doing, I will take a rope, throw it over those beams, and hang your sorry British neck from it." The pain in my shoulder was unbearable but he kept tightening his vise-like fingers. "Do you understand me?"

His eyes burned with the controlled rage of a mythical monster and I could almost feel him draining the blood from my face with his stare. I wanted to run, I wanted to hide, I wanted to throw up. I wondered how on earth I'd gotten myself into this mess and how in the hell I was going to get out. It wasn't supposed to be this way and none of this was supposed to happen. I was an English gentleman. I should have been attending fancy parties and the theatre in London, or heading up some fabulous corporation. I went to private schools and lived a life of privilege and excess. Where did it all go wrong? My life was a mess and if I screwed up this job for Brian, it was going to get a whole lot messier.

"Do you understand?" he repeated. I could barely breathe but managed a weak yes. He released my shoulder, slapped me on the back, and with a hearty laugh said, "Welcome to Ireland!"

He gave me a few more instructions and then ushered me to the door.

So laddie, I just have one final question for ya." I turned to face the Irishman. "Is she good in the sack?"

"Excuse me?" I said.

"Is she good in bed...you know a good screw?" asked Brian. His eyes were bearing down on me and I felt the hairs on my neck jump to attention.

"I'm not sure who you're talking about?" I replied. I tried to stay calm but I could sense a quiver creeping into my voice.

"Don't fucking lie to me boy. I told you what happens when you lie to me did I not?" He was full of rage and I thought his fist would strike my chin at any moment. "Tell me...is she a good fuck?"

"Yes...If you mean Michelle, yes I am sleeping with her."

"Now that was easy to answer wasn't it?" he said. Then

I heard him whisper something under his breath that almost knocked the air out of my chest. "Fucking Action Directe…fucking French…fucking English."

In one fell swoop, Brian had revealed the missing piece of the puzzle and it was a bombshell. Michelle belonged to the Action Directe, a French terrorist group, intent on overthrowing the French Government. They were responsible for a series of assassinations and violent attacks all over France, and I think they had connections with the even more notorious German group, "Baader-Meinhof". The Action Directe attacked government buildings, property management buildings and anything or anyone that happened to disagree with their "anti-imperialism" mantra.

I couldn't believe that Michelle was one "of them". That was her connection to Brian – the IRA. The crates were probably filled with weapons and explosives, and the profits from the drug sales were financing the violent attacks. That's why Michelle became so upset at the farmhouse when I told her I was a Conservative, and she accused me of not caring about the poor people. And that would explain the guns at the farmhouse she didn't want me to see. Good God! Simply put, I was sleeping with a French terrorist. I must be mad! My family would be so proud. Unfortunately finding out the truth didn't change how I felt about her. I loved her – terrorist or not – and I would stand by her no matter what.

Somewhere over the Irish Sea, Barrington put down his magazine and turned to me.

"I have some instructions from Brian that I need to pass along to you," he said. Barrington had been in a bitter mood the whole weekend and I wasn't quite sure why. I hope it didn't have anything to do with me, and my increased involvement with Brian's activities.

"I'm listening," I replied.

"First you need to arrange the shipment from Hong Kong. Here are the details." He handed me a piece of paper. "Call the agent from a phone booth and then destroy the paper."

"Done."

"In a few days, drive out to the house in Middlesbrough and personally tell Martin to expect the consignment within the next eight weeks. We'll let him know the exact date when the time gets nearer. If he needs to rent extra space to store the shipment, then go ahead. Then Brian wants you to go to Jersey and give the same message to Michelle."

I tried to hide the excited grin that was creeping up in the corner of my mouth. Just the mention of her name sent my heart pounding.

"Do you have any questions?" asked Barrington.

"No I think I've got it straight."

"Good. I don't know about you but this plane ride has given me a bloody headache," he complained. "You got any Aspirins or anything like that?"

"Sorry I don't," I answered.

"Well I'm going to go see if I can round something up. Maybe that sweet little blond up there in the third row could help me out." He smiled and gave me a wink.

That was Barrington, finding every opportunity he could, to get in some woman's pants. I read over the slip of paper a few times, then safely tucked it in the inside pocket of my jacket. Atwood was going to love this little piece of information. I tried to enjoy the last part of the flight by focusing on Michelle. I couldn't wait to see her again, to touch her, to hold her, and just spend time with her. So she was Action Directe – that was politics and it certainly didn't affect me. I fell in love with her because of who she was, not what she did. I'll admit, it wasn't an ideal situation, but then again, who was I to judge what was ideal and what wasn't.

That night, I drove out to Townfield to update my father about the forthcoming shipment, and to let him know I arrived home safely from Ireland. I showed him the slip of paper and he immediately copied the shipping details and phone numbers onto a separate piece of paper.

"I want to have all the evidence John," he said. "You can never be too careful."

I stayed for a wonderful supper and enjoyed being in the company of my parents. They were good people and I loved them dearly. I knew they wouldn't approve of Michelle and her political leanings, so I thought it best just to keep that part out. I wasn't worried about Michelle and knew she'd never betray me. And while technically, I was betraying her by working undercover for the British government, I was doing my best to keep anything she told me private.

The next day I found a phone booth and called Atwood. He was pleased with the shipping information and generally seemed in a good mood. That was a change. I gave him all the instructions Barrington had given me, including telling him about having to go to Jersey. I didn't tell him I was meeting Michelle though, I just said Brian wanted me to go.

"Well that's somewhat strange," he said. "And you're not sure who you have to meet?"

"No. But I think Barrington will be there as well, so he likely knows."

My next call was to Nigel, and he too was delighted with my work. He made me go through things at least five times, and asked if I happened to recognize any of the men or places from the photographs he'd shown me.

"Sorry, I didn't," I answered.

"That's okay John. You've done a brilliant job just the same."

I told him the same story about Jersey as I'd told Atwood. Since Nigel had already suspected I was sleeping with Michelle, I didn't want him to know I was going to see her. I told both government men I would call them back once I'd called the Chinese agents, set things up and returned from Jersey.

Next on the list was the Chinese Shipping Agents, who turned out to be a subsidiary of the Chinese Government Shipping Agency. As instructed by Brian, I told them I represented the Royal and Standard Shipping Company, and that they were due to ship some goods to the United Kingdom. The man on the other end of the phone told me to wait a minute, while he found the proper representative.

"Hello can I help you," said the new man in perfect English.

"Yes," I said. "I'm from the Royal and Standard Shipping Company. You're due to ship some goods to the United Kingdom."

"Yes sir, I know all about the shipment you speak of. Do you have the code number?" I gave him the code number from the piece of paper. "Excellent. Now the funds for payment have already been sent to the sellers account and the containers are ready to ship. If you have a pen and paper, I'll just give you the shipping vessel and container marks and then I'll send copies to your offices."

"Offices?" I said. I was confused. I didn't have any offices.

"Yes your offices," replied the man in a voice clearly implying other arrangements had been made and I was an idiot for not knowing.

"Right then," I said hanging up.

Next, I made a call to an excellent shipping agent in the United Kingdom, whom I knew quite well through my work at Sim and Coventry. I asked them to handle the inward shipping, including customs clearance. I gave them the details and told them the containers would be filled with machinery parts needed for a factory being built by the Chinese and British in Middlesbrough.

"What's the size and weight of each container?" asked the agent. I gave him the information from the slip of paper. "That's great. I'm more than happy to help and can have this arranged for you very quickly."

"Splendid," I said.

"Where would you like the goods delivered after they clear customs in the United Kingdom?"

"I'll take delivery of them at the Manchester Airport. In the private area reserved for private planes." Lots of containers were parked there, and I figured Brian's shipment wouldn't look out of place. It also gave the appearance that I was going to fly the goods out of the country, not simply open the container, take the individual crates out, and load them into trucks and vans. It was a huge shipment and I was quite surprised Brian entrusted me with the job.

The last task before I could take off and see Michelle was a trip to Martin's house in Middlesbrough. I dreaded going there. It was always so dirty and disgusting, and I wasn't fond of Martin in the least. He was a pig of a man. Nothing had changed when I arrived at the house. It was filthy as usual, with a carpet of beer cans, empty food containers, and general garbage. The marijuana haze was so thick my lungs choked and my eyes watered. Martin was sitting with a girl on his lap when I walked in.

"John! Hello!" he said turfing the poor girl to the ground.

"Martin. How are you?"

"Fine, fine. Let's go into the kitchen and get this business out of the way shall we?"

I followed him into the kitchen and told him what was happening with the shipment and the subsequent deliveries. He took everything in and just kept nodding his head in agreement. My goal was to just give him the information and be on my way, since I couldn't stand being in his presence. The house stank, he stank, and the way he treated the girls with the caning, was absolutely appalling.

"Well I guess I'll be on my way then," I said.

"No, no," he said with a smile. "Stay for the night. You've had a long journey. Brian insisted you stay the night.

I smiled and thanked him for the kind offer, even though my insides were churning. I did not want to spend another hour in this place, let alone the night, but once again, I didn't have a choice. Brian's orders were Brian's orders. There was no going against them; he'd made that quite clear.

"Mind if I make myself a coffee then," I asked.

"No, not t'all," he answered. "Make yourself at home. I'm just gonna go visit with the girls again. Bring your coffee in when it's ready and we'll have a chat."

I took my time making the coffee and dreaded having to sit on any of the mangy furniture in the lounge. Stalling as long as I could, I took my cup and ventured into the sitting area. Martin was slouched on the couch and some blond girl, stoned out of her mind was sitting on his lap. She was kissing his neck and making these moaning sounds. It took me a few minutes to realize that Martin had his hand up her skirt and was giving her a nice little finger fuck. Such a classy guy.

Being incredibly bored and not amused by the shenanigans whatsoever, I made up an excuse about not feeling that great and retired to my room for the night. Martin offered me one of the girls but I politely declined. At first light in the morning, I was out of that shithole and on my way to Jersey in the Channel Islands. I was on my way to see Michelle. Nothing in the world could have made me happier.

CHAPTER FOURTEEN

Situated just off the French coast in the English Channel, the Channel Islands are British but govern themselves, which has allowed them to become a tax haven for the rich. Beautiful with long sandy beaches and a free and easy attitude, they are a popular destination for vacationers from all over Europe. Jersey, the largest of the islands with its capital city, St. Helier, was only a few miles from the airport. The winding road to the city passes through spectacular St. Brelards Bay, and the L'Horizon Hotel, a four star luxury palace like an oasis right on the beach. It was the perfect setting for my reunion with Michelle – a lover's paradise.

I could hardly contain my excitement as I sat in the reception area and waited for her to arrive. I didn't think it was possible for a grown man to feel this silly and giddy about a woman, but I did. The craziness of the whole situation was not lost on me. A regular English gent (now working undercover) flying off to a resort for a clandestine meeting with his girlfriend, who was wanted by the police and both British and French Intelligence. Certainly, this was not my life.

I checked in, surveyed the lush details of the suite, then tossed my luggage on the floor and headed back down to the lobby. All I needed was Michelle. The wait was excruciating. Every time the lobby door opened, I perked up in my seat, my heart pounding with anticipation of her vision of loveliness. She didn't disappoint, with a white blousy top that flowed with the movement of her body and a short black skirt, she breezed into the hotel like a movie star. But it was her smile, wide and infectious, and the way her eyes danced when she saw me, that captivated my senses. If you've never had someone look at you the way she looked at me, then you're truly missing out on something magical. Through the crowded lobby, this gorgeous and wonderful woman only had eyes for me.

We hugged and kissed all the way to the elevators, not giving a damn about the inappropriate looks and stares tossed our way. I held her in my arms as tight as I could, feeling the warmth of her breath and the firmness of her nipples beneath her shirt.

"I've missed you so much John," she said as the elevator doors sealed us off from prying eyes.

"I swear I've missed you even more." I planted a passionate kiss on her lips and she responded with full enthusiasm. The elevator reached our floor all too quickly and I picked up her luggage and led her by the hand to our room. We both couldn't stop laughing and giggling. The sensation of being together again was pure euphoria.

I gave the hotel door a donkey kick with my leg and it slammed shut as we fell together on the bed.

"So…" said Michelle in a very sexy and teasing way. "What should we do now?"

"How about some tea?"

She burst out laughing and began easing the buttons open on my shirt, letting her fingers touch the warm of my chest. "I have so many better ideas than tea…"

"I'm sure you do," I said showering kisses on her neck and in that little crook behind the ear.

"You're tickling me," she giggled.

"Am I? Well maybe I should tickle you here…and here. How about here?"

She did her best to squirm away from my attacking hands,

all the while laughing and pleading for me to stop. Somehow, amid all the tickling, we managed to discard our clothes and make love. It was a choreographed dance of passion, an intricate maneuver of mind, body and soul, where our hearts were a metronome keeping us in synch. We spent the next few hours lost in each other, living only for the moment, letting life's complications slip away like a raindrop rolling off a tin roof. Exhausted and spent, we fell asleep, locked in a naked embrace I wanted to last for an eternity.

I awoke to soft kisses on my cheek and the playful caressing of my hair.

"You're so handsome when you sleep," said Michelle.

"Are you saying I'm only handsome while I'm sleeping?"

"Of course not," she laughed. "I think you're handsome all the time. It's just that when you're sleeping, you look so calm and peaceful, like nothing in the world could hurt you."

"You worry too much my dear," I said kissing her on the nose.

"With you, I don't think it's possible to worry too much…so much you don't know…I just want to keep you in this bed, safe and protected forever."

"Well now, that's something I could definitely get used to," I laughed. "Before I forget, I need to tell you about a forthcoming shipment."

Michelle immediately put a finger to my lips. "Not here. We'll go for a walk on the beach and talk then."

"Okay…but do we have to go right now? This bed is awfully warm and it's been raining out…"

She smiled that sexy grin of hers. "No…we can wait a bit. I'm not quite sure I'm done with you yet."

We made love again, got dressed, then walked hand in hand on the beach, our footprints making deep imprints in the wet sand, just as Michelle had left a deep imprint on my heart. Finding a secluded spot, we sat down on the towel I brought from the hotel.

"Isn't this a beautiful place?" she said looking out over the water.

"It's more beautiful because you're here with me," I answered. I knew the line sounded somewhat cheesy but I couldn't help it…it's the way I felt.

"So let's get this business about the shipment out of the way," said Michelle. "Then we can just enjoy ourselves."

I told her about the shipment and relayed all the pertinent information. It felt weird talking to Michelle about business and I have to admit, the whole thing made me a bit uncomfortable.

"What's wrong John?"

"I don't know," I answered. "I guess maybe I am feeling like I've gotten myself in over my head. The trip to Ireland scared the shit out of me and some of the things Brian said and threatened…well…it really made me think."

"What did he say?" she said grabbing my hand. "How did he threaten you?"

I told her about the trip and about Brian saying he'd hang me from the rafters if I didn't do what he asked, but kept silent about knowing she was a member of the Action Direct. I wanted to hear those words from her. I didn't know when the moment would come, but I hoped after all we'd shared, she trusted me enough to tell me soon. I let it all out. My fears, my apprehension. How I worried about both of us. She didn't say a word, only stroked my hair, looking down at the sand, then back out at the waves.

"My poor lost virgin." Barely above a whisper, her voice was full of sorrow. She got up and held out her arms to help pull me up. "We should go get ourselves a good dinner from the hotel. You wore me out and worked up my appetite.

Besides, a good meal might cheer us up."

We lazed back to the hotel, showered off the sand, and got ready for dinner. I didn't pack many "dress-up" clothes but managed to smooth out the wrinkles in my shirt and throw on a blazer. Michelle told me I looked dashing, so that endorsement was good enough for me. She on the other hand, looked truly breathtaking in a blue chiffon dress. I felt like a God with this Venus on my arm.

Dinner was fantastic, the food superb, the atmosphere romantic, and the company invigorating. We kept the conversation light and didn't talk about Brian, the shipment or anything to do with business. It was just as it should have been - two lovers in love, basking in the candlelight, drinking wine and being merry.

She asked me questions about my parents, my brother and wanted to hear some childhood stories. She laughed when I told her about my Grandmother Poldy always standing at attention during God Bless the Queen and was sad about my brother and I losing touch and drifting apart. She loved every minute and seemed to hang on every word. I got the distinct impression that her childhood days weren't quite as happy and fulfilling as mine.

"So are you married?"

"God no," I answered. "Are you?"

"No."

The thought of her being married never even crossed my mind. In the beginning, it would have made complete sense though, all the sneaking around and secrets. Now that I knew the real reason for the surreptitious behaviour, I wasn't the least bit concerned.

"Do you think you'll ever get married?" she asked.

"I don't know. I hope to one day." I studied her face for a sign that perhaps one day she'd want to marry me, but her stare remained blank and forlorn.

"I don't think marriage is in the cards for me I'm afraid. Life is just too complicated to make that type of commitment."

"But I think if the connection is right, it can be a wonderful thing," I said. "I only have to look at my parents. After all these years, they seem as happy as ever. Somehow they just make it work."

"Yes but that is such a rare feat. You're lucky to have them." She reached across the table and gently clutched my chin. "You really are a hopeless, idealistic, romantic aren't you?"

"Is it wrong to want a happy ending Michelle?"

"It's not wrong," she said. "It's just impossible."

"Well I choose to believe differently," I said shrugging my shoulders. "We all need to hang onto some sort of hope don't you think?"

"Hope is futile John, it's action that matters."

She was talking in circles again. I figured her comment had something to do with "the cause" but I wasn't going to ask. For once, I just wanted a straight answer to one of my questions, not some philosophical phrase I needed to decipher.

"Look how the weather's cleared up," I said changing the subject.

"Let's go for another walk then."

Paying the bill, she took her soft hand in mine and we made our way back outside to the beach. The sun was midway in the sky, inching ever so close to setting with each passing minute.

"Why did you steal from the government?" she asked.

"Things just got out of hand in my life I guess…and I don't even know anymore why I did it…the money was the biggest reason I suppose." Michelle nodded. "I'd been pushed out of the family company and was sort of in limbo. I wanted to make a name for myself on my own. I just wanted to get enough money so I could get started in something else. I was tired of turning to my father. I wanted to show everyone I could make it on my own. But as usual, I messed it up. Seems to be the story of my life. It was a stupid thing to do and in all honesty, I can't believe I even did it. I was such a fool and have hurt so many people, especially the ones I love. But I have to say, it has made me do a lot of thinking and I've realized that it's time for me to grow up and stop relying on others for my life. It's time for me to be my own man."

Michelle laughed. "Don't be so hard on yourself." She tucked her arm in mine and leaned in close as we walked. "Besides...from what I've witnessed, I think you're nothing but man!"

I laughed and kissed her on the cheek. "That's not what I meant."

We found a large rock at the far end of the beach and sat down.

"Okay Michelle, now it's my turn to ask you some questions. I've told you everything about me, but you refuse to tell me anything about you." I gently took her face in my hands and looked straight into her eyes. "Who are you really?"

"Why do you want to know?"

"Because I love you Michelle! Do you hear me? I love you!"

The dying light glistened off the tears slowly trickling down her cheeks. "You can't love me. No...that's the one thing you cannot do."

"Why Michelle? Why? Why can't I love you? Why won't

you let me love you? It's such a simple thing…just let me love you."

"Because…"

"Tell me God damn it! I'm tired of playing these games with you. Tell me the truth!" She looked over her shoulder once and then again. "Nobody is here but us Michelle. The beach is deserted."

"I don't even know where to begin," she sighed. She started going on about politics and different beliefs and I felt myself getting cross.

"Quit changing the subject. I don't care about your politics."

"Well you should."

"Why? Why does it matter?"

Her voice went soft and quiet. "Because it is my life and it must be that way."

"Be what way?"

Like a bolt of lightning, she jolted forward, her eyes bursting with life. She grasped my hands. "John you must run…you must get out of all of this right now." She was very insistent and kept repeating the words.

"I'm not going anywhere," I answered.

"You have no idea what you are into. You just don't know..."

"Then tell me Michelle…please tell me. At least give me a chance…"

She closed her eyes and took a deep breath. For a brief second, the world stood still as I waited for her to speak the words, to trust me enough to tell me the truth.

"I work for a group," she said slowly. "No…there are a group of us who are going to bring France back to the people. The people need to be in control…" She kept going on and on about the people. It was all about the people and the cause. Her words jumbled together in an almost trance-like state. "We need to free the people from the tyranny and the governments. It's so important…it's for the people, my friend Verena Becker knows it all, she lives in Berlin, she has done and given so much for the cause."

"Verena Becker? You know Verena Becker? She belongs to the Baader Meinhof Gang doesn't she? And is in jail for killing some important German official? Jesus Michelle!"

"She was…but she's out now. And she didn't do it…"

"I don't give a fuck about Verena Becker Michelle! I just don't understand! All the violence in France, the attacks, the assassinations…is that you?"

"You do what you have to…to make your point."

"But Michelle…innocent people are dying."

"No one is innocent," she said. "Not you, not I…nobody." Our conversation opened the floodgates, and I held her close, letting her weep on my shoulder.

"Come away with me," I whispered in her ear. "We can go somewhere; just the two of us…start fresh…all that matters is we're together."

"That will never work," she muttered.

"Why?" I kept pressing. "It seems like a simple solution to me."

"John what you are suggesting can never be. I cannot leave with you."

"I don't understand Michelle. You say that you love me. Is that a lie?"

She cried harder. "No! I do love you. Don't ever question that. But I cannot just get up and leave…even if it means being with you. There are people John…people who would not take too kindly to me running off. I have commitments, I've made promises."

"What about the promises you made to me…the ones we

made to each other."

"I never made you any promises. I never said we'd be together forever. I know better than that."

"But all those times we made love…were those not promises?"

"No." She turned her head away. "I cannot give you what you want John…what you deserve."

"I don't want anything more than you…just to be with you. Please come away with me. No one will find us…we can live in peace and put all of this behind us."

"No," she answered again. "John, you are in your own worst nightmare."

"Tell me something I don't know."

"For your sake and mine, you must leave tomorrow and fly to South Africa. I can make all the arrangements. I have a friend there who will look after you."

"I won't go," I argued. "My life is with you."

"Do you have any idea what you're saying?" she asked. "You don't want my life. Always looking over your shoulder, always being suspicious of anyone and everyone. People will rat you out in a second, to save their own skin. These people don't play around John."

"I know that."

"I don't think you do," she replied. "You have no idea…no clue."

"You make me out to be so naïve Michelle. I may not know everything, but I'm not stupid."

"My darling John I never meant to imply you were stupid," she said kissing me. "That makes me sad you think that." We kissed for a few minutes and then she looked up at me with eyes so full of sorrow and pain. "Do you know who Brian is?"

"Not for certain," I answered. "But I'm starting to get a

good idea."

"He is IRA John…and let me assure you he doesn't just dabble in IRA activities. Killing you would mean nothing to him. He probably wouldn't even blink. I've seen what he's capable of…and that makes me very frightened for you. You mean nothing to him John…nothing…but you mean the world to me. Please listen to me. You must leave."

Having Michelle confirm Brian was IRA sent an eerie wave of nausea to my throat. I'd witnessed his temper first hand in Ireland and had the feeling he didn't like me or trust me much. Not a good combination. Maybe Michelle was right, maybe I should go to South Africa. I mean I was prepared to go from the beginning. Why wasn't I jumping at the opportunity now? The answer was standing in front of me, silhouetted against the setting sun.

"Did you hear me John? Are you listening to me? Brian is IRA. He's bad news."

"So are you part of the IRA as well then?"

"No…I belong to Action Directe…we work for the people of France, but have connections with the IRA and another group in Germany that supports the same ideals as us."

"Obviously it's the Baader Meinhof group if you know Verena Becker," I said.

"It doesn't matter."

"Are you kidding me Michelle? Of course it matters. You're connected to all these dangerous groups and you call me stupid?"

It was the first time I'd ever lost my temper with her. I guess the enormity of hearing the kinds of people Michelle associated with finally hit home – thugs, crooks, and murderers. They'd mow people down with machine guns, blow up buildings, and rob banks, never blinking an eye or caring who got hurt. Murder was second nature to these monsters…and Michelle was one of them.

"John…calm down. That is why it will never work. I will always be for the people. That will never change. I'm sorry." I needed a few minutes to myself and took off down the beach. "John! Stop!" she yelled after me. "Don't run away."

"Why?" I yelled. "Isn't that what you want? For me to run away from you? To be out of your life forever?"

She caught my arm and pulled me in close to her body. "It's not what I want. I swear to you…but I am in too deep to just walk away…you…you still have a chance to save yourself. Please let me help you do that." The wetness of her cheeks melted into the heated wetness of my own. She brushed back my tears with the back of her hand.

"Do you really love me?" she asked.

"Yes…I do. I love you more than I ever thought possible."

"If you love me that much…then you will go to South Africa. You will run far, far away."

"Fine. I will go." She kissed me long and hard on the lips and the tears exploded from my eyes.

"Thank-you baby….thank-you."

We snuggled in the sand for a bit in complete silence. I'm not sure either one of us knew exactly what to say. The waves splashed against the shoreline like the peaceful murmur of a sleeping child, shhh…shhh…shhh. I held Michelle in my arms, just content to feel the warmth of her body next to mine. She leaned back over her shoulder and kissed me under the chin.

"Come with me, I want to show you something."

She led me along the beach until we came to a small church. The purplish blue night sky and the granite tombstones rising up from the ground in the graveyard made the setting both spooky and beautiful. Michelle held my hand tight.

"You're not scared of a graveyard at night are you?" Michelle laughed.

"No. What makes you say that?"

"Because you're squeezing my hand so hard, I'm losing the sensation in my fingers."

"Sorry." I loosened my grip and we walked around the side of the church to a spot overlooking the shore. A rather large and ancient tree draped a portion of the beach. Helped by the moonlight, Michelle found a rock in the sand and walked over to the tree.

"What are you doing?" I asked.

"I'm carving our initials into this tree…to let everyone know we were here and we were together." She dug the sharp end of the stone into the bark and began chipping away. One letter, then another appeared as she diligently engraved our love forever.

"There," she said wiping away the chips with her hand. "Now, no matter what happens, no one can ever doubt our love."

"That's so sweet of you Michelle," I said with a smile.

She returned the rock to its sandy home, then took both of my hands, the moon illuminating our loving silhouette.

"I love you so very much. I cannot come with you…and I've already explained my reasons…but I want you to do something for me."

"I'd do anything for you Michelle."

She smiled a sweet but sad smile and set her gaze upon the stars. "One day, a long time from now, when you and I are at peace…and you are old," she laughed. "Will you come back to this very spot and think of us? Will you do that for me?"

I couldn't answer, the lump in my throat had paralyzed my words. She wiped her own tears and continued.

"One day, you will…I promise you…meet a wonderful girl, you will marry and have lots of children…and while you might not get the peace you need straight away, it will come."

"What are you talking about Michelle?" I said through my tears.

"Just promise me you'll come back here one day and look up at these stars for me."

"I promise. I promise. But I don't understand why you're talking this way."

"No more talk for now," she said. "Let's just remember this moment, remember each star in the sky, and remember our love for each other. I will make all the arrangements for South Africa in the morning…tonight we will just love each other."

And love each other we did, in the sand on the beach, and back in the hotel room. We both sensed the finality of our time together and wanted to savor every minute. That night I experienced the most intense lovemaking possible. Tears of sadness, tears of joy, tears of passion, and tears of sheer rapture. No matter what happened in my life, I will remember that night like it's yesterday. From sitting on the rock on the beach, to the moment at the church, to the frolicking in the hotel room – all of it burnt in my memory, locked away until the sky turns a purplish blue and the stars shine just a certain way. Only then do I allow myself to think about what might have been.

Michelle was back to her happy self in the morning. She handed me a coffee and jumped back into bed.

"I don't think I've ever seen such a sleepyhead as you," she laughed. "So I have made all the arrangements."

"Already?"

"Yes…I've been up for hours!" she laughed.

"Oh…sorry about that."

"You leave on Thursday. Do you have any money?"

"Yes…I have a bit."

"Okay, you must catch the South African Airways flight to Johannesburg on Thursday. It flies out of Paris. Will that be a problem?"

"No," I answered. "That gives me time to get some affairs straightened up in England before I go."

"What about a passport? Do you have one?"

"Well the police confiscated one but I have another one hidden away."

"Good little virgin boy," she laughed. "You must get on the flight. It's important. On that flight, a man named Brandon will contact you. Remember that name, Brandon. Repeat it for me."

"Brandon," I said laughing. "I got it."

"Good don't forget it. He is South African and a good friend of mine. I have made contact with him and he's agreed to look after you. You can stay with him until you get things sorted out."

"That sounds fine," I said. "Are you sure you won't come with me? Please…"

"John…I don't want to go through this all again. I cannot go with you. Please don't ask or mention it again. If you really loved me, you would just go…without any questions. Just be on that flight."

"Will I ever see you again?"

She nodded, "I hope so…one day…but I can't ever make you any promises." She paused for a moment. "I have a saying I rather like…and if anyone else ever says it to you…it's really coming from me. It'll be our little secret."

"What is it?"

"It's that line talked about after the American President Kennedy was assassinated, 'for one brief shining moment there was Camelot'. That's how we need to look at things. For us…one brief shining moment."

"For one brief shining moment there was Camelot," I said.

"Yes," she replied. "The words are beautiful don't you think?"

"I suppose they are…But is that it? For one brief shining moment…that doesn't give me much hope for the future."

"But our one brief shining moment…isn't that enough for you?" she pleaded.

"I guess it's going to have to be," I said hanging my head.

"Cheer up my little virgin boy…you never know which way the wind might take me."

We packed up our things and headed down the lifts to the lobby. I could barely speak. I didn't want to say goodbye. I knew it was coming but I still wasn't prepared. Michelle held my hand and stroked my hair as we waited for my cab. Through the tears she just kept repeating her instructions…be on that plane Thursday…be on that plane.

"I love you," I said softly. "I will always love you until the day I die."

"I love you too…forever my little virgin boy…I will love you forever."

The taxi pulled up and the driver honked the horn. "We'd better get going mate if you want to catch your flight."

I kissed Michelle as if it were my last breath and got into the cab. The sight of her standing on the curb with the wind blowing through her hair, and the tears cascading down her cheeks was more than I could bear. I turned away from the window, buried my head in my hands, and wept like a baby. I honestly didn't know whether I would ever see her again.

The experience was one of gut wrenching agony. I'd never felt so sad in all of my life. Finally, I'd met a woman, a real woman, someone I loved, someone I cherished, and now, because of that love we would be separated. "One brief shining moment" was all I got? Well it wasn't enough. I wanted more. I wanted a lifetime with this woman, not just a brief shining moment. That was bullshit.

I just couldn't fathom how my Michelle got mixed up with such a group in the first place. The danger she faced on a daily basis was unimaginable and I didn't want to know how "involved" in the activities she really was. I prayed to God she was a behind the scenes player, and not one of those on the front lines with the bombs and the machine guns. Probably best I didn't know.

For a minute, I thought about skipping the flight and staying in England. Atwood said he'd protect me and so far, everything had been okay. Maybe Michelle was just overreacting? As long as I kept on Brian's good side and did as he asked, he'd have no reason to pop me. At least if I was in England, there'd be a very good chance I'd cross paths with Michelle. She'd be furious with me for sure, but maybe I was willing to take that chance if it meant seeing her again. I just needed more time to convince her to come with me.

Then I remembered Nigel's ominous warning, "When it all shakes down, the cause is always more important. Just remember that." Maybe now I understood what he meant. Back then, I didn't know the cause was to overthrow the French Government. I didn't know the cause was associated with the violent Action Directe. Michelle had said it herself…she would always be for the people. She was willing to sacrifice our love and our relationship for the cause. Knowing that hurt me deeply. I wanted to walk away from her. I knew it was in my best interest to walk away from her…but I couldn't. I loved her and I made her a promise. Whatever it took, I'd be on that flight to South Africa.

CHAPTER FIFTEEN

I dreaded having to drive out to Townfield and face my parents. They'd been so good throughout this entire drama and I hated to cause them any more pain. The thought of saying goodbye broke my heart.

"Something's wrong John," said my father. "I can see it in your eyes and hear it in your voice."

"You know me too well," I said with a cheerless smile.

"You're leaving aren't you?" he said. I sat there frozen in my seat, not knowing what to say or do. "John, I will do everything I can to help you, you know that."

He picked up his car keys from the side table and jingled them around in his hand a few times. I was stunned. It was as if he'd read my mind. I needed some start-up money and I'd already thought about taking his car and selling it at the local dealers for cash. The money I did have was already safely out of the country. I was going to let him know after the fact, but I needed to make it look as though I took the car without his knowledge. That way he couldn't be accused of aiding or abetting me. There would be no paper trail and my father wouldn't have to lie. The less people who knew I was leaving, the better. Then they could honestly say they didn't know a thing. I never wanted to put anyone in a position where they had to lie to protect me. I'd already done enough lying for us all.

He jingled the keys and set them back down on the table. "What's mine is yours John. Do what you have to do."

"Thank-you Dad. Thank you for everything."

"Just be careful son…please in God's name be careful."

Just before dawn the next morning, I packed my bags, took the car keys from the table in the drawing room, and walked out the front door of my beloved Townfield. I couldn't bear to look back, it was all just too painful and the memories too intense. I knew my mother was going to be devastated I didn't say a proper goodbye, but Townfield would be the first stop for Atwood and the police when they came looking for me. It was better for everybody if I just disappeared into the early morning English fog.

I sold the car at a local garage and took a taxi to the airport in Manchester. Under a false name, I booked a flight to Paris paying cash for the ticket. Security was lax and the attendant's didn't even bother to check the flight registration name with the name on my passport. Therefore, any flight checks made by the Police, Customs, or the IRA would have come up empty for my name. That was the goal. In Paris, I changed from British Airways to South African Airways, again paying for my ticket in cash. For the moment, I was quite confident no one knew where I was. Once I bought my ticket to Johannesburg, South Africa, I understood there was no turning back. I found a payphone and called my father.

"I'm so sorry Dad but I took your car and sold it for cash."

"I know son," he said. "Where are you now?"

"I'm in Paris, but I'm leaving on a flight for Johannesburg in a few hours. I'm leaving father. I just can't take it any longer. I'm so sorry about the car but I needed the money to pay cash for the tickets and I didn't want to ask you, so you wouldn't have to lie to the police. You know they're going to come looking for me."

"It's all right...it's all right...I understand what you are doing...it's all right," he said.

"Please tell Mum will you? Tell her I'm sorry and give her a hug and kiss for me." I was doing my best to hold back the tears.

"I will son. Will you call us as soon as you can from South Africa? I just need to know you arrived safely."

"Of course Dad, as soon as I can. I will miss you."

"I'll miss you too, John. I'll miss you too."

I hung up the phone, filled with utter misery. I couldn't believe I was actually going to board a plane and disappear. This wasn't just a vacation where I could return to England whenever I felt like it. I was now a fugitive on the run. A wanted man. Atwood was going to hit the bloody roof when he found out. For that matter so was Nigel. That part actually brought a smile to my face, knowing I outwitted the great Mr. Atwood and escaped right under his nose. I'd done my job. I'd given them more than enough information to make some arrests or at least build a solid case. As far as I was concerned, my days as an undercover agent were over.

I should have been happy. I should have been jumping for joy. Instead, I'd never felt so lonely in all of my life. No parents, no friends, and no Michelle. I didn't know how I was going to survive. They say sheer loneliness can kill a man, and never did I believe it more than sitting in the airport waiting for take-off. Where had I gone wrong? Was this intense solitude the price I had to pay for a couple of dim-witted mistakes? I was filled with regret for what I'd done and the people I'd hurt. Knowing I was now alone in the world certainly took a few good swipes at my youthful arrogance and conceit. But I had no one to blame but myself and was humbled by my new circumstances. I suppose I was beginning to accept that I deserved my fate. At least I wasn't in jail – yet.

The departure lounge was full of people and I found

myself surveying the room for the man Michelle called Brandon. I had no idea what he looked like, but I thought I might be able to pick up a sign or at least get some sort of indication of who he might be. No luck. The loudspeaker boomed calling my flight, so I took one last look around then picked up my bag and boarded the plane alone.

Maybe something happened and Brandon had missed the flight? Or maybe I'd misunderstood Michelle and Brandon would be meeting me at the airport in South Africa and not Paris. Either way, I was on the plane and ready to begin the next chapter in my life. Buckling my seatbelt and preparing for take-off, I prayed the flight would depart on time. I just wanted to get the hell off the tarmac, into the air, and away from Customs, Brian, and the whole sorted mess.

"Hello there," said a man settling into the seat next to me. "My name is Brandon." Michelle had kept her word. I would have a friend with me on this long journey to Africa.

"Hello, my name is John."

"Nice to meet you John," he said holding out his hand.

Brandon stood about six feet tall and looked as though he was in his mid-twenties. He was on leave from the South African Defense Force, the equivalent of the British Army division. His chiseled physique rippled through his shirt and his welcoming soft blue eyes put me at ease.

"Please fasten your seat belts and see that your chairs are in an upright position. We are preparing for take-off," said a pleasant voice over the loud speaker.

"Well here we go," he grinned. "Nothing like taking off…love the feeling."

The pilot fired up the jets and the big bird soared off into the sky. I was actually excited about the flight itself. Brandon said it would be long, but you got to fly over the Mediterranean Sea, then into Africa crossing over Egypt, following the Nile River all the way down until you got to the mountain ranges of the Great Rift Valley. On a clear day, he said you could see Mount Kilimanjaro, the highest mountain range in Africa.

"If you don't mind me saying," I said. "The flight doesn't seem to be all that direct."

"That's because many African countries won't let a South African aircraft in their airspace. Once we hit African airspace, have a look out the window, and you'll probably see a South African Air Force jet escorting the plane the rest of the way to Johannesburg."

"Why? It's seems rather odd and expensive."

"Let me assure you John that the situation in South Africa is quite different than you're used to in England, especially when it comes to race."

Apartheid was law in South Africa and the whites ruled over the blacks in every sense. By the early 1990's, sentiment was brewing in the country for an end to "White Rule" and I got the feeling that apartheid was on its last legs. Being a Boer, Brandon was part of the upper class, and afforded certain privileges and rights. From our discussion, I don't think he disliked the black people, he just believed that blacks and whites shouldn't live together in a society. Blacks and whites were tribes and each tribe should evolve on their own. To him, that's the way things had always been and that's the way they should remain.

"See here's the thing John," he said. "I'm all for the government building homes, hospitals, schools and such for the blacks…I actually think they should be doing more to help them…I really do. I just don't believe that blacks should ever have a say in the running of South Africa. I'm not against Nelson Mandela, I just don't think he'd be able to run the country. I fear civil war."

"Why is that?" I asked. "You don't think blacks are capable enough?"

"I don't think they're educated enough," he responded. "You have to remember…the white race has been educated and developed for hundreds of years now…but the blacks…well they've only just begun. I'm not saying it's their fault…I'm just saying they're so far behind us. They just need some time to catch up."

Everyone was entitled to his own opinion and I didn't think any less of Brandon for his. Sometimes it takes generations and generations to change attitudes on social issues. What one person thinks is right; the next sees as a total injustice. I didn't believe in Michelle's cause, but that didn't stop me from loving her.

"I'm not sure you're aware that South Africa possesses nuclear weapons, has the largest Armed Forces in Africa and many, many lucrative gold and diamond mines. In the wrong hands, with incapable leadership, these powerful weapons could be used in a very destructive manner."

"I suppose," I answered.

"Take the issue with the South African Townships…especially Soweto. Have you heard of it?"

"I know the name."

"Okay…well Soweto is a black township located just outside Johannesburg. It's probably the most dangerous place in all of South Africa…filled with violence and poverty. The Army is forever having to go to the township to keep the peace and quash disturbances. I've been there numerous times myself as a member of the Defense Corp and as a private citizen. The blacks will kill any white man if given the chance…unless you're there to buy diamonds." A huge grin crept across Brandon's face.

"Buy diamonds?" I said.

"Ya. I'll tell you about it another time though…too many eyes and ears on this plane if you know what I mean."

"I think I do."

We chatted on and off some more during the flight, just briefly discussing my situation, but not going into any detail. I had no idea what Michelle had told him about me and figured we had plenty of time to talk about it in the future. Much to my surprise, the airline served us a wonderful dinner, complete with some very nice South African wine, chosen by Brandon. First class does have its perks.

"So you should stay with my parents and I…at least until you get yourself settled in. I know they'd love to have you and so would I," said Brandon.

"Only if it's not any trouble," I answered.

"It's no trouble at all. I promise. My parents love company. Besides, they're rarely even at home and I think you'll find there's plenty of space."

I was thankful for Brandon's offer but I didn't want to impose. "Honestly, I can stay at a hotel," I said. "I don't want to put you out in any way. You hardly know me."

Brandon laughed. "Nonsense, I know you just fine and I insist you stay. So it's settled then. You'll come and stay?"

"Yes of course. I'd be delighted. At least now I don't feel quite so alone in a foreign country."

Brandon and his family lived in a fairly wealthy suburb of Johannesburg called Edenvale. The house was at the end of a cul-de-sac and boasted a nice front yard with a good-sized garden. His parents, like him were Afrikaans or Boer's, and were extremely welcoming to me, an absolute stranger from far off England. I was shown to my room and spent some time getting settled before Brandon called me for a bite to eat. After that, it was off to bed for the both of us.

The following day, Brandon took me to several different

estate agents to see about getting an apartment. We also swung by a bank so I could open up an account and deposit what cash I had left. With a favourable exchange rate of almost ten Rand to one British Pound, I increased my wealth in a hurry.

That night Brandon treated me to a meal at a restaurant in the city.

"So you're a close friend of Michelle's then is that right?" he asked. It was the first time her name had been mentioned in any of our conversations.

"That's right," I said.

"By the smile on your face and the redness in your cheeks, I'd say you are very, very close friends." Brandon laughed.

"I guess you could say we're close," I laughed back. "How do you know her…and please don't tell me you're an ex-boyfriend or anything like that."

"No, no…not to worry," said Brandon. "I've known her older sister for many years. She lived in South Africa for a while and we met at school." I hid my embarrassment at finding out for the first time that Michelle had an older sister. "It was her sister who rang me up to see if I could help you out."

"Do you know Michelle at all then?" I asked.

"Oh sure," he replied. "I guess you could say we're friends. I help her out with a few things from time to time. She's a firecracker that one."

"Tell me about it," I grinned. I could only assume Brandon knew Michelle was Action Directe, but I kept my mouth shut, just in case. I wasn't going to be the one to bring it up and break Michelle's confidence in me.

"So I was told that you'd gotten yourself into a wee bit of trouble back in England with the government or something like that? It must have been pretty bad for you to want to run from your own country."

I told him the story about the Department of Trade and Industry Fraud but went no further. He didn't need to know the part about me working undercover for the government and ratting out people like Barrington, Martin, Brian and his IRA friends. I figured it just might complicate our newfound friendship.

"So you escaped to South Africa," he said with a smirk.

"Yes I did."

"Wow man! You certainly have some balls!"

If he only knew the whole story. He might not think I was so fearless and full of gumption.

"Would it be all right if I gave my Dad a call when we got back to the house?" I asked. "I haven't yet had a chance to let him know I arrived safely."

"Of course, of course," said Brandon. "You should have said something sooner."

Back at the house, Brandon let me use the phone in his father's private office.

"Dad, it's me John."

"John! I'm so happy to finally hear from you."

"Yes...sorry it's taken me so long."

"Where are you," he asked.

I was unsure how to explain Brandon to my parents. I couldn't tell them he was a contact of Michelle's since they didn't know the nature of our relationship, and I wasn't about to explain it to them over a telephone from the other end of the world.

"I met a chap on the plane. His name is Brandon. A military man. He said I could stay with him until I was able to find my own place."

"Well that was awfully nice of him John," said my father. "You're sure he hasn't befriended you for other reasons are you?"

"Positive," I answered. "Besides I doubt that anyone knows where I am right now."

"Not for lack of trying," replied my father.

"What do you mean?"

"We've had some visitors out to the house…The Department of Industry investigators and the police. I told them I didn't have a clue where you were and hadn't heard from you in ages myself. I'm not sure they believed me though."

"What did they say?"

"They threatened to put your face all over the newspapers and on that television crime show if they didn't find you soon. They gave me their number to call in case I heard from you."

"Those bastards." Having my name splashed over the news would cause considerable embarrassment to my parents and my entire family. I couldn't let that happen. "I'll take care of it Dad. What's the number? I'll call and let them know where I am. They shouldn't have any need to bother you again."

"Don't do it if it's going to put you in harm's way." He sounded worried.

"Legally, there's nothing they can do to me down here Dad. I'm safe." I heard a heavy sigh on the other end of the phone. "In spite of all that, how are you and mom?"

We chatted for a bit about this and that and I asked my father if he could gather my things from the apartment in Chester and bring them home to Townfield. There was no need paying for an apartment I wasn't living in.

"I've already paid for the last month, so there won't be any money owing," I said. "All the furniture stays as well. There's just some clothes, my toiletries and some personal belongings."

"I'll stop by tomorrow and take care of it."

"Thanks Dad…and as soon as I get my own telephone, I'll give you a ring so you have the number. If you need to speak to me before then, you can get a hold of me here."

I gave him Brandon's number and we said our goodbyes. I didn't want to call Atwood or Nigel from Brandon's home line so I asked him if he'd mind taking me into town the next day.

"I've got some errands to run anyway John. Where would you like me to drop you off?"

"Anywhere is fine," I answered. "I just want to get a feel for the city and walk around a bit. I can take a taxi home when I'm ready."

Brandon dropped me off in front a row of local shops and I waved goodbye. I found the nearest hotel and dialed the number my father had given me.

"Hello, this is John Coventry calling."

"Where the hell are you?" said the voice on the other end of the line.

"I'm in South Africa if you must know."

"Nice try Mr. Coventry. But according to our records we have your passport and we've already checked all the outgoing flights from England…your name was not on any of the flight lists."

Were these people stupid? Surely, I was not the first criminal to escape from England using a second passport and a fake name. This whole conversation was quite funny.

"Well if you don't believe me then why don't you call the number back and see for yourself."

"Fine."

I gave them the international number and waited for the phone to ring. "Hello, John Coventry…What can I do for you?" I couldn't help but be smug. It was about time those bastards got a taste of their own medicine. "What's wrong?" I said.

"This is a South African number…," said the man.

"That's what I've been trying to tell you. I'm in South Africa at the moment."

"We can easily have you arrested there."

"May I remind you there are no extradition treaties between the United Kingdom and South Africa? Not to mention, Africa itself is one hell of a huge continent." I could feel them ready to explode with rage at the other end. "You have a good day now."

I didn't bother to call Atwood or Nigel, they would find out where I was soon enough. In fact, I'm sure the officer was making a few phone calls right away. Atwood was going to be pissed. True he'd saved me from jail…for the time being…but he also got me involved with IRA terrorists and made me fear for my life. I didn't necessarily think that was a fair trade-off for stealing money, although it wasn't Peter Atwood's fault I was all alone in South Africa. He didn't commit the crime…I did. I was the one responsible for the mess of a life I was living. How long was I going to keep blaming others?

I was nothing short of a thief, and a liar. I'd lied to my family, my friends, the Government – all the people who tried to help me the most. I thought I'd been fooling them, but really I'd only been fooling myself. This person standing here in South Africa was not the man I wanted to be, someone who was unable to face the truth and the reality of his actions. Working with the government was a chance to right my wrong, yet here I was running away and avoiding my responsibilities once again. What the hell was wrong with me? Would I ever learn?

CHAPTER SIXTEEN

I managed to find a nice little apartment in Johannesburg and settled into my new life. Brandon insisted I get a maid, so not long after I moved in, Bertha showed up at my door with her printed headscarf and apron. A charming, incredibly kind black woman from the Matabelle tribe, she was short on formal education but could speak and understand a fair amount of English. Such a hard-worker, I almost felt guilty paying her the ten Rand per week wage, which amounted to around one English Pound. You couldn't even buy lunch, once a week, back in England for a pound.

Other than a few mishaps early on, Bertha and I got along famously. The first day on the job, Bertha arrived promptly at seven am.

"Good marwning bass," she said.

"Umm hello," I responded. Bertha had walked right into my bedroom, while I was still half-asleep in my shorts. That would teach me not to lock my apartment door.

"Here's ya juice," she said handing me a glass of freshly squeezed orange juice. She was quite oblivious to my half nakedness and just kept chatting away. "Nice marwing out der today." She threw open the curtains and the blazing sun quite near blinded me. She waddled out of the room, closing the door behind her. A few minutes later, I heard the water running in the bath.

I really hadn't planned on getting up yet, but it seemed as though Bertha had a strict schedule she was intent on keeping. Sitting up in bed, I drank my juice, letting the deliciousness of the sweet liquid jolt my taste buds from a long night's sleep. Maybe this early morning ritual wasn't going to be so bad. Bertha knocked, then walked in carrying a large fluffy towel

"Bass…your bath is ready."

"Thank you Bertha, you can just set the towel down on the chair for me. I'll get it on my way into the bathroom." She looked confused. Surely to hell she didn't think she was going to bathe me? Was that the custom here? I could feel her chocolate brown eyes watching as I timidly pulled back the sheet, exposing my bare chest and black knickers.

"I'm fine now Bertha. Thank you for your help."

She didn't move. Snatching the towel from the chair, I made a beeline for the bathroom with Bertha hot on my trail. For a large woman, she had the surprising quickness and agility of a cat. Dear God! She was planning on bathing me. I stopped just inside the bathroom door and turned abruptly.

"Bertha, thank you so much," I said trying tried to be as polite as possible. "But really I can bath myself. I'm all right."

"Yes sir Bass," she answered. I closed the bathroom door and was just about to drop my drawers, when Bertha busted through the door carrying a large sponge.

"Bertha please!" I said raising my voice. "No! I'm fine. I do not need you to bathe me."

She gave me a slightly dirty look, then turned and walked out, mumbling in her native language, as she went. I couldn't imagine Helen, the housekeeper back at Townfield, suggesting she give my father or me a bath. Just thinking about it made me laugh. While in the tub, I heard Bertha banging around in the kitchen with the pots and pans. I guess she figured that if she couldn't give me a good scrub behind the ears, she'd at least fix me breakfast.

After a few days, we fell into a morning routine and I was happy to have her around. We didn't talk much, but she was at least another presence in the house and I was grateful for the company. Bertha lived with her family in the Johannesburg Township of Soweto, an incredibly violent area, well known for riots and causing trouble for the white police and South African Government. I was very curious about the place and asked Brandon if he might take me there.

"Are you sure?" said Brandon. "It's not the nicest place in the world...I can assure you of that."

He picked me up in his Jeep and right away, I noticed a handgun tucked down by his leg.

"You never can be too careful," he said. "Whatever you do, stay close to me."

The Township was very dirty and insufferably poor. People lived in a combination of mud huts and sheds, a horrid stench filling every droplet of air. The streets were relatively quiet at the time, with only a few groups of kids hanging around.

"Look over there," said Brandon pointing over the right side of the dashboard.

"A film crew from the United States...What are they doing here?"

"International television crews hang out down here all the time...just trying to be first in line to catch any skirmishes. Must be a slow news day today, they're all just sitting around looking bored."

All of a sudden, we saw one of the American production guys take a wad of money from his pocket and walk over toward a group of children. He waved the money around so the kids could see it, and then threw the bills into a nearby trashcan and strode off. Of course, all the kids stormed over to the trashcan and began frantically searching through the refuse to find the money. Possessing even one American dollar would have been a small fortune to these children.

"And roll…" a voice said from off to the side.

The television crew started filming the activities, which of course they broadcast later as a report about poor South African black kids rummaging through the trash for food. It was quite a disturbing and disgusting scene and I felt sorry for the children, not just because they were poor and hungry, but because they were being used as pawns in a much larger capitalist game.

The tour of Bertha's hometown really opened my eyes at how lucky I was to be born white, and to be born British. Sure, I had my difficulties, but I never wanted for the simple things in life like these people did. I always had a warm place to sleep, a solid roof over my head, and a plate full of food. It made me count my blessings and be thankful for the things I did have.

Brandon was a great friend and we spent a lot of time together just hanging out at his place or going out on the town for a few drinks with his buddies. There really wasn't much else for me to do and I welcomed the company as a respite from my extreme boredom. While sounding exciting and adventurous, kicking my heels and just touring around the country was getting stale. I wanted my life back and I wanted Michelle. I couldn't plan anything permanent or put down any roots because I had no idea what my future held. It was driving me crazy!

"So are you up to taking a little drive with Thomas, Henry and I?" Brandon asked me one day as we were sitting on his patio having a beer. "Henry and Thomas have some business to attend to out in one of the black settlements. I always like to go along just in case."

"Just in case of what?"

"Well you've been out to Soweto before. It's not the safest place in the world, especially at night. But don't worry you'll be safe with us."

"Oh why not," I said. "I suppose I haven't got anything better to do." I was curious as to what sort of business Thomas and Henry were into, but knew better than to ask too many questions.

We picked up Thomas and Henry and left for Soweto later that night. The dreadful actions in 1976 by the South African Defense forces in killing almost 600 blacks in Soweto had made this place the most dangerous township in all of South Africa but I was a little unnerved to see all three men armed with handguns and knives. Thomas reached into his bag and pulled a very small revolver.

"Brandon told me you don't have a weapon," said Thomas shoving the gun into my hand. "Just take this one. Hide it in your jacket or something. Just in case."

I looked at Brandon dumbfounded. They didn't seriously expect me to carry a gun did they?

"Thomas is right," said Brandon. "Just take it John. I'd feel better knowing you had something. I don't anticipate you having to use it…but it's there if you have to."

"You do realize I've never fired a revolver before in my life," I said.

"Just aim and pull the trigger," Henry laughed. "It's really not that difficult."

The car sped off into the South African night and with each passing moment, the tension mounted in my veins. I came to this country to escape all the guns and the violence. Now I'm holding a weapon. It just didn't seem right. I slipped the gun into my coat and out of sight. Lord help me if I actually had to use it.

"So does anyone mind if I ask why we're going to the

settlement tonight?" I said.

"Diamonds John…beautiful expensive diamonds," answered Henry.

I cast a glance at Brandon. "It's not my gig," he said. "I just go along for the drive."

"See John…diamonds are a great commodity," continued Henry. "Especially if you buy them cheap and sell them high."

"Well how is it you can get the diamonds for cheap?" I asked.

"The blacks nick them from the mines. They're quite good at it. It's a whole industry here in South Africa. Then they sell the diamonds to us and we sell or trade them on the black market. I don't give a shit about collecting diamonds. I only care about the money or goods those diamonds bring us."

"Sounds like quite an operation you've got going on there," I said. "So what sorts of goods would you trade for? Art? Paintings?"

Thomas laughed. "No…we give the diamonds to people like our mutual acquaintance Michelle and her friends…after taking our cut of course…then they take the diamonds to Amsterdam to sell…and that is what makes the world go round John my boy!"

"Oh I see." It was as clear as day. The blacks steal the diamonds, Brandon's crew buys the diamonds, and Michelle and her friends smuggle them into Europe. Amsterdam…of course…it's the diamond trading capital of the world. The money the Action Directe and the Baader Meinhof gang made from the diamonds went to buy the arms and explosives! Another piece of the terrorist puzzle clicked into place. Was my pure chance meeting with Baader Meinhof member Verena Becker at a bar in Amsterdam back in 1977 a coincidence? She said she and her friends kept an apartment there when they needed to get away from Germany, but perhaps she was in Amsterdam on business? This was almost more than I could comprehend.

"Like I said John, diamonds are a beautiful thing. We maybe could find a spot for you somewhere if you're interested."

"No, no…thanks for the offer…but I'm already in enough trouble."

"Ya Brandon mentioned you were wanted back in England," said Henry with a smile. "Well the offer stands if you change your mind."

The last thing I wanted to do was get mixed up with stolen blood diamonds. Despite the undercover work, I really wasn't the type of person who enjoyed danger all that much. Not if I had a choice. This time I was confident I'd made the right decision saying no.

Brandon slowed down and pulled the car down a narrow, sunken road. Illuminated by the glow of small fires outside the huts, I could see faces peering out of uneven window frames and standing in doors. I felt like such an intruder, my pale skin standing out amongst the sea of black. Passing a group of unruly young men yelling, drinking, and tussling around, I instinctively moved my hand closer toward the gun hidden in my coat. I didn't like being here one bit.

"Ha, ha, ha," laughed Brandon. "Look at those two over there by the water barrel. They don't give a fuck who's watching them."

I peered over Brandon's outstretched arm with my eyes and came upon a man and woman, buck-naked having sex up against the side of a hut, while three little children played in the dirt only a few meters away. The car turned to the right and Brandon pulled up alongside one of the huts. This one seemed larger than the others, but it was hard to tell in the darkness.

"Maybe I should just wait in the car," I said.

"That's really not a good idea John," answered Brandon. "It's best if you come with us. Just stick near me and you'll be fine."

I followed them out of the car, staying as close to Brandon as I could. Three surly black men with machine guns strung over their shoulders guarded the entranceway to the hut. Thomas said something to them in their native language, and they stepped back and let us all enter. The candlelight danced off the many different and unique tribal carvings and handcrafted woven blankets, creating magnificent but spooky shadows on the dried mud and cow dung walls.

Thomas and Henry walked up to the man sitting at the small wooden table while Brandon and I hung back by the door. Every once and a while, Brandon would give a quick check out the door. Bare-chested and wearing a long beaded necklace that bounced off his rippling abdominal muscles with every breath, the man reached over and picked up a carving of an elephant from a small shelf. Carefully tapping one of the legs on the corner of the table, he dislodged the elephant's leg. From inside the leg he pulled out a small crushed velvet bag and handed it to Thomas. Thomas poured the contents of the bag into the palm of Henry's hand, the diamonds sparkling in the reflection of the lantern sitting on the table.

"They look good mate," Henry smiled.

"Yes they do," answered Thomas. "Let's make the deal."

Henry put the diamonds back in the pouch and the two turned their attention back to the man.

"They're trying to settle on a price," Brandon whispered

in my ear. "Right now he wants more than Thomas and Henry want to pay."

"Will they leave without the diamonds if he doesn't come down in price?"

"Oh God no...they'll just try and get him down as low as they can. You don't walk away from diamonds like those, no matter what the price. Look...they just settled it."

Thomas handed the man a thick wad of notes as Henry shoved the bag of into the inside pocket of his coat. Just as the men were shaking hands, the pounding staccato of gunshots roared through the night air.

"Police! Police!" yelled one of guards.

"Goddamn it!" yelled Brandon looking out the door. "Let's get the fuck out of here! They've got the full arsenal tonight!"

With guns drawn (not mine) we made a run for the car and took off down one of the back roads. One of the armored police cars spotted us and gave chase. My heart leapt out of my chest as Brandon maneuvered down the narrow paths like he was driving on the Autobahn. Still, he couldn't quite lose the police car.

"Hold on everyone!" he yelled turning the car sharply to the left and down an embankment. He cut the engine as Thomas hopped out of the car and belly flopped into a secure lookout position halfway up the bank. We all waited in silence. I was too afraid to breathe. Suddenly the police car whizzed by without stopping. Thomas poked his head up and looked both ways down the road. Then he waved his hand in the air.

"There's the signal," said Henry.

Brandon turned on the engine and hit the gas. The car spun up the hill and back onto the roadway.

"That was bloody close," said Thomas diving back into

the car and slamming the door.

"Too close," answered Brandon steering the car down another passageway.

"You have to admit…it was kind of fun though," said Henry laughing. "Nothing like a little Saturday night excitement for ya, eh John?"

I took the revolver out of my coat and handed it back to Thomas. "You can say that again," I sighed. "Good God! I think I almost shit my pants! Next time you guys have some business to attend to…I think I'll just stay home if you don't mind." The car erupted in laughter.

"You're a good sport," said Henry. "It's all in a day's work for us."

"Why did the police come?" I asked. "Were they tipped off?"

"The police continuously raid the settlements. They know what goes on but really can't do much to stop it. Tonight they just happened to interrupt us. It's not the first time and it certainly won't be the last!" Thomas took a small flask out of his coat pocket. "Anyone need a drink?"

"Yes please," I said taking the flask and putting to my mouth. The burning sensation of the liquid managed to numb my senses just enough for the car ride home. Brandon dropped Thomas and Henry off at a pub in Johannesburg before driving me to my apartment.

"Sorry about tonight John," he said. "I should have never asked you to come. I put you in danger."

"Don't worry about it Brandon. It wasn't your fault and as much as I hate to admit it…it was exciting."

Brandon laughed. "Well I'm glad we got away safely."

"Can I ask you a question?"

"Sure."

"Is it true that Michelle takes the diamonds over to

Amsterdam, and then uses the proceeds to buy guns and explosives? I don't want to be nosey but is the IRA involved in all of this?"

"I don't know for sure about the IRA," answered Brandon. "But I wouldn't doubt it. The IRA would kill to get their hands on some of those weapons. Why do you ask?"

"Just curious really. Being from England and being a first-hand witness to all the IRA violence...I always wondered where the guns and explosives came from."

"Ask Michelle...I'm sure she can tell you better than I can. Good night buddy!"

As I walked into my apartment, I wondered if Brandon really meant to say that about Michelle or if it had been a slip of the tongue. She'd always been so careful and guarded about her actions. I'm not sure she would have appreciated Brandon revealing any secrets...even to me.

I loved South Africa, the people, both black and whites, could not have been kinder. Then there was the scenery. There's nothing quite like watching an "African Sun" rise or set. The sheer beauty and majesty of the orange and yellow filled sky was enough to take your breath away. I toured around much of the country and became enthralled with all that I saw. The rhinoceros standing by the side of the road, or the elephants watching your every move from the safety of the bush, it was all such an incredible potpourri of pleasure for the senses.

But as time wore on and the weeks turned into months, I became restless for my own land and country. I missed bandying about in the lush green fields of the English countryside, and visiting the village pubs for a pint of English ale. Most of all, I missed my parents and I missed Michelle. I hadn't heard a word from her since we parted in Jersey and

I was lonely and lost. Talking to my parents on the phone wasn't the same as sitting in the drawing room at Townfield sharing drinks, stories and a great many laughs. I even missed the gloomy English rain.

"John, I have an idea," said my father one day while we were chatting on the phone. "Why don't we meet in France for a visit? You can fly in from South Africa and I'll fly in from England. We can meet at the airport and maybe stay a few nights at a hotel."

"I would love that Dad but I'm not sure if…"

"Don't worry about a thing. I'll set everything up and pay for the ticket. I think it would be a great help to your mother…if I could tell her I saw you in person and you were alive and doing well. She worries you know…I worry."

"I know you both do and I'm sorry…I truly am sorry. I would love to have a visit. Oh you don't know how much I would enjoy that."

"Okay son, give me some time to make the arrangements and I'll get back to you."

The next week I was sitting in Charles de Gaulle airport in Paris having coffee with my father. I cannot even express how happy I was to see him. He smiled, gave me a hug and for that brief instance I felt like I was home. It seemed so close, just across the Channel. In an hour or so, I could be back on English soil. Of course, the minute I set foot on that glorious English dirt, authorities would snatch me up and throw me in the deepest dungeons to rot until the last days of hell. Well maybe that's being a bit dramatic but I knew that's what Atwood and Nigel would want to do. That's not to say I didn't deserve it.

My father brought me up to date on all the family happenings and I was pleased to hear there hadn't been any further visits from the police. Seeing my father in person was bittersweet. One day was not near enough to make up for the time we'd lost, time we'd never ever get back. My parents weren't getting any younger, and the thought of something happening to them while I was so far away consumed me.

"Go back to South Africa John," advised my father. "Let some more time pass...let those people like Brian and Martin forget all about you. Just give it some more time son."

"I'll try...but I honestly don't know how much longer I can last. I'm dreadfully lonely."

His eyes filled with sadness and he gave a sympathetic smile. "I know John. It must be painful for you." He paused and took a sip of his coffee. "So let's change the subject. Tell me about South Africa. What's it like?"

I told him about Bertha and our various miscommunications, and that made him chuckle. I'm sure I'd already told him everything over the phone on different occasions, but it was nice to hear his laughter and see his reactions. I didn't dare tell him about my escapade with Brandon, Thomas, and Henry. I think that would have been too much for him to bear.

"Well son," he said looking at his watch. "I'm sorry this visit has to be so short, but I've got to get back to England and you've got to get back to South Africa. Remember, France does have extradition treaties with the United Kingdom, so even sitting here, you're not safe." He took a large manila envelope from his coat pocket and passed it across the table to me. "I want you to have this."

I opened the package. "Dad, this is too much money. I can't accept it."

"Nonsense John. Family comes first. Don't ever forget that."

"Thank you so much. It's greatly appreciated."

"Give Mum a kiss for me will ya?" I asked.

"I certainly will."

I gave him a hug and watched him walk away. It was one of hardest moments of my life. I loved my father with every fiber of my soul and I hated knowing I'd caused him and my mother so much anguish and despair. I caught my flight and readied myself for a long and boring trip. This time I didn't have Brandon to keep me company, I was stuck with my thoughts, and they weren't very pleasant.

Life settled back into a routine, and more and more I contemplated returning home to England. I couldn't run forever. If Michelle were with me, things would have been different, but she seemed to have abandoned me. What was I waiting for? Nigel was right; the cause would always triumph. She was off living her life, and I was stuck here in a foreign land, just counting down the days until I could begin to live mine.

I didn't even have a timeframe. I didn't know where Michelle was, what she was doing, and I had no way of finding out. I started to believe that she sent me to South Africa as a way to get me out of her life. I didn't want to think that way, but her lack of communication was beginning to skewer my brain. She obviously had no desire to speak to me on the phone. Brandon had my number; she could get it if she really wanted to. She could make the call. If there's a will, there's a way. I guess the frustration and loneliness was starting to build, and I didn't know how to control it or make it go away. That's really what I wanted, to make it all go away.

I'd been back in South Africa for a number of weeks when Brandon called the apartment.

"Got some news I think you're going to like." I could hear the excitement in his voice. "Michelle is flying in to see you."

With those words, all my anger and disappointment

vanished like the mist on a summer's morning.

"When?" I asked.

"A few days. Think you can last till then?" he laughed.

"I'm gonna have to aren't I?"

Brandon and I met her flight at Jan Smutts International Airport in Johannesburg. I could hardly contain my enthusiasm. It'd been so long since I held her in my arms and kissed her sweet lips. I just wanted to be with her, talk to her, tell her how much I missed her…tell her how much I loved her.

Stepping off the plane, she was a vision of unparalleled beauty and I froze in my tracks.

"John!" she screamed. "My little virgin boy!" The sound of her voice shocked me to attention and we ran toward each other, not caring who or what was in the way.

"Oh my God! I missed you so much," I said hugging her tight.

"Not any more than I missed you," answered Michelle.

As soon as our lips touched, the passion re-ignited and it felt like we hadn't spent a minute apart.

"How are you?" I said breathlessly. "Let me look at you. My God you are beautiful." I kissed her again.

"I want to introduce you to my friend," said Michelle backing away slightly. "John, this is Rondell."

"It's a pleasure to meet you Rondell," I said holding out my hand.

"I've heard so much about you," said Rondell.

"Really?" I said with a smirk. "Good or bad?"

"All good," she answered. "All good."

In truth, Michelle had never mentioned Rondell to me. From her accent, I presumed she was German but I wasn't sure. She was pretty enough, then again, anyone standing beside Michelle paled in comparison.

"What are the plans?" said Michelle.

"Well," I said taking her by the hand. "We're going to stop by my apartment so you two can freshen up and change if you like, and then we'll all go out for dinner." I leaned in and whispered in her ear. "Although I'd much rather nibble on you for dinner."

She laughed and playfully swatted my arm. "I see you're still as bad as ever."

"Oh how I've missed you Michelle," I said. "Your voice, your laugh. I even missed you calling me your little virgin boy. How long can you stay?"

"For a week," she answered.

"That's it? Can't you stay longer? It's been months and months…one week isn't enough for me," I pleaded.

"I'm sorry…but it's all the time I can spare."

I found myself a little put off by the comment. "Well I'm glad you could *spare* any time at all. I mean you're off doing what you do and I'm stuck here…doing nothing."

"John, please. I don't want to argue. I'm sorry it's been so long, I really am…it's just that I haven't been able to get away. It's not as easy as you think."

"I'm sorry too," I answered. "I've just been so lost and lonely without you. You have no idea."

She kissed me on the lips, then smiled. "Well I'm here now. Let's enjoy the time we have together."

Michelle loved my little apartment and I kept thinking what a happy couple we'd make living out our days together in the South African sun. I knew better than to bring the subject up again. At least not on the first night.

Dinner was wonderful and we all had a fabulous time. I caught myself just staring at Michelle as she talked to Brandon and Rondell, and wondering how someone as dynamic and passionate as her, ends up getting mixed up in something as terrible as the Action Directe. I don't think it's something I'd ever understand.

The dinner conversation was light and casual, with no mention of any type of "business" dealings. I'm certain Michelle didn't tell Brian she was off vacationing with me for a week. I could only imagine his reaction. It was very late by the time we finished dinner and Brandon dropped Michelle and I off at my apartment. Rondell had booked herself a room at a nearby hotel, not wanting to feel like three's a crowd I suppose.

Having Michelle naked in my arms again was exhilarating. We spent the night making love and just being as one. The next morning, Bertha arrived at her usual seven am and immediately began running the bath. Today I would let a woman bathe me, but that woman would be Michelle. To be honest, there wasn't much bathing going on, just a lot of playing and splashing around in the water. Poor Bertha…having to listen to all our hollering and laughing. Oh well. I could have cared less. Michelle was here.

After a hearty breakfast, Brandon showed up with Rondell and the four of us set off for Durban, where we were going to stay for a few days. Our hotel, the Holiday Inn, was a modern day skyscraper with this huge swimming pool jutting out from the side of the building. The bottom of the pool was made of glass, so you could look right through and see all the people below. It was beautiful, but also a little scary in a "what happens if the glass cracks" sort of way. Situated on the main road running parallel to Durban's world famous beach, the hotel had a panoramic view of the South Indian Ocean.

The beach was glorious, with golden sand leading down to the sparkling shoreline. I wasn't too pleased seeing the shark nets out in the water though. Sharks weren't on the top of my list for "most wanted pet". Just thinking about them gives me nightmares. Michelle of course, thought it was hilarious and goaded me into visiting the beachfront aquarium, where huge hungry sharks swam about, just waiting for someone like me to fall into the tank.

"C'mon John," she said pulling my hand. "They're only fish. It's such a better view looking down into the tank."
"They're more than fish Michelle, and I'm really not comfortable being up here." I could feel the dampness of my cold sweat seeping into my cotton t-shirt.

"What if I promise to hold you tight like this?" She wrapped her arms around my waist. "I won't let you go. I swear on my life."

"Well that won't mean much if the bloody shark jumps out of the water and bites my head off."

"First of all, sharks can't jump out of the water, only whales and dolphins can do that. Second…see that big protective barrier there?" she said sarcastically.

"I'm pretty certain Jaws jumped out of the water when he attacked the boat," I answered.

"John…Jaws was a movie…he was a machine." She clasped both sides of my face in her hands and pulled it towards her. "Listen to me. Jaws wasn't real. He was make-believe. Do you understand?" Her voice was firm and sweet, as if she was trying to convince a child there was no such thing as monsters under the bed.

"Sorry…don't care what you say," I said cheekily. "I'm not buying it. If I stick my head over that tank, some shark is going to jump up and bite it off."

"Fine," she said pretending to be angry. "You stay here…I'm going to go over and look at the sharks. Have fun standing there all by yourself." She walked over to the barrier and started yelling. "Here Mr. Shark…C'mer Mr. Shark."

I just shook my head and laughed as I watched her, falling deeper in love with every passing minute.

Brandon and Rondell were very kind to let Michelle and I go off together. I was glad. I didn't want to share her with anyone. Michelle was very generous, took me to the best restaurants, and paid for everything without question. She never seemed short of money, and I knew the only way for her to get that kind of cash was through her connections with the Action Directe. I buried the thought and enjoyed my plate of shrimp.

"Let's just spend the afternoon lying on the beach," she said as we left the restaurant.

"That's fine with me." We were both feeling happy from the wine and the mood was gay.

We found a spot on the beach to spread out the blanket and lie down. Even though the beach was crammed with people, I had this feeling of absolute freedom and serenity. Michelle sat down on the blanket and began to undo her bikini top.

"What are you doing? Why are you taking off your top?" I said quickly holding up a towel.

"It's ridiculously hot and I don't want suntan lines."

"Michelle, you can't go topless here. No one else is…and…I don't know what the local rules are. We don't want to get in trouble."

Grumpily, she let me re-tie her straps. "Well it's a stupid law in my opinion. If a woman wants to take her top off, she should. Men do it all the time."

"That's different," I said.

"How is it different?"

"It just is."

"Well I don't think it's fair or right. Have you seen some of the men here? There should be a law requiring them to keep their shirts on!"

"Come and lounge on the blanket with me," I said with a smile.

She lay back down and we spent a glorious afternoon chatting and relaxing, like a normal couple would. As the sun began to set and the beach cleared of people, Michelle had an idea.

"Let's get naked and go swimming! I love skinny dipping!"

"Absolutely not," I said. "I'm not getting naked on a beach. You can go, but I'm staying here."

"You're no fun," she pouted. Her mood changed and she actually seemed perturbed with me.

"Michelle…why are you upset with me?" She refused to talk. "Because I don't want to go skinny dipping? I'm sorry if I don't feel as brazen as you do."

"You just don't want to have any fun with me today."

She stormed off down the beach, leaving me speechless. I had no idea what had gotten into her or why she was acting this way. After a half an hour or so, she came wandering back with her usual cheeky grin. I didn't say a word. She sat down on the blanket, leaned over and whispered in my ear.

"Okay my little virgin boy, enough with the beach and swimming. Let's go back to the hotel so I can fuck you silly."

Michelle certainly had a way with words, blunt and straight to the point. I think the combination of her frankness and her French accent, made me adore her so much more. I could never stay angry with her and she knew it. She dragged me off the sand and we walked hand in hand across the street to our hotel room. Dinner was put on hold as we made love for hours and hours, in every corner of the room. Her appetite was ravenous and I could barely keep up.

"The best times of my life are when I'm with you," I said cradling her in my arms. She smiled but did not say a word. "I miss you so much and you see how good we are together…why can't it be like this always."

"John…we've already had this conversation. I cannot stay and you cannot come home." She paused for a moment, then her voice got very quiet. "Brian is looking for you."

"What? Why?"

"He's angry that you've disappeared. He keeps asking me questions and I keep lying. I told him we had a big fight, broke up, and I haven't heard from you since."

"Why is he so angry?" I asked. "I did everything he asked. I set up the shipment."

"He thinks maybe you're not really who you say you are."

I could feel the air deflate from my lungs as I struggled to find the breath to speak. "What do mean I'm not who I say I am?"

"Remember the bodyguard interviews?" she asked.

"How could I forget," I answered.

"That was a set up. Brian set you up. He paid those men to say those lies about you assaulting them."

I was in shock. "Why would he do that?"

Michelle looked away for a minute. "You are so naïve John. He wanted you arrested and sent to prison. Brian has contacts everywhere. With you behind bars, he could keep his eye on you…keep you in line…or even worse."

"I don't understand," I said.

"I warned you that Brian was a dangerous man. If he thinks you've betrayed him, he will kill you. Nothing will stand in his way. English prisons are filled with IRA sympathizers. All it takes is a single word, a single instruction from the outside…and you're a dead man. Nobody in prison helps a man with any sort of sex charges. If you're killed in prison, Brian's hands are clean."

"Killed? Brian wants me dead?"

"It appears so. I'll do everything I can to protect you but…" Her voice trailed off and she kissed my cheek. "Why did you have to get involved?" she said softly.

I couldn't believe what Michelle was telling me. Had Brian somehow figured out I'd been working undercover all this time? Did he tell Michelle?

"Why does Brian think I betrayed him?" I asked.

"He can't figure out why you weren't arrested?"

"I was arrested…and I was charged," I replied.

"Yes but he said you were released right away…and didn't even spend the night in jail. He can't understand why."

"I don't know why," I said in a panic. "The judge said there wasn't enough evidence. Maybe I have a good lawyer."

"I believe you John. It's not me you have to worry about."

"You're not in trouble with Brian because of me are you?"

"I can handle Brian and I promise I'll do my best to stop his hunt. Let me talk to him when I get back. I can be very convincing when I need to be." She kissed me again and I held her close.

"What should I do?" I asked.

"Just stay here in South Africa. You'll be safe here."

"For how long though?" I said. "You know I can't stay forever, especially if you won't stay with me."

"Give things some time to settle down. Someone else will come along and Brian will forget all about you."

"I hope so," I answered.

"Wait until you hear from me. I'll give you the okay to come home."

"You promise?"

"I promise."

"I have one other question," I said. "Do you or your organization ever buy Blood Diamonds from the blacks in South Africa? Is that the connection between you and Brandon?"

"Why do you want to know?" Her voice was guarded.

"It's just that I went on a little business venture with Brandon and his friends out to Soweto a while back…and they mentioned something about selling the diamonds for guns and explosives. I just wondered if any of those guns or explosives ended up in your hands?"

"Why does it matter John? We get supplies from all over the world…if some of the money comes from the diamonds, then it comes from the diamonds. It's not really that big of deal. Why the concern?"

"I guess I just want to know if the bullet Brian wants to put in my head came as a result of the transaction I witnessed in Soweto," I answered sarcastically.

"Of course the IRA benefits from the diamonds, we all do…but Brian isn't going to put a bullet in your head. I won't let him!"

"Michelle…now you're the one being naïve. There's not much even you can do to stop a bullet."

"Shh!" she said putting her hand over my mouth. "No more talking about bullets, Brian, or diamonds. It is what it is. Now make love to me again my little virgin boy!"

The week with Michelle flew by, and as we spent our final night together, I pleaded with her once again to stay. I was desperate.

"Will you at least give me a phone number where I can reach you, so when I'm lonely I can at least call?"

"I can't John. Telephone lines can be tapped…in my business I just can't take any chances…not even for you."

"Well that makes me feel so special."

"Don't be like that."

"How else am I supposed to be? Nothing is more important to you than the cause! Not me, not anybody!" I was getting angry. Michelle said she loved me, yet I was always playing second fiddle.

"I believe what I believe John…and I've dedicated my life to making those beliefs come true. I wish you could understand."

"Well I don't. I don't understand. I don't understand how your group can bomb buildings or assassinate someone with a machine gun and then call yourselves an instrument of the people. It doesn't make sense and I'll never agree. It's mad and you're mad to believe it!"

"You don't know what you're saying John," she snapped.

"Fine," I said. "I'm done arguing about it. It's obvious that I'm never going to change your mind and you're content to keep me here in South Africa and out of your life."

"I'm not *keeping* you anywhere. I'm trying to protect you and make sure you're safe but I guess that means nothing to you."

"Michelle stop…I appreciate everything you're doing but it's so hard for me because I'm always in the dark. I don't know when I might see you or even hear from you again. I hate living like this. It's not you…I'm just frustrated by the whole thing. If only we'd met under other circumstances." I hugged her close and kissed her on the ear. "Maybe in a little cafe in Paris…I'm there on vacation…and I see you sitting at a table reading the paper. You look up and our eyes meet…then the love story begins…only that story would have a happy ending. I'm not so sure I see a happy ending for our story Michelle, and it scares the hell out of me. It really scares the hell out of me!"

"Don't be scared." Her voice was soft and gentle. "Whatever happens happens."

"How can I not be scared? I read the papers Michelle. I know what the Action Directe and the IRA are capable of. Not to mention your friend Verena and the damn German's. What happens if you get arrested? What happens if you get killed? What the hell am I supposed to do then?"

She ran her fingers through my hair and kissed me delicately on the neck. My defenses were down and she knew it.

"You go on…that's what you do. You go on and live your life…and you remember. You remember me, and the love we shared. That's all I ask."

"There's not a chance in hell I could ever forget you Michelle. Not a chance in hell."

The talk drifted away into passionate lovemaking. For some strange reason, I had the sense this would be the last time I would see Michelle for quite a while. I didn't know why, but the night had a feeling of finality and we clung to each other with all our might, holding onto what we had, me longing for what might never be. We got little sleep, preferring to spend the hours locked in an embrace of love, happiness, and pure unabated joy.

The scene at the airport the next day was the complete opposite. Once again, Michelle was leaving, and there wasn't a thing I could do to stop her. Michelle and Rondell checked in for their flight and sorted their luggage. There was still a bit of time before take-off, so Michelle and I went outside and left Brandon and Rondell in the lounge having a coffee.

It was a beautiful afternoon. The sun was shining bright, with just enough breeze to keep the air refreshing.

"I'm going to ask you one last time," I said. "Please stay with me in South Africa. Just think of what our life could be like. Quit the Action Directe…just walk away. You can do it…I know you can. Please Michelle please. Think about it."

She paused and looked at me with sad eyes. "It's all I have been doing. I would love to have a life with you but…I just can't. At least not right now." She hugged me very hard and put her head on my shoulder. "I have something for you." She reached into her purse and took out an envelope. "Don't open this until I'm gone."

"What is it?" I asked.

She opened my coat and tucked the envelope in the inside pocket. "Just read it after I'm gone."

Rondell popped her head outside the door. "Time to go Michelle, they just called our flight."

I took her in my arms one last time and held her close. "I can't stand that you're leaving Michelle," I said. "It's always so hard to say goodbye."

She smiled a sad smile then whispered in my ear. "Remember your promise to me in Jersey?"

"Yes, I remember," I said softly. "You want me to go back there one day."

"Yes," she replied. She turned her face and gazed hard into my eyes. "Do not forget me, my virgin boy. Do not forget me."

I shook my head in reply, for no words could express the profound sorrow I was feeling. Michelle turned away and with a final wave was gone. Back to France and back to a life that didn't include me. I was devastated and honestly didn't know how many more of these farewells I could take. Yes, I wanted to be safe, but I also wanted Michelle. I'm not sure she fully realized how hard it was for me to be a thousand miles away from her.

As I watched her plane take off, I knew I'd have to make a decision before long. Either stay in South Africa forever, or take my chances back in England. Judging by experience, I couldn't count on Michelle getting back to me about Brian any time soon. I know I promised her I'd wait, but the odds were good I'd be waiting forever. I couldn't help but wonder why he was so suspicious of me. I did everything he asked and never caused any trouble. Did he have contacts in the government or with the police? How could he have known about the undercover work? I'd been so careful...so very, very careful.

Maybe Brian just didn't like the fact I ran out on him before he said I was finished. I don't suppose many people did that and then lived to tell about it. I was such a meaningless little fly in his operation, just a worker bee. Surely, he had more important things to worry about, didn't he?

"You look like shit my friend," said Brandon putting his arm around me. "Let's go grab some dinner and a drink...or two.

"That sounds like a good idea to me," I answered.

We drove into Johannesburg, and Brandon took me to a nice restaurant, where we ordered some food and I drowned my sorrows in drink – lots and lots of drink. By the time Brandon dropped me off at my apartment it was late. As I stumbled into my bedroom and took off my coat, the white tip of Michelle's envelope caught my eye. I sat down on the bed and tore it open, revealing a card with a picture of a horse grazing in a country field.

"With love to you, for being my little virgin boy. You will find peace one day soon. Never forget <u>our</u> time in Jersey and what I asked you to do for me one day. I do love you.

Michelle XX

I was, I am, I will be.

I read the card over several times, trying to figure out the underlying meaning. It sounded like a farewell card…a farewell forever card. Did Michelle know something I didn't? And what did that last line mean, "I was, I am, I will be?" Why was Michelle using it? I had no idea, and couldn't for the life of me, understand what she was getting at. I loved the card anyway, and kissed it gently, holding it to my nose, breathing in any lingering scent of her sweet perfume. She said she loved me and I believed her. That's all I needed. Just something to hold onto until the day we met again. Whenever that might be.

CHAPTER SEVENTEEN

Time continued to tick away and I spent my days just being lazy and lounging around. Sounds like a great life until you have to live it day after day. Alone. Without Michelle there, the beach wasn't as playful and the sun didn't seem as bright. I hadn't heard a single word from her since she waved goodbye on the tarmac. No phone calls, no letters, not even a message sent through Brandon. I was worried about her. She promised she'd let me know after she spoke to Brian. I hoped to God Brian didn't do anything to her out of his hatred for me.

I often found myself sitting at night in my apartment, just thinking. Thinking about the past, the present, and the future. I kept Michelle's farewell card on my night table. It was the first thing I saw in the morning and the last thing I looked at before I went to bed. I knew the contents by heart. I also had this sickening feeling in my stomach that I would never see Michelle again. Asking me to remember her…like there would be a chance I could forget. She wanted me to find peace in my life, but that could only happen if I returned to England and faced the consequences of my crime. I finally realized I needed to stop portraying myself as a victim. Whatever the punishment was, I would take it and be thankful it wasn't longer. I was the one who'd broken the law, run away, and disgraced my family and myself. It was time for me to grow up, be a responsible adult, and go home to the people who loved me.

As much as I didn't want to admit it, Michelle had abandoned me. I know she didn't mean to, but in her mind,

I don't think she had any other choice. I wasn't part of the Action Directe and therefore could never fully be a part of her world. I thought her involvement in the whole faction was ludicrous and suicidal. She was either going to end up on the run, in jail, or dead, and none of those prospects boded well for our future together.

While I still had enough money for now, my funds would eventually run out, and there was no way in hell I was going to ask my father for more. He'd already done so much to support and stand by me. The last time I spoke with him on the phone, he seemed tired and worn out. He wasn't getting any younger, and I began to feel guilty about being away from both him and my mother for so long. They'd been there through thick and thin, and now, here I was abandoning them and putting them through more strain and worry than they desired or deserved. My father lived by the motto, "family first". It was time I heeded those words, headed home, and faced my future, whatever it may be.

"I think I want to come home," I said to my father on the telephone. "It's time."

"Are you sure?" he answered trying to mask his excitement.

"I can't hide forever," I said.

"But you'll be facing a certain jail sentence."

"I know but I'd rather do the time…just get it over with. That's the only way I'm going to be able to put this all behind me and move on with my life."

"Well I have to say, both your mother and I will be glad to have you back home. Things haven't been the same since you've been gone. We've missed you…we really have." He let out a heavy sigh.

"I've missed you both too."

"So I can't imagine you just hop on a plane tomorrow and

fly back to England do you?"

"No," I replied. "I'm going to give the lawyer a call and ask him to begin negotiations with the police for my return. Who knows, maybe I can still cut a deal."

"You never know John, you never know."

"I'll give you a call as soon as I hear something okay?"

I hung up the phone and immediately made the call to my lawyer.

"I think it's a wise decision John," he said. "The longer you stay free and on the lam, the harder it's going to be for me or any other lawyer to negotiate any favourable terms."

"What do you think you can get?" I asked.

"Honestly, I have no idea. I'll just have to talk to them and explain you ran to South Africa not to escape the charges, but because you feared for your life."

"And that was because of the undercover work I was doing for the government. Trust me, I don't normally associate myself with the IRA."

"That should help some John. Now your government contact knows all about the IRA connection don't they?"

"Yes sir, I told them everything I knew. My main contact was a man named Peter Atwood. He worked for the Department of Customs and Trade. There was also another man…Nigel was his first name…he worked in British Intelligence. He knows more about Brian and the IRA."

"Do you know Nigel's last name?"

"Come to think of it…no…I don't think he ever told me. Atwood knows who he is and I have both their phone numbers."

"Great. I wouldn't mind having those. I think it's going to be important to stress to the police and prosecution, just how much work you were doing on behalf of the government and the high level of risk involved. Might soften their stance a bit…and the judge's as well."

"Whatever you think you can do…I'd really appreciate it."

"I'll get back to you as soon as I can."

"Thank-you," I answered.

A few days later, my lawyer called back.

"Okay John, here's what's going on. There is a warrant out for your arrest in the United Kingdom on the Deception charge. However, the police have agreed that if you return, they will not meet your flight, handcuff or arrest you the minute you step off the plane, which in itself is quite odd. They would give you three days, unmolested by them or anyone else, for you to get your affairs in order and do whatever you had to do. At ten am on that third day, you would go to the police station in Liverpool and surrender yourself. You would then be formally arrested and would appear in front of a judge the same day for sentencing."

"Three days? Why are they giving me three days?"

"I'm not exactly sure," he said, "but I'd take it if I were you. I don't think you're going to get anything better."

"What about the sentence? How long?"

"That's up to the judge. I'll only be able to speak to that once we're in court."

"So that's it then?"

"That's it," said my lawyer. "You just need to give me the information for your flight home, and I'll let them know."

"Can I have a few days to think about it?" I asked.

"Of course," he answered. "The decision is totally yours. If you want to stay in South Africa for the rest of your life, you can, but if you ever want to come back to England for any reason, then you need to take this deal. Like I said, it's totally up to you."

The next couple of days were agony, trying to weigh both

the pros and cons of staying in South Africa or returning to England. Michelle still hadn't contacted me and I really had the feeling my life with her had reached a dead end. The choice was clear. I booked a flight and made the call to my lawyer.

"Please inform the police that I'm ready to come home." It felt good saying the words out loud and knowing they were true. After ten long months, I was going home.

Brandon thought I was nuts to give up my freedom.

"It's a definite prison sentence John," he said the next afternoon over coffee.

"I know Brandon, but I can't hide out here forever. My home, my family, my friends…except for you of course…are all in England. I miss them and I miss England."

"I understand," he answered.

"Now if Michelle had stayed with me in South Africa, things would have been very different. But without her, I'm lonely."

"I can only imagine."

I packed up all my belongings and said goodbye to Bertha. I'd become quite fond of her over the past year and would miss her. I felt bad about throwing her out of work on such short notice, so I gave her a nice parting bonus to tide her over until she found something else. Brandon offered to pick me up and see me off at the airport.

"I can't believe you're leaving," he said with great sadness. His large arms smothered me in a friendly embrace. "I'm not sure what I'm going to do without you. We've had some great adventures haven't we?" His eyes were glossy and holding back tears.

"I just have to thank you for everything you've done for me since I got here. You've been more than a friend…you've been like a brother and I'm grateful. You have no idea."

"I was glad to help John and if you ever need anything in the future, you know where to find me," he smiled.

"I do," I replied. I stuck out my hand. "Good luck with things Brandon. I wish nothing but the best for you always."

To my surprise, Brandon threw his huge arms around me again. "Farewell buddy. Hope you have a nice, safe flight."

"Thanks Brandon. You take care of yourself."

I picked up my carry-on bag, gave him one last wave, and headed down the boarding tunnel. Since the flight was overnight, I decided to spend the extra money and fly first class. At least then, I'd have a good meal, a bit of legroom and some extra comfort. Sleep did not come easily. My mind kept replaying the events of the past couple of years like a video loop. Reconciling where my life had been, and where it was headed, was not a welcome task.

I've done good things and I've tried to be a good person. Back when I was still the Managing Director of Sim and Coventry, Liverpool was chosen as the host of what was called the International Garden Festival. The City of Liverpool wanted to use the opportunity to clean up the old and derelict land by the docks, which had laid in disarray since the heavy, heavy bombing in World War II. The rebuilding project would feature pubs, restaurants, and a whole number of separate gardens with waterfalls and other elements. The goal was to not only beautify the land but also regenerate the area and the city.

Of course, the project wasn't going to be cheap, so calls for corporate investment and donations went out. Personally, I thought it was a wonderful idea. Liverpool desperately needed a kick in the pants and since Sim and Coventry had been a very successful fixture on the City's business scene for generations, I felt it only right to pay the people back in any way we could.

My father and Max weren't as enthusiastic with the idea of giving a sizable donation to the Garden festival. Father was a huge saver and hated giving money to anyone or anything outside of the family. My brother just hated to spend the money period – giving it away meant less for his own pocket. After many, many long discussions, my father finally agreed, and I committed Sim and Coventry to a substantial donation. Max hated the decision but since I was Managing Director, I didn't need his approval.

A few weeks before the festival, I received an envelope in the post, stamped "Buckingham Palace". Inside was a letter from the Lord-in-Waiting to the Queen asking if I would accept an invitation to be in the welcoming party at the opening of the Garden Festival. I was truly honoured. They were even going to put a plaque in the ground on a pathway near the pier with my name on it, as a remembrance of the part Sim and Coventry and I made to the festival and the people of Liverpool.

My mother, father, and all my family joined me for opening day. We toured the Gardens, which had turned out spectacular. The Queen and Prince Phillip arrived standing in the back of an open jeep, waving to the crowds. They visited every part of the Gardens and the Queen appeared to be really enjoying herself. I was nervous and excited when the royal group approached the welcoming committee.

She smiled and nodded her head to each of us, while Prince Phillip, with his arms together behind his back, walked a few paces behind. I never realized until that moment, how tiny in the stature the Queen was. It was a glorious day and the Festival turned out to be a great success. The plaque with my name on it, still sits in the ground outside the Britannia Pub in Liverpool. Maybe I'd have to go re-visit that plaque once I was back on English ground, just to remind myself that not everything I've done in my life was a mistake or turned out like shit.

The flight was long and boring, especially since the nighttime darkness prevented me from even looking out the window. I passed the time flipping through a magazine and drinking. Probably too much drinking, but I was nervous about returning home and wondered if the police would keep their end of the deal. I wondered what people were going to think of me once this all came down, especially since there was no way I'd be appearing before a closed court this time. The press would be there, along with public spectators. All ready to ridicule and throw scorn my way.

How would my friends and family react, those who didn't know? I'm sure Max wasn't going to be pleased with the newfound attention attached to the family name, that was a given, and there would be friends and acquaintances who would suddenly disappear or look the other way if we passed on the street. Those were the "other" consequences of my mistake. I'd just have to live with it.

I also wondered how much, if any, of my undercover work with the government would be revealed during the trial. Maybe it wouldn't even be mentioned. I had no idea how these sorts of things worked and could only surmise. The flight attendant came by and took my empty glass.

"We'll be landing in thirty minutes," she said with her never-ending cheeriness. I don't know how they do it. After more than twelve hours of serving people in a cramped space, I'd be ready to rip someone's head off.

I put away my magazine and settled back in the chair. In thirty minutes, I would set foot in England for the first time in many, many months and in a couple of hours, I would be home again at Townfield. Driving up the lane and seeing the lush gardens and the orchards would be a welcome sight.

South Africa was wonderful but I did miss the familiarity of home.

The police kept their promise and I sailed through Customs and Immigration upon arrival at London's Heathrow Airport. At first, I was worried because there was a pack of officers waiting outside the terminal exit, but they paid no attention to me as I walked past. I took a cab to the train station and was lucky to catch the train to Liverpool without having to wait too long. From the Liverpool station, I hailed another cab, which drove me home to Townfield.

I had such a feeling of nostalgia as the taxi carried me up the laneway to the front door. It was hard to believe I'd almost missed an entire year. No watching the roses bloom or the fish swimming in the pond. The place looked beautiful. First thing in the morning, I was going to go for a nice long walk around the property and re-acquaint myself with the trees, flowers, and misty English breeze.

I was just about to knock on the front door, when it swung open with a flurry. The enormous smile on my mother's face instantly made me feel welcome and at ease.

"Oh John!" she said wildly. "You're home!" My mother was never one for tears, but at that moment, we both had a few dribble.

"Mom…hello," I said dropping my bags and giving her a hug.

"Is that him?" said my father racing down the hall.

"Yes it's me Dad."

Like my mother, he was grinning from ear to ear. He grabbed me in his arms and squeezed me tight. "Dear God John…I'm so glad you're home."

"Me too. Me too."

"Come to the drawing room son and we'll all have ourselves a drink," he said.

"Just let me take my bags upstairs," I said.

"Later," said my mother. "Take them up later. Right now your father and I just want to sit and have a chat."

We sat in the drawing room for hours, talking and catching up. Mother wanted to know all about Africa and my many adventures out into the bush. I told them about the trip Brandon, Rondell, Michelle, and I took to Botswana and Sun City. Of course, I didn't mention Michelle by name; I just said Brandon and a couple of friends. I'd been so careful hiding my relationship with Michelle from them, the last thing I wanted to do was blow the cover now.

My parents were fascinated with the stories and sightings from my South African adventure.

"The elephants crossed the road right in front of you?" said my mother.

"Yes there were two of them. It was quite a sight."

"Go on," she said.

"Well…everywhere you looked, you saw animals. Sometimes they were hiding in the bush, but most of the time, they would stand there looking at you for a minute, then just continue about their business like it was nothing. We drove through some little villages, where the women would inevitably be sitting outside the mud hut cooking over an open flame."

"Dear Lord," said my mother. "A mud hut."

"We watched one lady toss a whole chicken into a boiling pot."

"A whole chicken?" she exclaimed.

"Head, feet, feathers and all," I said laughing. "Didn't look all that appetizing to me, but the people didn't seem to mind. It truly is amazing to see the native people in the outlying areas and watch the way they live…so different from you and I…even in the worst circumstances."

"Did they seem happy though?" asked my mother.

"Oh yes…full of smiles and laughs all the time. They didn't know any different and really didn't seem to care."

Helen cooked up a wonderful steak and kidney pie for dinner and I was delighted. It had been a while since I'd feasted on one of my favorite meals. By the time she brought out dessert, I was ready for bed.

"John, you look exhausted," said my mother.

"I am," I answered. "I tried to sleep on the plane but couldn't get too comfortable. So yes, it's been a long day."

"Why don't you have a nice hot shower, then go to bed. We can visit again in the morning."

"How long do you have before you have to turn yourself in?" asked my father.

"Three days."

"And then what?" asked my mother.

"He has to turn himself into the police station in Liverpool, so he can appear before a judge and be sentenced," said my father.

"Oh John, I'm so worried for you. I don't want you to have to go to prison," she said.

"It's all right," I answered. "The sooner I get this over with, the sooner we can all move forward with our lives. That's really what I want most…to just put this nonsense behind me. I am so, so sorry for what I've done and I'm finally ready to own up and take responsibility. It's something I should have done from the start and knowing the pain I've put you both through…nothing I can ever do or say will make up for that."

"I think that's a good attitude to take son…and please don't worry about us. I'll admit this whole ordeal has been somewhat difficult but hopefully it will soon be over," said my father. "We both support your decision to come home.

I know this next little while isn't going to be easy for you, but you'll make it through. We have faith in you."

I smiled. "I'm glad someone does. These days I don't have much faith in myself. I've made some bad decisions in my life…decisions that have affected your life as well…and for that I am truly sorry. I haven't been a very good son and am in fact quite disgusted with myself."

My mother gave me quick hug. "Nonsense John. You're just talking like that because you're plum tired. Go have that shower, freshen up, and get a good night sleep. You'll feel better in the morning."

My mother was right. I woke up the next morning feeling relaxed and refreshed. There's nothing quite like coming home and sleeping in your own bed. We all sat down for a big breakfast of bacon, eggs, toast, and coffee.

"What are your plans for today son," said my father.

"Nothing really. I thought I'd go for a walk in the garden and just relax."

"You don't have to visit with the lawyer beforehand?"

"No," I answered. "He said everything can wait until I turn myself in. At this point, there's really not much he can do."

We finished breakfast and I spent the morning outside walking through the gardens and sitting by the pond. The slight breeze brought a chill to my spine, but I think my body was acclimated to the intense heat in South Africa, and not the dampness of the English air. My mother brought me out another cup of coffee and we sat together by the pond.

"Things really grew this year," she said just making conversation. "The roses in the front have gone wild. Grandmother Poldy would be happy…of course she probably would have hacked them all down to the roots already," she laughed.

"She was fond of doing that wasn't she?" I replied with a smile.

"Yes she was. Don't get me wrong, I loved the lady dearly, but boy could she drive you to drink sometimes."

"I wonder if it's like that with all mother-in-laws." I said.

"I suppose there's always some sort of friction," she laughed.

We shared a few more Grandmother Poldy stories as I watched the sun try to burn through the light grey cloud.

"You should have seen the sun in Africa," I said. "There's nothing quite like it. Like a big ball of flames setting over the horizon. It was amazing."

"John…are you sure you should have come home?" she asked quietly. "I'm glad you did because I missed you but…"

"I know…I know," I answered.

"Are you frightened?"

"I think I'm more frightened not knowing what's going to happen tomorrow. Or maybe I'm not frightened as much as nervous."

"Do you want us to come with you?"

"No," I said firmly. "I don't want you or Dad to be there. I appreciate the offer but I'm sure the press is going to be scavenging around and I just don't want to put you in an uncomfortable position."

"It's fine John."

"No mother, it's not. I've already caused enough trouble for you, there's no need to have you sit all day in court. I'll have the lawyer call you and let you know what's going on as soon as I'm sentenced."

She was trying to be brave, but I could see the hurt etched in every wrinkle on her beautiful face. I can't imagine it's too easy knowing you have a son that's about to be carted off to jail, for a crime he definitely committed. Deep down inside, she must have been disgusted with my actions and with me. I know I was. I wondered if the shame would ever go away.

"Well let's not talk about this anymore," she said patting me on the knee. "Come inside and have some lunch."

"It's lunch time already?" I said looking at my watch.

"Yes it is."

"I must have spent more time puttering around in the gardens than I thought." I felt a sense of panic grip my heart. My hours as a free man were slipping away much, much too quickly. I wanted to reach out and stop time, not forever, just for today.

After lunch, the three of us settled into the drawing room for another afternoon of socializing and reminiscing. It was nice to be able to sit back, relax, and be myself. No worrying about Brian, Atwood or being undercover. Those days were officially over. Once I served my sentence, Atwood and Nigel would be a distant memory and I hoped I'd never have to lay eyes on them again. Too many bad memories.

Oddly enough, I found myself wondering how the operation was going. Maybe British Intelligence had arrested Brian based on the information I supplied about the shipping crates. That would be sort of cool to know I had a hand in bringing down a member of the IRA. And what about Barrington? Surely, he'd been arrested for dealing drugs. I gave Atwood the exact location of the stash. I felt sort of bad about Barrington; he was generally a good guy. Martin, the guy in Middlesbrough could rot in hell for all I cared. What he put those women through was nothing short of disgusting and cruel. He was a very, very sick man.

Unfortunately, I had no way of knowing what happened to all my old "friends" and I wasn't about to pick up the phone and start inquiring. Michelle was never far from my mind and it pained me like holy hell not knowing where she was or what she was doing. I just prayed she was safe, and keeping herself out of trouble. I knew it was wishful thinking.

After a fitful night sleep, it was the morning of the third day. I shaved, showered, and put on a suit. A respectable appearance in front of the judge could only help. My parents were both up and waiting at the breakfast table.

"I don't think I can eat," I said.

"You have to John," my mother worried. "I'm sure it's going to be a hectic day and I'd feel better knowing you at least had a good breakfast."

"All right, if you insist. Despite an appetite ravaged by butterflies, I managed to finish my eggs and toast, and a couple cups of coffee. I had a few minutes to spare before the taxi would arrive to take me to the police station.

"Are you sure I can't give you a lift?" said my father.

"I'm sure. I'd rather say our goodbyes here at home, and not in front of an audience."

"It's not goodbye John," said my mother.

"Yes, we'll be in touch," added my father. "The lawyer is going to call and fill us in as soon as he knows the sentence and where you'll be serving your term."

"Good. I asked him to."

"Stay strong darling," said my mother. "Stay strong."

"I will mother," I said giving her a hug. "At least I'll try."

The taxi pulled up and honked the horn. We gave our final hugs and said our final adieu. It was a moment of extreme pain for all of us. But unlike leaving for South Africa, I knew someday I'd return to Townfield, and my parents would only ever be a car ride away if I needed them. That was reassuring. The uncertainty lay once the prison guard placed me in a cell and locked the door. In there, I was completely on my own. And that scared the bloody hell out me.

CHAPTER EIGHTEEN

I made the taxi driver pull over a ways down the street from the police station. I wasn't in the mood for any accusatory stares or questions. Besides, I wanted a few minutes alone to clear my head and the walk would help. I stopped before the main doors of the station, straightened my tie and took a deep breath. This was it. The moment of truth.

A large police officer, with broad shoulders and a chiseled jaw line, sat behind the reception desk. He looked up from the newspaper as he saw me approach.

"Can I help you?" he asked.

"Yes," I said. "My name is John Coventry. I believe you are expecting me?"

He sort of laughed. "Why? Should we be?"

"I was told by my lawyer to arrive here at ten am today. You have a warrant out for my arrest."

He shuffled the newspaper to the side and began flipping through a stack of notes. "I say...here you are." He paused for a minute as he kept reading. "We're not quite ready for you at the moment. Would you be able to come back in an hour?"

He was kidding right? It's not as if this was a trip to the dentist. Here I was turning myself in and they weren't ready? And me being a fugitive on the run no less. That gave me faith in our wonderful justice system. The folly of it all shocked me.

"I suppose I could come back," I said trying not to laugh.

"Oh that would be splendid," he said. "See you then."

"Well that was somewhat anti-climatic," I thought walking out the door. Never in my right mind did I expect to be turned away. Clearly, my case didn't interest them all that much. Maybe it was a good sign and I'd be treated with a light sentence.

There was a little cafe I knew of down on Water Street, not far from the station, and across the street from my father's bank. He loved the place, and would often meet his business associates there for a lunch of Welsh rarebit and coffee. I opened the front door and carefully descended the steep stairs into the basement teashop. Not yet midday, the place was fairly empty. I found a table, ordered a coffee, and sat the hour out. There was nothing else to do.

I took my time walking back to the station and ambled up toward the reception desk. The police officer saw me coming and nodded his head in my direction. Suddenly, two new policemen rushed in, pushed me up against the desk, and handcuffed me in a display of over-the-top police drama. I guess the fact this was the second time I'd voluntarily turned myself in, in the last hour, slipped their mind.

"John Coventry, you are under arrest," said one of the officers. "Come with me."

Like I had a choice. They took me down the hall and threw me into a very gray and dingy cell, with two other men.

"Wha' they nab you for mate," asked one of the men. He had a scruffy face with shoulder length greasy hair.

I didn't really feel like talking but figured it'd be advantageous to be cordial. "Oh…I borrowed some money from the government and forgot to return it. Kind of pissed them off I guess."

The men laughed. "Serves the fuckers right, cheap incompetent bastards," said the greasy one. They were both on the greasy, grimy side but one had dark hair and the other was more of a strawberry blond.

"They got us fer burglary," said the second one. "We almost got away with it too, until dickhead's girlfriend over there starting yaking like a fucking bird. He knows how to pick the women let me tell you."

"Oh fuck-off Jones," said the blond one. "At least I was getting laid. No woman wants to fuck your sorry ass."

"Well I hope they don't want to fuck me ass," he said laughing. "It's my job to fuck them up theirs!"

Both men roared a disgusting dirty laugh and I joined in to keep up appearances. I felt like I was back at the house in Middlesbrough, listening to a conversation between Martin and Barrington. Was every criminal a filthy pig? Soon after, the three of us were moved out of the cell, placed in a security van, and driven off to the courthouse. This time I was locked in a cell by myself and I was glad. I could hear the other two morons cackling away a few cells over.

"Would you like a coffee and the morning paper," said one of the guards.

"Yes please," I answered. "That would be great."

"You can have a smoke if you like too," he said passing me the paper. "Be right back with the coffee."

I was surprised at how well I was being treated and never expected coffee. I must have sat there for a couple of hours, reading and smoking, before the guard came back to get me.

"Time to go upstairs," he said unlocking the door.

He led me to the courtroom and told me to stand on the small platform. The usher went over the formalities like my name, address, and date of birth. Then he read the charges.

"How do you plead? Guilty or not guilty to the charge of deception."

"Guilty."

Since I'd already fled once, the judge remanded me into

custody and denied bail. I was expecting it and frankly didn't care. Every day spent as a guest of her Majesty on remand, was a day taken off the sentence. I would have just spent the time sitting around Townfield anyway, so it made sense to start serving my sentence as soon as possible. Moreover, there was no way I was going to ask my father to put up bail money again.

After my brief court appearance, I was escorted down to the holding cell to wait for all the court proceedings to end for the day. Then all of us prisoners remanded to custody would be tossed in the security van and carted off to the Remand prison. The Remand prison reminded me of a school dormitory, with billiard rooms, televisions and the morning papers. Of course, each night we were locked away in a cold cell, but at least there was something to do, and other people to talk to during the day.

The other prisoners seemed nice and were really quite friendly towards me. We talked about what I had done, and what they had done, but it soon became clear to me that one or two of the fellows were a bit too interested in my business, especially when the subject of Ireland and Customs came up in the general conversation. From then on, I kept my mouth shut and refused to talk about my personal life or problems. I couldn't remember whether or not I'd inadvertently mentioned Ireland or the Customs to the guys, and I chided myself for not being more careful. The less people who knew the better.

My main trial date was fast approaching and I was getting nervous. While the Remand prison wasn't horrible, it was just a pre-cursor to the real thing and I wasn't looking forward to the prospect. Many of the prisoners in Remand were repeat offenders and were only too happy to share some of their prison stories. Stories that made me cringe with fear and anxiety.

"You've got to toughen up John, if you're going to last a day," said Stephen. He was on his third trip back to prison. This time he beat the shit out of some guy who happened to hit on his girlfriend during a night out.

"It was an accident," said Stephen laughing. "His head just kept hitting my fist. Not my fault his nose broke or he cracked his ribs. He should a known better. I gave 'im fair warning." Stephen seemed like a pretty good guy, if he was on your side. "That's the key," he said. "Make friends with the right people and you'll be okay. Fuck the wrong ones over…and well expect to be fucked over yourself."

"I don't have anything to hide," I lied.

"That's good then. Just mind your own business and you should be fine. Oh…and be wary of the Irish. They can be mean sons of bitches. Crazy bastards those ones are." Not the most encouraging words in the world. I'd been praying night and day that Brian had forgotten all about me.

When my trial date finally arrived, I woke up with my whole insides turning faster than a roller coaster on full throttle. I wanted to vomit. One of guards took me from my cell and loaded me back into the security van.

"Good luck to ya," he said slamming the back door shut.

Another guard met the van and escorted me to the Crown Court. This time both the press and spectators packed the courtroom. The usher called my case identification number and the guard led me to the dock. Standing there with all those eyes thrust upon my back, was one of the most humiliating experiences in my life. I could almost hear the whispers and the mocking laughter.

"How you holding up," said my lawyer.

"All right I guess." He was standing with some other man.

"This here is a representative from the Department of Trade and Industry," said my lawyer. "I believe you spoke to him on the phone once while you were in South Africa."

Shit. He was the one who'd visited my parents at Townfield, and who I talked to on the telephone. I'd rubbed it in his face that I was in South Africa, and basically told him to go screw himself. Great start to the trial John. Way to go.

"Coventry," said the man. He wasn't very friendly and ignored my outstretched hand.

"I spoke to the Customs people about helping you and well as you can imagine, they're not too pleased with you at the moment," continued my lawyer. "Things were said…and now really isn't the time to get into it."

What things were said? I had no idea what the hell he was talking about. The man from the Department of Trade and Industry set some papers on the table and pushed them towards me.

"Do you agree to these?" he asked.

I looked at my lawyer for an explanation. "It's fine, I've already looked them over. You can sign them."

I signed the papers and the government man took his seat back in the front row. Court was called to order. The usher ran through the formalities and once again, I had to state my name, address, and date of birth. He then read the charges. They seemed to be slightly different from when I was initially charged, and he went on and on about deception and corporate fraud. I didn't care about any of it anymore. I just wanted the judge to pronounce my sentence so I could get on with it.

The judge stared at me with stern and demanding eyes. "Well this is a most serious crime and from looking through these papers here, I see you still haven't told anyone where all the stolen money is." He shuffled the papers through his long pointy fingers. "Do you have an answer Mr. Coventry?"

"I don't have the money anymore sir," I answered. "I've spent it all."

"You've spent it all?" he said with a smirk. Clearly, he was being facetious. He shrugged his shoulders and continued. "Of course this is a white collar crime that cannot go unpunished in the eyes of the law. Therefore I sentence you to fourteen months, less time already served."

The prosecution lawyer stood up behind his desk. "Your honour, I ask that you take into account the sexual assault charges that have been made against the defendant in Chester."

I almost fainted right there and then.

"I will not take them into account," answered the judge in a firm voice. "Nor do I think there is evidence to even substantiate this." The prosecution lawyer pouted but sat back down in his chair. The judge turned his attention back to me. "You will go to prison. The length of your sentence will depend on my further examination of your case. This court is adjourned." He slammed his gavel and walked out.

I wanted to protest but knew it would only make matters worse. First, he sentences me to fourteen months, now he seems unsure and my sentence is indefinite? What was that all about?

"Calm down John," said my lawyer. "I'll make some calls. It could mean a lighter sentence. I don't know for sure. I'll be in touch though." The guard came to take me away. "Stay strong John."

"Please call my parents," I said.

"I will. I will."

That was it. My trial was over and I was headed off to jail for a period unknown to me or even the judge himself. What a goddamn joke! Could nothing in my life work out properly? I mean holy shit. Once again, I was at the mercy of someone else. They'd be the ones to tell me when I could leave and finally get on with my life. What if the judge forgot about me? Lost my file maybe or decided to be a prick and use my case as an example to parade his power. That would be just my luck.

So there I was, loaded back into the security van, and taken off to prison. I'm not saying I didn't deserve to go to jail for my crime. I most certainly did. I defrauded the government out of a substantial amount of money and I deserved to be punished. If I didn't believe that, I would have never come home from South Africa. My problem was the open-ended sentence. It's not like I killed anyone or perpetrated violence of any sort. Why keep me in jail indefinitely? It served no purpose but to waste the taxpayer's money.

Arriving at the prison, I was placed in a cell with two nasty looking thugs. It wasn't an auspicious beginning. The guys again reminded me of Martin - dirty, foul-mouthed and looked like they'd spent their lives crawling through the sludge of Liverpool's back alleys. From the first glance, I knew we all weren't going to be lifelong friends.

I tried to keep to myself, but it's sort of hard to do in a jail cell. One of the guys kept asking me questions about who I was and what I did to end up in jail. I said as little as possible, and pretended to be nice. The whole while, the two men kept looking back and forth at each other, grinning. I prayed to God they weren't gay. I wasn't in the mood to be anybody's bitch ever again, but there was no way in hell I'd be able to fight them off if they came calling.

I was scared. The men made me nervous. The way they talked, the way they walked, the way they ogled me with creepy, sinister eyes, like I was an outsider who would never belong in their world.

"So how long you in for?" said the man with the moustache. He was a big fellow, with large biceps and a number of tattoos.

"Around fourteen months," I said. I really didn't want to go into any detail. It was none of their fucking business.

"Aye, that's not so bad," said the other guy. He was somewhat shorter with a thick neck and receding hairline.

They kept firing questions and I kept trying to duck the answers. When the mustached guy brought up the subject of drugs, I could feel my hands begin to shake. Why the hell were they asking me all these questions? Maybe they knew I had connections to Barrington. He dealt drugs, so maybe my name had been tossed about. People talk, far too much, it would seem.

"Got a cigarette mate?" said Mr. Moustache.

"Ya sure," I said trying to be friendly.

As I opened the pack to pass him one, a monumental blow struck the side of my head and I crashed hard against the brick wall. Another blow landed on my face and my nose exploded, spewing blood like an erupting volcano. Both of the men were taking turns with their fists and their feet. I thought I was going to die.

"This'll teach you to be a fucking rat!" said Mr. Moustache.

I saw his fist fly toward my face and I froze. Time shifted into slow motion and I could see the intense rage burning in his eyes and exhaling through his enlarged nostrils. Beads of sweat dripped down his face and moistened the breadcrumbs that'd been stuck in his moustache since lunch. As his fist lurched forward, the crumbs propelled into the air like spitballs, shooting straight for my face, adding insult to injury.

The force of contact sent me spiraling to the floor in a haze of darkness. For a minute I couldn't see or hear, excruciating pain ripping through my body. Blow after blow after blow. To my ribs, to my head, to my back. I couldn't move. I opened my eyes and saw one of the guards standing over me.

"Grab my hand!" he yelled.

I tried to take hold of his hand and I heard him screaming for help. Somebody grasped a tuft of my shirt and dragged me across the floor, warm and wet from my own pooling blood.

"Coventry! Coventry!"

I heard them yelling but I couldn't respond. My mind was back in Jersey. Michelle and I were standing underneath the old tree, looking at the stars. If I was going to die, that was the image I wanted to take with me to eternity. I wondered if she'd even know I died. Who would tell her? She'd been the best thing that ever happened to me. She was the flame in my heart that would never go out, my cool breeze on a scorching summer's day, and the flowers that blossomed in the garden at Townfield. She was everywhere I looked, yet nowhere to be found. Like an apparition of perfection haunting me until the end.

"Well hello there Coventry," said a gentle and kind voice. "You had us all scared there for a moment. We didn't think you'd ever wake up." It was one of the prison guards.

"So I'm not dead?" It was hard to talk. Every breath sent a searing pain through my lungs.

"No you're not dead. You're in a bad way…but no you're not dead. Do you remember what happened at all?"

I shook my head. "Not really."

"They bloody well tried to kill you son!"

"It feels like they did kill me," I answered. "Where am I

anyway?"

"You're at the hospital and your parents are on the way."

My poor parents having to see me like this. When was it all going to end? I hadn't even been in the main prison for a night before someone attempted to kill me. I guess my undercover work wasn't much of a secret anymore. Once you're labeled a rat, you might as well commit suicide because one way or the other, I was going to end up dead. A triumphant ending to a triumphant life. The sarcasm made me smile.

My stay in the hospital lasted just over a week, and I was still experiencing pain when I left. The only good thing about having the shit beaten out of me was having each day I spent in the hospital, in a nice comfortable bed, count as one day off my sentence. I had to find some sort of positive aspect. I dreaded going back to prison and hoped this time, I'd at least be put in my own cell or with someone who wasn't a goddamn psychopath.

"You're not going back to that prison," said the officer escorting me to the car.

"I'm not?" I was surprised and relieved. "Are you setting me free then?" I had to try.

"No, sorry, I can't set you free," he smiled. "You're going to have to discuss that with the judge."

"So where are you taking me?"

"It's another prison just outside of Liverpool. More of an open setting and you have quite a bit of freedom to roam around. I think you'll like it."

"I'll like it when I can leave," I said.

Right away, I knew I'd be happier at this prison than the last. The grounds looked more like a school camp, and instead of being locked in a cell at night, the prisoners lived in little huts all about the grounds. Things were definitely looking up. My prison escort led me in the main building so I could get registered and outfitted in my new prison wear. Not the most stylish clothing I'd ever worn, but I wasn't in any position to comment or complain. Another guard showed me to my hut and explained the rules and regulations.

"When the siren sounds, it means everyone back to their huts immediately."

"So other than that, we're free to wander around?"

"That's correct. Some of the huts are social rooms and have televisions in them. You can hang out in there and do what you please. Well here we are. Looks like your roommates are all out for the evening. I guess you can meet them at lights out."

"Thank you for your help," I said.

He smiled and walked away. I was still quite weary and sore from the beating, so I found my bed and laid down for a nap. I must have been tired because I slept right through dinner. No matter, I didn't have much of an appetite anyway and it hurt to chew and swallow. Mr. Moustache had an accurate right hook. I was happy in my new environment. At least I wasn't cooped up inside and could enjoy a nice walk around the perimeter. Perhaps the time would go by quickly, and if I stayed out of trouble, I'd be eligible for early release. I hoped the judge wouldn't count the attack as a strike against me because it was totally unprovoked. They came after me and I had nowhere to run.

Feeling a bit more energized, I decided to do a bit of exploring and familiarize myself with the surroundings. As daylight descended into darkness, I came upon one of the social huts with a television. I had just made myself comfortable on one of the couches when a younger looking prisoner walked in and glanced my way.

"What's your name?" he asked.

"Who wants to know?" I said. I promised myself I was going to be more careful this time.

"I'm delivering a message for the Prison Governor, now what's your name?"

I didn't want to get off on the wrong foot with the governor. "John Coventry."

The young man grinned. "Then my message is for you. The Prison Governor wants to see you right away."

"He does?" I asked. "What about?"

"Don't have a clue, but I do know he doesn't like to be kept waiting. So you'd better follow me."

I shrugged my shoulders and got up. It seemed a little strange the governor wanted to see me this late in the evening, but maybe it had something to do with the beating. With some effort (my ribs still ached), I got off the couch and followed the young man outside.

"Over here," he said leading me toward some other huts.

"Are you sure this is the correct way?" I asked. We seemed to be going in the opposite direction of the main buildings.

"We're just taking a short cut," he smiled.

Like a rabbit about to step on a snare, my senses jumped on high alert. It was too late. A bear of a man sprung from the darkness and grabbed hold of my head, twisting my ear like a pretzel toward his mouth.

"Do you remember what ye were told about the rafter's lad?" he said in a hoarse, satanic whisper.

"I have no idea what you're talking about," I screamed. The pain was intolerable.

"Don't lie to me you fucking little bastard!" His breath was hot and wet in my ear. "You were warned about the long rope we'd string around your neck, if you opened your mouth. Or did you happen to forget about yer little trip to Ireland?"

Holy mother of God! I was a dead man for sure. This wasn't going to be any sort of beating; I was going to a shit kicking IRA style. Apparently, Brian hadn't forgotten about me and had his thugs primed to send me a message. If I was going to survive this attack, I needed a plan and I needed it fast.

Kicking the man in the leg hard enough to release his grip on my ear, I took off in a dead run. That didn't last long. Four strides in, I was tackled to the ground by a mob of six or so guys who proceeded to pound me with homemade clubs. Who knew torch batteries shoved in the bottom of a sock would make such an effective weapon? Blow after blow struck my already weakened body, and I was sure this time I wasn't going to survive. Primal screams leapt from my throat as I felt the blood pool up around my head. I tried to fight them off as best as I could, but there were just too many of them and I was in so much pain. Once again, I resigned myself to death.

The big bear man stood over me laughing. "You sorry piece of English ass." Poised in the air, he began to swing his club, picking up speed and momentum. "Brian says hello…and goodbye!" he cackled.

Like a cobra, he struck - a direct hit across my head. The blood gushed with the strength of a raging river and I could feel my life slipping into emptiness. I heard the faint sound of screams and laughter, and oddly enough, it was my own voice doing the laughing. Laughing at what my life had been, and how it was going to end. Beaten, defeated and alone. When the laughter died, my world went dark.

Apparently, God wasn't quite ready for me in heaven, because I woke up in a hospital room attached to a multitude of machines.

"How are you feeling John?" said the nurse.

"Not so good," I replied. "I'm having trouble breathing."

"That's because three of your ribs are broken and well…your nose is a frightful mess. They broke that too, and smashed all the cartilage inside. You'll have to wait and see how it heals, but I bet you'll have to have an operation to reset your nose and open up the passageway. Right now, everything is so swollen, it's hard to tell."

"Splendid…just the news I was waiting to hear."

"It's good you have a sense of humour about it," she smiled.

"How can I not?" I replied. "Two major beatings within a couple of weeks? That has to be some sort of record doesn't it?"

"Well at least you're still alive to talk about it," she said.

"Maybe, but there's a big part of me that figures I'd just be better off dead."

"Don't ever say that," she scolded. "I see death all the time and you sir need to be thankful you're alive."

She was right and I was thankful. I guess I was just feeling a little down and dismayed about what had happened. And I don't think the mountain of pain medication sourcing through my veins helped my mood. Everything on me hurt like a son of a bitch, even more than the after the first beating. I had gashes on my head, cuts on my face, and bruises all over my body.

Not only were several ribs broken, my liver, kidneys and abdomen were swollen from the blows. The doctor said I was real lucky to have made it out alive, and praised the quick reaction of the prison guards and ambulance team. A couple of plainclothes officers wanted to ask me a few questions, but I told them I was feeling too shitty to answer. I wasn't about to rat out the guys who beat me, especially if I had to go back to the prison. Maybe next time they'd leave me alone, if they knew I'd kept my mouth shut to the authorities.

Of course, the hospital called my parents and it broke my heart they had to see me in this sort of shape again. My mother tried to be brave but I could see pain in her eyes as soon as she walked into my room. My father was furious.

"How can this happen twice?" he said. "I thought prisons were supposed to have security?"

"They do and they came as quick as they could," I answered, "but it all happened so fast and there were so many of them. There wasn't anything the guards could have done to prevent the attack. They had no idea."

"Well at least they've increased security here in the hospital for you," said my mother.

"They have?"

"Oh yes," said my father. "They've put you in a private room and stationed a police officer outside your door...round the clock even."

"Are they afraid I might make a run for it?"

"No, no," replied my father. "He's there so no one can get in without proper identification and authorization."

"That makes me feel better."

My recovery took quite a bit longer than before, and I was glad to spend the time in the hospital and not the medical ward of the prison. Really though, I just wanted to go home. Hadn't I paid my dues? Not in sheer time but definitely in blood and agony. I dreaded going back to that prison. The stress of always having to look over my shoulder and not trusting a soul, was weighing heavy on my mind. I wasn't sure I could last a day in that atmosphere, let alone another twelve months or so.

I stretched my recovery time out as long as I could, and I

think the doctors and nurses knew I might have been milking it a little bit those last few days, but they were good sports and played along.

"How's your pain today John?" said the nurse.

"Still sore and having some trouble taking a deep breath," I replied.

"Still? Well I'll let the doctor know. I'm sure he's not going to release you until you're feeling tip top."

"Thank-you," I said.

"Just doing my job," she smiled.

Upon recuperation, the prison officers escorted me from the hospital to a waiting car. For the first time, I wasn't placed in handcuffs, only surrounded by guards. They needn't have worried, I wasn't going to run - I had nowhere to hide – and my ribs hadn't fully healed, which I presumed would make running fast quite difficult. I noticed the tall policeman who guarded my hospital door during the day, was trailing behind our car in a regular police car. Our vehicle was unmarked and non-descript.

The car steered out of Liverpool and headed north at a rapid pace.

"Am I not going back to the other prison?" I asked.

"No, you're not," answered the guard.

"Where are we headed then?"

"Somewhere you can serve your sentence out in peace," he smiled.

The officers were all very nice and friendly toward me, a marked difference from when they first slapped on the cuffs. Arriving late at night in the city of Preston, I was placed in a room with a bed, a good meal on a tray, some cigarettes, and a television. By the morning, I was in a much happier frame of mind and ready to get to my final destination. Besides, each travel day was another day off my sentence. We could drive all the way to Scotland for all I cared, as long as it lessoned the time I had to spend in a cell behind bars.

I was given a generous breakfast of bacon, eggs, toast, and coffee before we piled back into the cars and took off down the road. Watching out the window, I began to notice a familiar route, one I'd taken many times before. The car travelled east across the country and over the Yorkshire Moors. Thank God, we didn't move north toward Middlesbrough but stayed on a more southerly path toward Harrogate and a small village called Weatherby.

Like the second prison in Liverpool, this one was very open with little security. Prisoners roamed about at will and had wide-ranging privileges. Upon arrival, I was taken to the Prison Governor's office.

"Coventry," said the governor. "In light of your recent problems at the other two prisons, it's been decided that you will spend your days, from sunrise to sunset, here in my administration offices. That includes meals. They'll be brought up to you and you can eat them in the little kitchen area over there. At night, one of the guards will personally escort you back to your cell. That way we shouldn't have any incidents."

"Thank-you sir," I said relieved. "I just want you to know, I did nothing to provoke either of the attacks, so you don't have to worry about me causing any trouble."

"I know you were jumped on both occasions and I'm not worried about you causing any trouble. My job is to keep you safe and alive while you're in my prison. That's my only concern."

Spending my days in the governor's offices was almost like spending the day at home. I was free to read or watch television and could make myself a cup of coffee or tea whenever I wanted. Sometimes, the governor would put me to work sorting through papers, rearranging books or getting him a cup of tea, but generally I was left alone and the days passed quickly.

Even the nights weren't so bad. The bed in my cell was lumpy like coal and my pillow smelt musty - a small price to pay for a peaceful night's sleep, knowing my only roommate was an old stained toilet that rattled the pipes every time I flushed. Life became routine and I settled in quite nicely. I kept to myself and didn't go out of my way to make any new friends.

One morning the governor called me into his office.

"Well Coventry, it seems our time together is almost up." I didn't know what to say, I was so excited. "All you have to do is write a letter saying how sorry you were for defrauding the Department of Trade and Industry and then you can go."

"I'll be free?"

"You can just walk out the front door and put all of this behind you."

"Do you have a pen and some paper I could borrow?"

"Of course," he laughed. "Right over here."

I sat down at the table and looked at the blank pages in front of me. It was like these pages were giving me a chance at a full confession. A way to wipe the slate clean and start fresh as a new man, with a new attitude. I wrote non-stop for nearly an hour, and the words on those pages were perhaps the most honest and candid words I'd ever written.

"I, John Coventry admit my wrongdoing and am extremely remorseful for deceiving Her Majesty's Department of Trade. I committed a crime and have no excuse except to say that greed and sheer arrogance clouded my judgment. I admit my guilt and wholeheartedly believe this experience has made me a better man…

It was all true. I was terribly sorry for what I'd done and extremely embarrassed. I wasn't that same young, brash, "I can do anything I please" sort of man anymore. I'd learnt my lesson, and the shame and heartache I'd brought upon my family was almost indescribable. The tears welled in my eyes as I signed my name to the bottom of the page. With that signature, I'd finally accepted without qualification, that I was the only one to blame for *everything* that had happened to me. I was never the victim. I couldn't change any of it but I could use the experience as a stepping-stone to a being a better person and living a better life. The next day, I walked out the front doors of the prison a liberated man.

CHAPTER NINETEEN

Although I was free, I never felt free. The beatings had scarred my psyche and I found myself jolted awake at night with dread, lying in a pool of cold sweat. I strived to put everything behind me, but the task proved difficult. I hated walking alone, especially in the dark, and constantly listened for footsteps lurking in the shadows. I was still a prisoner, trapped beneath layers of trepidation and horrific memories, fear paralyzing my every move. I felt stuck in a vacuum of time, unable to move forward and powerless to shed the skin of my past.

My parents were very gracious in letting me come home to stay at Townfield for as long as I wanted, and I was delighted to spend time in their company. Much had happened in the family since my incarceration at Weatherby. After becoming (actually my father gave it to him) the majority shareholder in Sim and Coventry Ltd, my brother Max up and announced he was going to sell the business. To add salt to the wound, the name would be changed from Sim and Coventry to Murphie Walker Limited. My father attempted to hide his disappointment but I knew he was devastated. The company and the pride of the family name meant everything to him. I tried to talk to Max, but he wouldn't return any of my calls and really wanted nothing to do with me.

I found Max wasn't the only one steering clear. Except for a few close and life-long family friends, very few people even acknowledged my existence and I was shunned. I guess there was just a general rule now that you didn't talk to or associate with John Coventry. I heard the whispers and saw them smirk when I walked past.

"Oh there goes that guy who robbed the government! Oh the scandal! You know he used to run a big company and used to be so successful…look at him now!" (Cue the laughter). The words did sting, but I had no one to blame but myself. I caused this mess and I would have to live with the consequences the rest of my life. Honestly? I wasn't unhappy. I enjoyed meeting my friend Mark for a drink and spending time with my father. He was getting on in age. I'd already lost the year I was in South Africa and the months I'd spent in prison. Time was a precious commodity.

Thoughts of Michelle still filled my head and I wondered where she was or what had happened to her. The memories of our time together in South Africa played in my heart like a never-ending film. I pictured the way she walked down the beach, constantly flipping her hair back as she smiled and chided me to hurry up. How the subtle wrinkle on her forehead deepened when she pouted or didn't get her way. But most of all, I remembered the way she felt when I held her in my arms, and how she would bury her head into the crook of my shoulder and fall asleep, her warm breath gently swaying the sensitive hairs on my neck.

Many times, I had a notion to try and find her but I didn't even know where to begin. The mere thought of having to stick my head back into that lion's den of a world made me queasy. True love or not, I wasn't that courageous. Brian proved once he wasn't the type to forgive and forget and I wasn't about to push my luck. I busied myself working in the gardens at Townfield and trying to decide how I was going to piece my life back together.

"You know you're welcome to stay here for as long as you like," said my father.

"I know that and thank you, but at some point I'm going to have to figure out my future. I can't rely on the two of you forever."

Finding a job with my track record proved impossible, so like it or not, I was stuck hoping the passage of time would heal the wounds and soften all the hardened hearts. People can be so unforgiving and unwilling to give someone a second chance. I knew I messed up, but I was sorry and was trying to move on. I just needed someone to believe in me and give me that opportunity.

One day out of the blue I received a phone call.

"John, hi it's Rondell. How are you?"

"I'm fine! How are you?" I was so pleased to hear from her. She was my one safe connection to Michelle.

"I'm coming to Liverpool in a few days," she said. "Can we meet?"

"Of course we can," I answered. "Just tell me where."

"The Atlantic Tower Hotel, say at two pm."

"I'll be there and I look forward to seeing you. I have so many questions."

Hanging up the phone, I could hardly contain my excitement. Maybe Rondell had some information about Michelle. She had to…why else would she want to meet? I prayed it would be Michelle waiting at the Tower Hotel and not Rondell, the phone call just a precursor to a secret meeting. Oh how I wanted that to happen. To see her smiling face and hear her engaging laugh.

"Who was that on the phone?" asked my father. Since my release from prison, he'd developed an annoying habit of listening to my conversations and wanting to know the details of everything I said and did in my life. I understood his concerns, but it infuriated me nonetheless.

"Just Mark," I lied. "We're trying to set up a coffee date

down in Liverpool."

"Oh that seems nice," he said.

There was no way I was going to tell him I was meeting with Rondell. He didn't even know who she was since I'd conveniently left both her and Michelle out of my South African stories. I'd always been so protective of my relationship with Michelle, like she was mine alone. My parents just wouldn't understand how I could have fallen in love with a terrorist. To me, she wasn't a terrorist at all; she was just Michelle.

The next couple of days dragged on forever. No matter how hard I stared down the clock, the hands refused to move any faster.

"I've never seen you so anxious John," said my mother. "Is everything all right?"

"Yes, everything is fine," I replied. "I guess I'm just looking forward to getting out of the house for an afternoon and heading into Liverpool." It was a lame story but all I could think of on short notice.

My mother laughed. "Well maybe you should take that as a sign you need to get out more."

The day of the meeting, I puttered about the garden until early afternoon. The gardener needed some assistance tackling a deluge of weeds that had taken hold along the south fence, and I was more than happy to lend a hand. The physical labour helped burn off some of the adrenaline coursing through my veins. Having completed the task, I headed into the house for a shower and shave. I wanted to look my best for Michelle. She had to be there, she just had to.

The lobby of the Tower Hotel was bustling with people but I noticed Rondell right away. She looked tired, upset, and was clearly alone.

"Rondell!" I said with a wave.

She walked over and put her arms around me. "I'm so sorry, I'm so, so sorry."

"Sorry about what?" I asked. She could hardly look me in the eye.

"I'm just so sorry John." She just kept repeating the words over and over again.

"Rondell," I said pulling away from our embrace. "What's wrong? Where's Michelle. I thought she'd be here with you."

"Michelle is dead." Rondell barely got the words out before bursting into tears.

"She's dead?"

"She's dead John, she's dead."

The words hit me like a bolt of lightning and I had to steady my legs so they wouldn't collapse beneath me. My Michelle was dead. I knew all along it was a distinct possibility, but to hear the words and have to face the reality was almost too much to bear. Rondell was inconsolable. I gave her another hug and felt the weight of her body collapse against my arms.

"How did it happen?" I whispered.

"She was shot," she answered.

"When? Where?"

"It was at the farmhouse."

"I don't understand?" I said, still in total shock.

"Let's find a seat and talk for a bit," said Rondell.

I'm not sure how I was still functioning. I think my body must have shifted into survival mode, where instinct and intuition takes over for reasonable thought. I didn't remember ordering two cups of coffee, yet two arrived at the table, along with two pieces of pie. I wasn't even hungry. Rondell's lips were moving back and forth and I assumed she was talking to me, but my mind was back in Jersey, under the old tree and under the stars.

Michelle made me promise to go back there one day. Why did she do that? Why did she have to go and jinx things? I didn't want to be angry with her for dying, but the overwhelming feeling of hurt and despair encompassed every fiber of my soul. Why couldn't she have walked away from the Action Directe? It wouldn't have been that hard. Between the two of us, we had enough money to start again in South Africa or even somewhere else. Why? Why? Why Michelle? Why did you have to die?

"I'll be right back Rondell," I said getting up.

I needed a quick trip to the washroom before I vomited on the bar floor. I splashed some water on my face and the back of my neck and that seemed to help. For the longest time, I just stood looking at my sorry face in the mirror. The circle was complete. I'd officially lost everything. My job, my friends, my self-respect, and now Michelle. The one person who truly made life worthwhile was dead. She wasn't coming back. Not now, not ever.

"Unfortunately John…that's not all. Oh my God I don't even know how to tell you this."

"Tell me what? Rondell…please…just tell me…whatever it is."

"She had a baby…a son…your son. His name is Pierre."

"What? A baby?" I could hardly breathe.

"I'm so, so sorry. I begged her to tell you but she would have none of it."

"Why? Why did she not want me to know?"

"I don't know…I honestly don't know. Michelle was like my sister and I loved her dearly…but something changed after our trip to see you in South Africa. She became so distant and distracted…not the Michelle I knew. I don't know if it was the hormones from the pregnancy or just the years of stress catching up to her but she became increasingly odd. She spent most of her time alone in her bedroom at the farmhouse, drawing on the walls with coloured rocks she found on her walks through the woods. As time went by, her mood got worse and she became lazy and violent. She'd draw a knife or gun on anyone who even slightly annoyed her…and that included me. I kept trying to get through to her…to find out what was wrong…but I couldn't. She wouldn't talk about it."

I didn't even know what to say or how to react to what Rondell was telling me. The Michelle she was describing was not the Michelle I knew.

"She had such a difficult pregnancy John," continued Rondell. "Bleeding, cramping, and a lot of pain. There were several times Michelle thought she was going to miscarry, but little Pierre hung in there. She used to hold her stomach and walk around her room just repeating your name over and over."

"My God Rondell, I could have been there for her…why didn't she contact me. I would have come to France right away. My God, my God, my God…"

"That's exactly what she didn't want…you coming to France. It was too dangerous and she knew you'd come."

"Damn her!" I was so angry at being kept in the dark. I felt betrayed.

"Pierre was born in her bedroom at the farmhouse."

"No hospital?"

"Oh God no John, she couldn't risk going to a hospital. She would have been arrested for sure. She did have help from a sympathetic midwife and the birth went quite well considering…"

"Well I'm at least glad to hear that."

"I asked Michelle again after Pierre was born if she wanted me to contact you directly and her face went white with anger. Under no circumstance were you to be told about Pierre."

I buried my head in my hands. I understood Michelle was trying to protect me but it didn't make it any easier knowing I was totally excluded *on purpose.*

"Don't think that she forgot about you though John. After she found out you left South Africa and went back to England she did everything she could to find out what had happened to you. It's just all so complicated…you have to understand that."

"I do Rondell…I do understand. It just makes me sick to think she had to go through all of this on her own. I know she had you…and thank God she did but I could have been there." I just couldn't get the idea out of my head. I would have done anything for Michelle. I could have been there to hold her hand, to tell her everything was going to be okay. Maybe that's why Michelle kept me away, because she knew deep down inside that things were never going to be okay.

"So how did she die?" I asked. "I mean you said she was shot. Was it by the police? How did it happen?"

"Soon after the baby was born, Michelle was downstairs with a bunch of us, just sitting around. The birth of Pierre didn't seem to change her mood any. Yes, she loved the baby but she was still having these real 'dark' moments that she didn't seem to be able to overcome. I remember she was playing with a gun…just clicking it on and off with the safety latch on. There was a sudden unexpected bang outside the farmhouse and everybody rushed outside with weapons drawn thinking it was the police or god knows who else. I lost sight of Michelle as we all scattered to take cover. Poor Pierre was still upstairs asleep. I made for the cover of the bushes and just lay as flat and as still as I could. I heard several gunshots ring off then silence. I waited until I saw some of the guys reappear before walking back towards the farmhouse. I looked for Michelle but I couldn't see her anywhere. She was the only one missing from the group.

The guys found her lying just off the clearing with several bullet wounds. She was unconscious but still alive. They carried her back to the house and we tried to tend to her, but there wasn't a thing we could do. There was just so much blood. I tried to bind the wounds but it was just too difficult. I couldn't stop the bleeding. God knows I tried but she'd been shot too many times. She never regained consciousness and died a few hours later in my arms. It was horrible. I didn't even have anything to give her for the pain."

I could feel the stinging heat from the tears falling down my cheeks. She didn't deserve to die like that. Nobody deserved to die like that.

"Was it the police?" I asked.

"I don't know for sure. Whoever was there killed Michelle and then took off."

"You'd think the police would have raided the farmhouse and not just killed Michelle."

"John, who knows who it was…honestly…it could have been anyone. Michelle certainly had her share of enemies that wanted her dead."

"I guess they got their wish."

"After her death, we drove to the nearest hospital and quickly dumped her body by one of the exits."

"You what?"

"It was the only way John," she pleaded.

"Doesn't seem right. You just don't drop a body off at the hospital like it's a sack of garbage."

"Michelle would have done the same thing…in fact she

had done the same thing before." All I could do was shake my head in disbelief. I really didn't know this woman at all. "I called a few hours later pretending I was a relative and they said that she was indeed dead and the police were investigating. Eventually they released the body to me."

"So what did you do then," I said bitterly. "Bury her out behind the shed at the farmhouse?"

"Please John, this is hard for me too you know?" She was crying.

"I know Rondell…and I'm sorry."

She gathered herself and continued talking. "Her body was cremated. I pretended to be her next of kin, so I got her ashes, took them to the Channel Islands, and scattered them in the water at St. Brelards Bay in Jersey. That's what Michelle would have wanted. She made me promise if anything were ever to happen to her, I would find you and tell you as soon as I could."

"I do appreciate you making the effort Rondell. I hadn't heard anything in so long…I was beginning to wonder if I'd ever see her again. Oh God, I'm going to miss her."

"I miss her everyday…every time I look at Pierre."

"What about Pierre? How is he?"

"He's fine. He's still too young and will never remember anything."

"That's probably a good thing." I paused to collect my thoughts. "So what are your plans now?" I asked. "What are you going to do?"

"I'm going to live with my Aunt in Berne, Germany. It's a nice place, safe and secure. A good place to start again and raise Pierre."

"Start a new life Rondell and take care of my son."

"I will John, I will. Well it's getting late," said Rondell standing to leave. "I'd better get going." I stood to say my goodbyes when suddenly she sat down again and beckoned me to do the same. "I don't think we should see each other again." She paused and leaned in close. "In fact, we should not."

"Okay," I said nodding. "If you say so."

"I do. It's for the best." Rondell smiled, rose from her chair, gave me a kiss on the cheek, and walked away.

I must have sat in that chair for an hour, not moving, just thinking. Michelle was dead. The more I thought about it, the more I was in disbelief. She couldn't be dead, it was impossible even entertaining such a thought. Last time I saw her, she was so vibrant and alive, full of passion and ready to take on the world. What had happened?

"Are you all right sir," said the waiter stopping at my table.

"No I'm afraid I'm not," I said dazed. "Would you mind bringing me a Grouse Scotch?"

"Not at all. Be right back."

He returned shortly with my drink and I downed it in two gulps while the waiter stood by.

"Another please."

I couldn't stop drinking and I couldn't stop thinking about Michelle. Her death, the baby. I still couldn't believe Michelle had a child. It was absurd. Why didn't Michelle tell me she was pregnant with my child? Sure Rondell tried to explain but it was a lame excuse. Michelle would have known she was pregnant while I was still in South Africa. She could have easily called or set something up with Brandon. Damn her! Damn her for keeping it a secret and damn her for dying! It wasn't fair...it just wasn't fair. She thought she was protecting me, and realistically, she probably was. I wonder if Brian knew about Pierre.

By the time I left the lounge in the hotel, I was downright

plastered. Like a fool, I got into my car, started the ignition, and drove home to Townfield. My vision so impaired, I had to close one eye, just to get a glimpse of the white line on the road. By God's grace, I made it home in one piece without killing myself or anyone else. I wasn't in the mood to talk to my parents, so I avoided them and just went upstairs to bed.

Despite the amount of alcohol consumed, I had a hard time falling asleep. It was just one of those semi-sleeps, where your body is limp, and your eyes are closed, but your head is spinning a million miles a minute. The same questions, over and over again. I didn't have the answers. Most likely, I would never have the answers. And if I wasn't asking myself questions, I was thinking about all the times I'd spent with Michelle. Like the first night she came to see me in the pub at Darlish - this hot, sexy woman knocking on my door in the middle of the night. What a time that was!

In fact, all the time I spent with Michelle was crazy. Crazy with fun, crazy with passion, and crazy with love. I was a lucky man. She taught me things about life and about myself that I never would have known or figured out on my own. And if a child was consummated by our relationship, then I hope that child one day understands he was made out of pure and simple love. Maybe knowing that would give him some comfort growing up.

They say it's better to have loved and lost, then to have never loved at all. That's bullshit. The pain of loving Michelle, then losing Michelle haunted me like the mistiness of the Yorkshire Moors. I'd be going about my business, thinking I was moving forward, then I'd see her smile on another woman's face or catch her reflection in the bathroom mirror, laughing as I brushed my teeth. I'd never had someone make me so happy, yet so sad all in the same breath. Time is supposed to heal the pain, but that's bullshit too. It only makes it worse.

Because my parents didn't know about my relationship with Michelle, I had to hide my grief over her death. I could read the worry etched in their faces, but I didn't let on what was the matter. I spent weeks moping about the house, not really caring what I said or did. I drank too much, ate too little, and generally was an emotional mess. Sleep never came easy, between nightmares about the beatings and thoughts of Michelle, I spent the night time hours drifting in and out of consciousness.

I just couldn't let the matter rest. I needed closure. I needed to return to Jersey and keep my promise to Michelle. I told my parents I was going away for a few days to London to relax and clear my head. Instead, I took the train to Manchester and booked myself on the first flight to Jersey. Flying into the islands was heart wrenching. All the memories of the glorious time I'd spent there with Michelle came flooding back like it was yesterday. It was almost more than my fragile heart could handle.

I checked into the hotel, threw my bags in my room, and headed out for a walk along the bay. A misty rain swept down along the water, the clouds as grey as my mood. But there was no turning back. I pushed on down the beach, retracing the same steps that Michelle and I took so long ago. By the time I reached the church, the skies exploded in a downpour, Michelle's tears from heaven matching my tears on earth.

I ran for the cover of the church and huddled beneath an overhang in the roof, waiting for the heavy rain to subside. Despite the storm, the bay looked beautiful with the rain bouncing off the rumbling waves crashing against the shore. If only Michelle were here with me, then everything would have been perfect. It was hard to reconcile that I would never have any of those moments with her again.

I lit a cigarette, took a deep inhale, then kissed the wind with my smoke. Like Michelle used to say, 'I'll see you again…wherever the wind takes me'. Maybe she was standing right here beside me, sharing in the agony of our loss. I wanted to believe that…I needed something to hold on to, even if it was just an apparition. Something that wouldn't make me feel the intense loneliness and sorrow I was feeling right now.

With the let up of the rain, I made my way out from the shelter of the church and over to the ancient tree that held the symbol of our love. As I tenderly ran my fingers over the carved initials, I couldn't stop the flood of emotion bursting from within. I cried harder and longer than I had ever cried before in my life. I cried for what was…what is and what could have been. Maybe that's what Michelle meant in the card that she gave me in South Africa, "I Was, I Am, I Will Be." It was like a mantra to our love. Remember me as I was, remember me as I am and remember what could have been. That had to be it. She was documenting our love.

"Oh dear God Michelle," I whispered. "I'll never understand what happened. Why you just couldn't leave your life and be with me? It would have been so wonderful…like magic."

A cool touch on the back of my neck startled me and I turned quickly to see who was there. But the grounds were still, except for the gentle blowing of the wind. All I could do was smile. Michelle was with me. In my heart, in my soul, and always in the wind.

CHAPTER TWENTY

The months passed, and eventually I was able to convince myself that life does indeed move on, whether I wanted it to or not. I'm not going to lie and say it was easy, but as my mother would say, "sometimes you just have to gut it up and get on with it." I busied myself with odd jobs around the property and re-discovered my love of reading. Socially, I was still an outcast, but it didn't bother me too much anymore.

My parents still enjoyed having friends over for mid-day Sunday drinks, and I usually took that opportunity to drive to Mark's for a visit. Except when Ron and Cora Harrison stopped by. Cora knew much of what had happened and both of them were always so pleasant and welcoming to me. Actually treated me like a human being, which is more than I can say for some people.

The following Monday after one of the Harrison's visits, I was sitting in the drawing room reading the paper, when I noticed a dark car drive up the laneway. I wasn't expecting any company and both my parents were out. The car stopped and out stepped three men in dark suits.

"You've got to be kidding me?" I said.

The doorbell rang and I unwillingly opened it.

"Hello John," said Peter Atwood with a friendly smile. "It's been a long time."

"What do you want?" My mood had suddenly soured at the sight of the man who'd gotten me mixed up in this whole undercover mess.

"Can we come in?" he asked.

"I suppose," I answered. I led them into the drawing room but wasn't about to offer them anything to drink. Let them die of thirst.

They sat down without invitation and I just stared at him with a straight and angry face.

"Well I'll get right to the point John," said Atwood. "We want you to do some work for us."

My brain paused to let the words sink in and then I burst out laughing. "You want me to do some work for you? After everything that happened? You must be joking." The look on Atwood's face told me he wasn't. "No way," I said flatly. "No bloody way am I getting involved in this shit again."

One of the other men piped up. "You cannot just walk out on us John, that's not how things work."

"Look," I said, my voice spewing venom. "I did everything you asked me to. Actually, I did more than my bit and kept my end of the bargain. You thought nothing of getting me mixed up with the IRA, drug dealers and generally some very nasty people. I've had the shit soundly beaten out of me twice…almost to the point of death. I can't breathe out of one side of my nose and need an operation to fix it, and you have the nerve to come to my house to ask if I can help you out even more?"

"Yes," said Atwood. "But we got you protected and out of prison."

"Doesn't matter," I said shaking my head. "There's no going back."

"If it's money you want," said the other man. "We can make it better."

"No it's not about the money."

"We could get you employed full time…all tied up proper. You're not working now are you? See we're offering you a job."

I wanted to spit in his condescending face. "The answer is no. I will not work for you now. I will not work for you ever!"

"That's not a good attitude to take," said the man.

I turned to Atwood. "Who is this guy? Like he has any idea what I've been through? You people got me involved in things you knew were highly dangerous! I will always have nightmares. I will always be fearful of walking down the street. Money can't make up for all the things I lost!"

"Calm down John," said Atwood.

"I will not calm down. Listen…I kept my side of the deal. I kept silent and I told no one. I kept my end of the deal, but you didn't keep yours. You…did…not…keep…yours," I repeated very slowly.

"That's where our opinion differs I guess," said Atwood. "You knew the risks when you accepted the position and we kept you as safe as we could."

"I knew the risks?" I laughed. "You said you wanted some information on drugs. I gave you the stash in Peter Barrington's house but no…that wasn't enough. So I gave you shipping labels and told you about Martin in Middlesbrough. Still, you wanted more. You asked me to get close to Brian, so I did. You neglected to mention he was an operative for the fucking IRA! Or that Michelle was Action Directe." Her name slipped out before I could stop it. "Brian set me up on sexual assault charges."

"Which we got you out of," said Atwood.

"You're missing the point! I never should have been put in that position in the first place."

"If you remember correctly John, you never told me about the interviews until after they happened. You weren't always straight with me yourself." He did have a point but I still wanted to throttle him. "Then you ran away to South

Africa."

"I went to South Africa because I was fearful for my life," I said. "Brian was after me, I had to get away."

"We could have protected you," said Atwood.

"Like bloody hell you could have. I should have just stayed in South Africa."

"John," said the other man. "*You* don't just decide to leave us when *you* want to. No one does. You belong to us now"

"Is that a threat?"

"No threats," he said. "Just stating the facts."

"Well let me state these facts for you. I'm burnt out. I am no use to you and I don't want to get involved ever again. Now please just go away." The man was about to speak, but I quickly put up my hand. "I don't want to hear it."

Atwood got up off his chair and held out his hand for me to shake. I glanced at it, glanced at him, then walked out of the room. They saw themselves out the front door and drove away. Ignorant bastards thinking they could come to my home and threaten me.

My cover had already been blown? What were they thinking? If I didn't last a single night in jail without being in protective custody, how did they expect me to last a minute back in the drug world? Unless they sent me to another country. No, my time working undercover was over. Done. I'd already had enough excitement for a lifetime, thank-you very much. And as far as the threats went, they could shove their useless threats up their ass. I'd learned my lesson. I had no intention of tempting fate or breaking the law ever again. I put the visit behind me and purposely didn't tell my parents.

By this time, my father was getting quite old and was always worried about me. It broke my heart to see the pain and stress I'd put him through. One night, I was watching a television show with my mother, some show about the police catching criminals. Suddenly my father, (who had already gone to bed) appeared half-dressed at the sitting room door.

"Why are the police here?" he asked. "Are they after John?"

"No Dad," said my mother calming him down. "The sirens are on the tele. John is fine, he's sitting right here. It's okay. Everything is fine."

"Dad," I said standing in front of him. "I'm right here. The police aren't coming to get me. That's all over with remember? It's the television you heard."

After a while, we were able to calm him down and convince him that things were fine, but I felt absolutely horrible about the whole ordeal. Plainly, the events of the past weighed heavy on his mind. I hated that. I hated that because of me; he couldn't hear a police siren on the television and not be anxious.

Some months later, I was frightened out of my nighttime sleep by a knocking on my bedroom door.

"John, come quick," said my mother. "Something's wrong with your Dad."

I rushed out of bed and to my father's side. He didn't look well at all. His face was pale and his eyes had lost their luster.

"Call the ambulance," I said.

No sooner had I thrown on a pair of pants and a shirt, when the ambulance came screaming down the drive. They took him to the hospital and the doctors diagnosed his condition as grave.

"I'm not sure he's going to make it out of the hospital," said the doctor. "I'm so sorry."

My brother Max was out of the country at the time, so I

telephoned him and suggested he make plans to return right away. In the meantime, my mother and I, along with my Uncle Michael, took turns sitting by my father's bedside. We tried to keep the mood light, but with every passing moment, my father got weaker and weaker. It's not easy watching someone you love die. The process is slow and painful, and as much as you want to do something to help, or make it better, nature holds you powerless. What's going to happen is going to happen.

Max arrived home three days after I made the call, and right away he offered to spend the night with my father to give my mother and I a rest. I tucked the blankets under his arm, and gave him a kiss goodnight on the forehead. Suddenly he clasped my arm.

"I'm sorry. I'm sorry," he said.

I smiled back at him, not having really understood why he was apologizing. I was the one who should have been apologizing, not him. Then he turned to mother as she walked out of the hospital room.

"Au revior." That's all he said.

In the middle of the night, my mother received a phone call from Max.

"You'd better come back," he said. "I'm afraid Dad's taken a turn for the worse."

We rushed back to the hospital and as we approached my father's room, Max was coming out the door. The look on his face told the sad story.

"He just passed," he said hugging my mother.

Without hesitation, we entered his room. He looked so peaceful lying there, as if he didn't have a care in the world. I kissed him once again on the forehead. He was still warm to the touch.

"Do you mind John if I have some time alone with your

father?"

"Of course not mother. Max and I will be right outside the door if you need us."

I was crushed. My father meant the world to me. He'd been by my side and never once let me down. I know I'd tried his patience on more than one occasion, but he never gave up on me, even when I had given up on myself. He was the epitome of a generous man, a great leader with a heart of gold for his family and friends. Now he was gone. The finality was unbearable.

My father had a truly determined belief in God, heaven, and that we'd all be together one day in eternity. I'd never taken religion too seriously, so when my father once mentioned during a casual conversation that when his own father passed away, he felt a unique closeness, almost sensing his spirit, I didn't pay any heed.

But remarkably, after my father's death, I did feel his presence, very strongly in fact, and it has never left me. From that day on, I never doubted there was a God, or questioned if there was life after death. It gave me such a quiet comfort knowing one day we'd all be reunited. Me, my father, Michelle…anyone I'd ever loved. My father gave me many gifts in his lifetime, but that understanding was the biggest and most meaningful. I now had the gift to believe, the gift to hope, and the gift of forgiveness. Forgiving myself for past transgressions was the only way I could truly move forward, and moving forward was the only way to find peace. Michelle told me once I'd find peace. At the time, I didn't believe her. Maybe I should have.

My mother and I lived together at Townfield and while I was happy, I was restless. There was only so much gardening, reading, and watching television one could do before going batty. I tried to find a job, but all my contacts were gone, scared away by my past, and scared away by society's unwillingness to admit that everyone makes mistakes. I would never get a fair shake in England. Too much had happened and too many people had long memories. I'd been out of jail for fifteen months and nothing had changed. I wasn't sure it ever would.

"John," said my mother one night. "I think it's time you leave Townfield. Not that I don't love having you here…but you need something more."

"I've always wanted to travel to America and visit Los Angeles," I said.

"Why don't you then. I just hate seeing you cooped up here."

"Mother, you've already done so much for me. I can't ask you for anything more."

"Nonsense John. You're my son. Make the arrangements and pack your bags. You're still a young man. Go do something. Don't be afraid to live your life!"

She had a point. Maybe I wasn't afraid of my past; maybe I was afraid of the future. Maybe I just didn't trust myself enough. But I had to try. Going to America would be a fresh start, something I desperately needed. There I would just be some English guy, lost in the multitude of personalities. The only way anyone would find out about my past was if I told them, and that sure as hell wasn't going to happen.

"I'll only go on one condition," I said.

"What's that?" said my mother.

"That you promise to come visit me."

She smiled and gave me a big hug. "It's a deal."

London's Heathrow airport was as always heaving with masses of people. Since I was early and had already checked my suitcases, I decided to grab a coffee at Starbucks, have a seat, and kill some time. The coffee at Starbucks was always so bloody hot and I grimaced after the first sip.

"Little too hot is it?" said a well-dressed man in a pinstriped suit.

"Nigel? What are you doing here?"

His yellow tie coordinated perfectly with the silk handkerchief tucked neatly into his breast pocket. Nothing was ever out of place with this man. He epitomized poise and confidence.

"I just came to wish you well and see you off. Nothing more…nothing less." He took the meticulously folded newspaper from under his arm and set it on the table. "Mind if I have a seat so we can chat for a minute?"

I pointed to the empty seat and motioned for Nigel to join me. I didn't even know what to say. These days my temper had rescinded and I didn't harbour any ill will towards Nigel or Atwood. They had just been doing their jobs and were actually trying to help me out. In fact, I probably owed them a bit more respect or at least an apology.

"You know John…you haven't always been the most model citizen." I was about to interrupt him but he held up his hand and continued. "But since I've known you, I really think you've changed. I read the letter you wrote upon your release from prison and I found it thoughtful and sincere. And I am genuinely sorry about the beatings you received in prison…that was out of my hands." He seemed earnest and gracious – a side of him I hadn't seen before, speaking to me more like a father and not a government officer.

"I'm glad you're putting your life back together John."

"God knows I'm trying Nigel," I answered. "I will always regret what I did and I accept full responsibility for my actions…have no one to blame but myself. I was a fool to commit the crime and now I have to live with the consequences of being branded a thief. There's nothing more I can say except I am so very, very sorry."

"What's done is done," said Nigel.

"And I have changed. I'm not the same stupid, spoiled man you first knew. I guess that maybe I needed those bad experiences to force me to grow up and stop relying on everyone else. I'm ready to move on and take control of my life."

"Ah…" said Nigel. "You feel like an independent man now. I understand. I think working with us thrust you into an unfamiliar world…you saw how the other side lived…and met people who didn't always share your same views."

"You mean Michelle…" I could barely say her name out loud.

"Yes Michelle…pity about her."

I turned my head and took a sip of coffee. I didn't want Nigel to see how much her death still affected me.

"Have you been in contact with any of these people lately?" he asked.

I shook my head. "Of course not. I want nothing to do with them."

"Well let me know if you hear from any of them or if there's any information you think might be of interest to me. I'll be keeping an eye on you John Coventry…even in Los Angeles."

"Great," I laughed. "So Nigel what was the real reason you came to the airport? What can I do for you?"

Nigel smiled and looked me straight in the eye. "For the moment…nothing." He tucked the newspaper under his arm and rose to leave. "Take care of yourself and have a good flight. Call me anytime…and remember John." Nigel leaned in close and lowered his voice to almost a whisper. "You don't leave us." He reached across the table and straightened my tie. "*Ever.*" Then he turned from the table, smoothed out the creases in suit coat, strode across the terminal, and disappeared into the crowd.

The flight to Los Angeles was both exciting and troublesome. On the one hand, it felt great to be starting fresh. On the other hand, I had no idea what I was going to do when I got there. At least in South Africa I had Brandon to show me the ropes and get me acclimated. If I was going to survive in America, I'd have to stand on my own two feet.

I wasn't totally unfamiliar with the country, having taken a trip with the Young Conservatives to New York and Washington DC during the Nixon era. I remembered listening to Senator Robert Kennedy give an intoxicating speech at some event in New York. I was quite impressed, especially since we all got to meet him afterward. The best part of the trip was going to the White House, meeting and talking to President Nixon. I asked him what it took to be a good President.

"Son," he replied. "You have to be a real bastard to be President." He paused and then broke out in his trademark grin. "And I am a real bastard!"

The airline hostess brought me a drink, and I reflected on everything that had happened these last few years. It had been quite a journey, from the fraud, to the undercover work, to falling in love with a terrorist, to escaping to South Africa, Soweto and the blood diamonds, then coming home and going to prison. Not to mention getting almost killed by IRA thugs. It was even too much for me to believe.

But it was true, all of it happened. Thank God, my father was meticulous in writing everything down, or no one would ever believe me. I took a swig of my Bloody Mary, the strong measure of vodka kicking the back of my throat. I will never forget what had happened, the people I had met, and the shocking things I had done. But that was in the past. Now was the time to look to the future, learn from my mistakes, and be a better person. Nigel was right…I had changed.

My British Airways flight landed at Los Angeles International Airport. I'd already filled out the green visa entry forms on the trip over, so as soon as I picked up my baggage, I headed to Customs. I'd never seen so many silly questions as on that form. "Have you ever been a member of the Nazi Party? Have you ever used drugs? Are you a Communist? Of course, I answered correctly no to all.

I was a bit worried about going through Customs just because of Nigel's parting comments to me at Heathrow – you can never just leave. I didn't know if there was any way he could mess around with my passport or make my life difficult. The line-up was huge.

"Why are you coming to the United States," said the Customs Officer. He was rude and didn't offer a smile.

"For a visit," I answered.

"How long are you staying?"

"A couple of weeks or so," I had no idea how long I'd be staying.

"Fine." He nodded, stamped my passport, thrust it in my hands, and sent me on my way. Not the friendliest welcome, that was for sure, but I'd least I'd made it through without any problems. I caught a cab and headed off to the Beverly Hills Hotel, my hotel in Beverly Hills.

After a brief nap and a shower to ward off the jet lag, I found myself thirsty for a stiff drink. The hotel bar would suffice. I ordered a whiskey (never as good as at home I found out quite quickly) and settled into one of the bar stools to relax. There was a newspaper lying near the bar, so I picked it up and began to read some local story about pollution in the ocean, and garbage washing up all along the Pacific shoreline. It was all quite boring, so I flipped through the pages until I came across the World News Section. Right there at the top of the page was the headline:

"German Baader Meinhof Gang Ends Terrorist Attacks"

The notorious German terrorist group Baader Meinhof has decided to end their reign of terror on the German Government. Dated April 20. (How appropriate they pick the anniversary of Adolf Hitler's birth).

"It's about time that nonsense stopped."

The group has released a statement through the Reuters News Agency in Germany.

"Almost 28 years ago, on 14 May 1970, the RAF otherwise known as the Baader Meinhof Group arose in a campaign of liberation. Today we end this project. The urban guerilla in the shape of the RAF is now history. ***I was, I am, I will be.***"

My body froze. Those words were familiar. I threw some money on the bar and ran back up to my room. My head was racing as fast as my heart. I tore through my luggage until I found the card Michelle had given me back in South Africa. I knew I'd brought it with me; I just had to locate it. I opened zippers, checked pockets, and tossed out clothes.

"Thank God," I said finding it hidden underneath the sleeve of one of my sweaters. I opened the card and read her words once again.

"With love to you, for being my little virgin boy. You will find peace one day soon. Never forget <u>our</u> time in Jersey and what I asked you to do for me one day. I do love you.

Michelle XX

I was, I am, I will be.

"I was, I am, I will be," I repeated.

The words stung me like the tip of an arrow. When I first read her card in South Africa, I had no idea what the phrase meant. I thought she was just speaking poetics, like she tended to do. Then after her death, I thought they were a testament to our love and our relationship. But here in her card to me, she was quoting the fucking Baader Meinhof Gang? Unreal. Baader Meinhof were violent and acrimonious people, far worse than Michelle's beloved Action Directe. Nigel was right. Michelle certainly wasn't a "small fish". She had introduced me to Rondell and told me of her friendship with Verena Becker, who was very high up in the chain of command for the Baader Meinhof gang. She had her French Action Directe connections, Brian and the IRA in Northern Ireland, and Brandon and the blood diamonds in South Africa. Michelle seemed to be smack dab in the middle and the key that linked them all. Maybe the phrase, "I Was, I Am, I Will Be" was some sort of code?

"Oh Michelle," I said staring at the card. "Why? We could have had a brilliant life together. You, me…and Pierre. But no…you chose them. The cause was always more important. I should have known."

The hurt of reading those words in the newspaper and finally making the connection to Michelle's letter was painful. We could have been together; we could have been a family. Instead, Michelle is dead, Pierre is in Germany with Rondell, and I'm here in America. Was everything we ever shared together a lie? I poured myself a drink from the mini bar, loosened my tie, and flopped onto the bed. No. I had lived enough lies these past few years and while I believed in the love Michelle and I shared, I knew I had to put it behind me and move on. There would be no more tears, no more wondering what could have been. The past was the past and I was here in America ready for my future.

Suddenly there was a knocking on my hotel door. I didn't feel like talking, besides I had no idea who it could be. I hadn't ordered room service and I didn't know anybody in the States. The knocking persisted, getting louder and louder. I couldn't stand it any longer.

"What do you want?" I said flinging open the door.

"Hello John Coventry."

ABOUT THE AUTHORS

John Coventry

"I Was, I Am, I Will Be" is the true story of his life and is his first foray into the world of writing. His story is one of passion, intrigue, and secrets. At times, painful to write, it is glimpse into a dark and clandestine world few dare to enter.

John Coventry was born near Liverpool, England. He's led an incredible life, traveled extensively, met many interesting people and as Jackie Stallone says, 'John really has shaken hands with highest and the lowest from Kings, Queens, Presidents and Prime Ministers to drug runners, IRA terrorists and worse.'

John Coventry's life began to unravel as he began to mix with some unsavory people in an attempt to fraudulently remove a considerable amount of money from the British Government and having to work for them in an attempt to stay out of prison. The Customs offer was simple, "work for us, become involved with some of your friends who are druggies, find out who the dealers are"......It did not take long for his involvement to become much deeper as John enters the world of drug runners and terrorists and worse, and this starts the first part of his thrilling book .

In 1999, John left the clutches of the Security Services and arrived in Beverly Hills, California where he lived for the next 10 years, meeting and making lasting friendships with many celebrities both within and outside the movie industry. After the advice of several of these people, John left the United States in 2008 and moved to live in France, there in a a secluded farmhouse in Normandy and using the original notes, documents, photographs and secret recordings that his late father had made and placed in a vault, he started to write the first book, " I Was, I Am, I Will be".

John, the eldest of two sons, was brought up within an established English family dating back to 1460. He was sent away to boarding school when he was six. His school life was unhappy; while the school that he attended was owned by an Admiral of the Fleet and run by a Lord, he was sexually assaulted by the Masters (this is recorded in his book).

John met and had tea with British Prime Minister Harold Wilson while still at school and since then has met every Prime Minister from Wilson to Margaret Thatcher to Tony Blair. When John was 20 he led the first group of Young Conservatives ever to visit the then Communist Russian Soviet Union on an official engagement. During their stay John became friends with a young man from Leningrad (now St Petersburgh) University. The Young boy was called 'Putin' and he was, of course, to rise to become the Russian President.

The United States was his next port of call and again leading a British fact finding mission, was received at the White House by President Nixon. This was the first of a long list of United States Presidents, Governors and Senators that he was to meet.

Trish Faber

Trish Faber was born in Markham Ontario, Canada, the youngest of five children. She began to write at the age of five, using her family as characters in her first epic novel, "The Rabbit Family". Although never formally published, the single, handwritten, and self-illustrated copy of "The Rabbit Family" did make appearances at the local school, grocery store, bowling alley and bridge club meetings, courtesy of an enthusiastic mother and her large purse.

Trish is grateful to her family for allowing her to develop her imagination and creative flair without ever passing judgment. She realizes that at times this must have been difficult. Trish holds an Honours Degree in English and History from the University of Western Ontario, and a life degree in the trials and tribulations of being a restaurant owner, an academic tutor and life skills coach, as well as a business owner. She likes music, sports, tomato soup, and has secret aspirations of one day becoming a rock star. Most of all, she loves spending quality time with her friends and family.

"I Was, I Am, I Will Be", written in collaboration with John Coventry is her second full-length novel. "Pierre's Story" – the sequel to "I Was, I Am, I Will Be" is also available through Wonder Voice Press/

TITLES
"Songs About Life" (1st Edition 2006, 2nd Edition 2016)
"I Was, I Am, I Will Be" (2010)
"Pierre's Story" (2013)
"Ghost – The Rick Watkinson Story" (2016)

Connect with Trish Online:
Website: www.trishfaber.com
Facebook: www.facebook.com/pages/Trish-Faber-Writer
Twitter: @trishfaber
Wonder Voice Press: www.wondervoicepress.com

For updates and more information on both authors, go to www.coventryandfaber.com.

www.ingramcontent.com/pod-product-compliance
Lightning Source LLC
LaVergne TN
LVHW051110080426
835510LV00018B/1977